RELEASED

DEVELOPMENT AND UNDERDEVELOPMENT
Series editors: Ray Bromley and Gavin Kitching

*Development and Underdevelopment
in Historical Perspective*

POPULISM, NATIONALISM
AND INDUSTRIALIZATION

In the same series

Development and Underdevelopment in Historical Perspective

POPULISM, NATIONALISM AND INDUSTRIALIZATION

Gavin Kitching

Routledge

First published 1982 by Methuen
Revised edition published 1989 by Routledge
11 New Fetter Lane, London EC4P 4EE
29 West 35th Street, New York, NY 10001

© 1982, 1989 Gavin Kitching

Printed in Great Britain

British Library Cataloguing in Publication Data
Kitching, G. N. (Gavin N.), 1947–
    Development and underdevelopment in historical
    perspective: populism, nationalism and
    industrialization.—Rev. ed.
    1. Economic development. Effects of
    Populism, ca. 1800–1981
    I. Title
    330.9'034

    ISBN 0–415–03448–5
    ISBN 0–415–03449–3 Pbk

Library of Congress Cataloging-in-Publication Data
Kitching, G. N.
    Development and underdevelopment in historical perspective:
populism, nationalism, and industrialization/Gavin Kitching.—
Rev. ed.
        p.   cm.—(Development and underdevelopment)
Bibliography: p.
Includes index.
    ISBN 0–415–03448–5.   ISBN 0–415–03449–3 (pbk.)
    1. Economic development.   2. Developing countries—Economic
conditions.   3. Populism—Developing countries.
    I. Title.   II. Series.
    HD82.K53 1989   338.9—dc 19

Contents

'London going out of town – or – the march of bricks and mortar' by George Cruikshank, 1829

Series editors' preface

Development studies is a complex and diverse field of academic research and policy analysis. Concerned with the development process in all the comparatively poor nations of the world, it covers an enormous geographical area and a large part of the modern history of the world. Such a large subject area has generated a varied body of literature in a growing number of journals and other specialist publications, encompassing such diverse issues as the nature and feasibility of industrialization, the problem of small-scale agriculture and rural development in the Third World, the trade and other links between developed and developing countries and their effects on the development prospects of the poor, the nature and causes of poverty and inequality, and the record and future prospects of 'development planning' as a method of accelerating development. The nature of the subject matter has forced both scholars and practitioners to transcend the boundaries of their own disciplines whether these be social sciences, like economics, human geography or sociology, or applied sciences such as agronomy, plant biology or civil engineering. It is now a conventional wisdom of development studies that development problems are so multi-faceted and complex that *no* single discipline can hope to encompass them, let alone offer solutions.

This large and interdisciplinary area and the complex and rapidly changing literature pose particular problems for students, practitioners and specialists seeking a simple introduction to the field or some part of the field with which they are unfamiliar. The Development and Underdevelopment series attempts to rectify these problems by providing a number of brief, readable introductions to important issues in development studies written by an international range of specialists. All the texts are designed to be readily comprehensible to students meeting the issues for the first time, as well as to practitioners in developing countries, international agencies and voluntary bodies. We hope that, taken together, these books will bring to the reader a sense of the main preoccupations and problems in this rich and stimulating field of study and practice.

RAY BROMLEY
GAVIN KITCHING

Preface

This book has been written as a textbook for undergraduates in development studies and in economics, politics, sociology and history courses where development issues are the primary concern. Its first duty, therefore, is to be clear, to explain the thinkers and theories it examines in a way which can be readily understood and can provide a sound basis for further reading and study.

However, when I was an undergraduate, the books I most enjoyed reading and found most instructive were those which, while presenting information and theories about some subject matter, also had an argument, a point of view of their own. For this reason I always preferred books by a single author to collections of 'readings' on a subject. Trying to be true therefore to my own preferences, I have written a book which, while presenting information on the development process in China and Tanzania, or introducing students to the ideas of the ILO on employment, or of Michael Lipton on 'urban bias', also both tries to set that information and those theories in an historical tradition of thought about development (i.e. to provide a theme which binds them all together) and attempts to evaluate them from my own point of view. Obviously I hope that students will find the single tradition ('populism') which I identify interesting and convincing, and that they will also agree with my evaluation of it, with my point of view. But in the end this is less important to me than that the thinkers with whom I deal should be clearly understood, and the student be stimulated to read further both about them and about development issues generally. For at the beginning at any rate, it is less important to have a point of view of one's own about development, or to accept the views of others, than to recognize that the issues with which 'development studies' deals are some of the great issues (of justice, of equality and inequality, of the nature of the 'good' life) with which human beings have been preoccupied since the days of Plato and Aristotle.

Those issues were given a new urgency and political explosiveness with the Industrial Revolution, because for the first time the real possibility of ending material want and suffering among human beings seemed to present itself. As a result an enormously rich and varied debate arose about the forms which industrialization should assume, its relationship to earlier pre-industrial ways of life, and the kinds of future which it made possible. The populist tradition which I have focused upon in this book was only one strand in that enormously complex and intellectually rich debate, in which Karl Marx came to be (whether supported or opposed) the dominant figure. If at the end of this book the student has at least some sense of the richness of the intellectual inheritance on which development studies draws, and can glimpse, even fleetingly, the ways in which so many of the ideas and preoccupations to which the nineteenth century gave birth still echo today, then it will have more than fulfilled my hopes for it.

My intellectual debts in the writing of this book are many, and some I am sure are not even consciously known to me; but of those that are, I must mention Terry Byres, whose review of Michael Lipton's work led to this book being structured around the themes of populism and nationalism, Michael Cowen, to whom, like many other people, I owe thanks for ideas subjected to the scrutiny of a fine mind, Robert Bideleux, who supported my inexpert bunglings in the world of Russian populism, Noel Thompson for sharing the golf course and the Ricardian Socialists with me, and Henry Bernstein and Ray Bromley, whose careful comments on the original manuscript have made this book better than it would otherwise have been.

PREFACE TO THE REVISED EDITION

In the seven years since this book was written, there have been important changes in the Third World, especially the rise of monetarist economic policies and the development of the so-called 'debt crisis'. I have also received considerable comment about the book over those years, both from students and from colleagues in the field.

The postscript to this edition is therefore concerned with both these issues. It is at the same time a comment on recent trends in the Third World and on their implications for the leading themes of the book, as well as a reply to criticisms made since its publication.

Overall, however, I feel that the book has stood the test of time well – a not inconsiderable achievement in this rapidly changing field – and that its major themes remain as relevant today as they were in 1982. I hope that new readers will agree with this judgement and that they will continue to find the book both enjoyable and instructive.

Gavin Kitching, 1988

Acknowledgements

The author and publishers would like to thank the copyright holders for permission to reproduce material from the following publications.

Ujamaa Villages in Tanzania: Analysis of a Social Experiment: copyright © 1979 by Michaela von Freyhold; reprinted by permission of Monthly Review Press and Heinemann Educational Books. *Small is Beautiful: Economics as if People Mattered* by E. F. Schumacher (London: Blond & Briggs, New York: Harper & Row, 1973); copyright © 1973 by E. F. Schumacher; reprinted by permission of the publishers. *Modern Economic Growth: Rate, Structure and Spread* by S. Kuznets (Table 1), by permission of Yale University Press. *World Bank Development Report 1980* (Tables 1 and 4), by permission of Oxford University Press. *Beyond Ujamaa in Tanzania: Underdevelopment and an Uncaptured Peasantry* by G. Hyden (Tables 2 and 3), by permission of Heinemann Educational Books and University of California Press. *Economic Growth and Employment in China* by T. G. Rawski (Table 4), by permission of Oxford University Press. *China's Economic Revolution* by A. Eckstein (Tables 4 and 5), by permission of Cambridge University Press.

For my mother

These people and movements, then, are populist, and have much in common: the Levellers; the Diggers; the Chartists (Moral and Physical Force); the Narodniki; the US populists; the Socialist-Revolutionaries; Gandhi; Sinn Fein; the Iron Guard, Social Credit in Alberta; Cardenas; Haya de la Torre; the CCF in Saskatchewan, Poujade, Belaunde; Nyerere. The list is . . . long but still very incomplete. No historian can neglect the concept as a tool of understanding.

Peter Wiles

Introduction

When the colonies of the European powers in Asia and Africa became independent in the 1950s and 1960s, they looked firmly away from their past and towards the future. They regarded the colonial past as at least best forgotten, a history of exploitation and humiliation which had left their people poor − 'the wretched of the earth'. Their attention was rather turned to the future, to planning for economic development and prosperity. Consequently, a lot of the academic writing in 'development studies' has echoed that orientation towards the future, much more concerned with solving present development problems, in measuring current development performance, and in projecting future trends, than with examining the history of development either in the west or in the Third World.

It was not always like this. In the late 1950s, just before decolonization became a worldwide phenomenon, a number of writers in the west attempted comparative histories of economic development in Europe and North America and tried explicitly to draw lessons for the new states from this history (Clark 1957, Youngson 1959, Rostow 1960). However, in the late 1960s and 1970s in particular, these writers themselves came under attack for being 'ethnocentric' in expecting the Third World merely to repeat the development patterns of the west, for neglecting the role of 'imperialist' exploitation in western development, and above all for failing to understand that the very development of the west and its present domination of the world economy foredoomed the new states to 'dependent' or 'peripheral' status within the world economy and made repetition of western capitalist development impossible. Western economic history was now seen as an irrelevance for the Third World; the only way forward was revolution and socialism (Baran 1957, Frank 1971, Rodney 1971).

I would argue, however, that this 'writing off' of western economic history as irrelevant to the Third World was premature, and that there is a place for the comparative historical study of development. This would embrace the economic, political and social history of Europe and North America, the colonial and post-colonial history of the Third World, and the history of the 'world system' (Wallerstein 1974) or the world economy itself. However, such a study must avoid the ethnocentrism which weakened the earlier literature, and it must also be centrally concerned (as the earlier literature was not) with the relationships of economic and political domination and subordination in the world economy which have marked it since its emergence in the sixteenth century.

However, these are very large tasks, and in a short textbook I do not intend to attempt all or even most of them. My aim rather is to select one central theme, which I call populism, and which has run through the theory and practice of development since the early nineteenth century. I also try to show how and why it has recurred again in recent literature and debates on the subject. It was a biblical writer who first suggested that 'there is nothing new under the sun', and the aim of this book is to suggest that, if not wholly true, it is at least apposite in the context of development theory. Ideas in this field are often dressed in a new vocabulary and hailed as original, when often they are little more than elaborations of or slight variations on ideas a century or even two centuries old. By tracing these continuities behind apparent originality, and by examining the outcome of earlier debates in which 'modern' concerns were prefigured, one can often see the contemporary development debates in a new light.

POPULISM

Hostility to the suffering and dehumanization brought by industrialization and rapid urbanization began among intellectuals almost at the same time as industrialization itself. Poets and artists like Wordsworth, Shelley and Blake in England lambasted the 'dark satanic mills' of the first Industrial Revolution and turned to a celebration of the countryside and rural life which was qualitatively new in its conscious rejection of industry, the city and even of scientific rationality itself (Williams 1973). But this literary and artistic 'romanticism', though it continued through the nineteenth century and very much influenced social and economic theorists and politicians, is tangential to the doctrine which I will call populism. For the economic and social theory of populism proper does not reject material progress, the increase of material prosperity and well-being (as some romantic literature does); rather it is argued that this can come about without large-scale industrialization and urbanization. In particular such progress, the increase of material

well-being – 'development' as we would say – is seen as perfectly compatible with preserving a society and economy in which small-scale agricultural producers (peasants) and non-agricultural producers (artisans)
remain in a large majority. The second chapter of this book looks at the
intellectual origins of this doctrine in the early nineteenth century, its
development through the century and the social and political movements with which it was identified. The third chapter then looks at the
resuscitation of this doctrine in somewhat modified forms (which I call
'neo-populism') in 1920s eastern Europe. Four modern variants of neo-
populism are examined in Chapter 4, in the writings of President Julius
Nyerere of Tanzania, in the World Employment Programme of the
International Labour Office (ILO) and in the recent academic work of
Michael Lipton and E. F. Schumacher.

However, populism in the nineteenth century and neo-populism in the
twentieth century were and are counter-doctrines, minority oppositional
creeds, to the dominant social and economic belief of those centuries,
and indeed of development itself, the belief in the necessity of
industrialization in order to produce a continued rise in living standards.
Chapter 1 of this book therefore sets out the fundamentals of the theories
which have sought to equate development with industrialization, and
presents some of the empirical evidence which has been thought to
'prove' the correctness of these theories. A central issue in this first
chapter is how far industrialization necessarily implies large-scale production and concentration of industry in large towns and cities.

Having thus in the first four chapters set out the fundamentals of
orthodox theories of development and their populist and neo-populist
critiques, Chapter 5 of this book attempts an assessment of neo-populist
development strategies by examining two developing countries which
are often regarded as 'successful' examples of non-industrial development – Tanzania and China.

NATIONALISM

Although a great deal of modern development studies literature states or
implies that the main aim of development should be the relief of poverty
and/or the reduction of inequality, it is doubtful whether this has ever
been the main aim of the politicians and statesmen who have en-
deavoured to stimulate development from the nineteenth century
onwards. For them, the primary goal of development, or more exactly of
industrialization, was to protect or enhance the power and independence
of the nation-states over which they ruled. In particular, without an
advanced and efficient industrial structure it was not possible to produce

the new armaments required for defence or conquest, and thus one was likely to fall prey to more powerful industrial powers. This was a particular preoccupation of the Meiji rulers of Japan (Allen 1972). And not only the direct production of armaments was involved. The 'railway boom' in nineteenth-century Europe which produced such a large upsurge in investment and capital formation, and also provided the most powerful stimulus to the European iron and steel industry (Landes 1969), was stimulated as much by military and strategic concerns (the ability and need to be able to move troops and equipment quickly and in large numbers) as it was by strictly commercial or economic needs.

But nationalism is not simply involved in the actual practice of development. It is also at the centre of much development theory, sometimes in a very obvious way, sometimes in more subtle or disguised forms. Adam Smith and the first generation of classical political economists in Scotland (who, along with the French Physiocrats, can be regarded as the first development theorists) framed their writings as advice to rulers on how best to manage the affairs of state so that national power and prosperity should be enhanced. In more modern literature on development a national perspective is so deeply ingrained, even in the basic concepts and tools of measurement, that we may simply take it for granted or fail to recognize it. Thus for example the 'national accounting' measures which are at the centre of economic statistics are all precisely that – 'national' accounts. They give figures for national investment, national imports and exports, and above all, the still supreme measure of development, national growth rates of income or output. It is no accident that the World Bank's annual Development Report has the 125 countries of the world meticulously ranked in terms of per capita income, so that everyone may know where they are in the world league table of development.

If nationalism has been at the centre of the theory, practice and even of the measurement of development since the onset of industrialization in the world over 200 years ago, then it is scarcely surprising if there has been a recurrent debate over the extent to which national development requires national autonomy. To put the matter simply: is it best to pursue national development using as far as possible only 'national' resources, manpower and finance (a policy of partial or total 'self-reliance') or is it necessary or acceptable to rely on 'foreigners' for some or all of these things? And if one does have to rely on foreigners, how can one ensure that this does not lead to loss of independence or of national identity?

As well as their preoccupations with the peasantry and with agriculture, the nineteenth-century Russian populists, living in a poor and backward country in close proximity to a rapidly industrializing western Europe, were also concerned with such nationalist issues. Chapter 6 therefore looks critically at the nationalist dimension of populist thought, and follows some of those themes through into modern development theory and in particular to the Latin American tradition of 'dependency theory' which – mainly through the work of André Gunder Frank – has also had enormous influence in Africa, India and elsewhere. A final chapter reiterates my arguments for regarding both populism and nationalism as inadequate bases for theories of development or underdevelopment, but stresses that economic theory is not everything, and that it is the broader political and social appeal of such ideas which gives them their force. It is suggested, however, that if social and political aspirations are not disciplined by careful theory and analysis, they will lead to false prescription and to development policies which fail. Theory is not therefore a mere intellectual indulgence, but, at its best, the most 'practical' of activities.

1

An old orthodoxy

We are concerned in this chapter with an apparently simple idea – 'if you want to develop you must industrialize'. We can think of this idea either as a theoretical proposition derived by logical reasoning from some set of assumptions or as a historical or empirical idea, a comment upon or generalization from events which have happened in the real world. However, there is a difference. For if the proposition were only historical or empirical, it would carry no force of necessity, i.e. even though we can show that almost invariably as the per capita incomes of countries have risen, so the importance of industry in their economies has increased, while the importance of agriculture has diminished, there is no logical necessity for this to be so in the future just because it has nearly always been so in the past. We cannot preclude the logical possibility that there might be ways of raising per capita incomes over the long term without industrializing. Historical or empirical evidence (which we present in Table 1) can never be absolutely conclusive proof or disproof of any theoretical proposition.

There is, however, a very powerful theoretical argument which seems to suggest that there is a definite limit to the levels of prosperity which can come from agricultural production alone. The argument runs as follows. If we imagine a society consisting entirely of small-scale peasant producers of food who are not exporting to or importing from any other economy (i.e. a closed economy), then:

1 at first they will be producing mainly for their own consumption of food, and will therefore produce a wide variety of food crops; but in due course, they begin
2 to trade among themselves (we can either think of this as barter of some foods for others, or sale for money). As they do this, so
3 individual peasants or groups of peasants begin to specialize in the production of particular crops (say crops for which their land or

Table 1 Shares of agriculture and industry in the economies of selected developed and underdeveloped countries c.1800–1985 and their per capita GNP in 1985

Country	Share of agriculture (%)	Share of industry (%)	GNP per cap. 1985 ($)
UK			
1801	32	23	
1901	6	40	8460
France			
1835	50	25	
1962	9	52	9540
Germany			
1860	32	24	
1959	7	52	10940
USA			
1869	20	33	
1963	4	43	16690
Japan			
1878	63	16	
1962	26	49	11300
USSR			
1928	49	28	
1958	22	58	4550*
Bangladesh			
1960	61	8	
1985	57	14	150
Kenya			
1960	38	18	
1985	41	20	290
Thailand			
1960	40	19	
1985	27	30	800
Bolivia			
1960	26	25	
1985	17	30	470
Ivory Coast			
1960	43	14	
1985	21	26	660
Turkey			
1960	41	21	
1985	27	35	1080

Sources: Kuznets (1966, Table 3.1, pp. 88–92) and World Bank (1987, Tables 1 and 3, pp. 202–207).

* 1980 figure (from *World Development Report* 1982, Table 1, p. 111).

local climate is particularly suitable). As a result, they become more skilled at specialized production and their productivity grows (they produce more crops from the same total land and perhaps even more crops with less input of labour). As a result of this

4 they are able to barter for or buy more and more food from each other, i.e. their individual incomes and their total income grow along with their total output. However, it is obvious that

5 this process must have a definite limit, for the need of human beings for food is finite, and after a while the need of the peasants (as consumers) for food will not grow as fast as their output and income is growing. Economists express this by saying that the 'income elasticity of demand' for food is limited, i.e. as income rises past a certain point, so the demand for food rises less and less with each subsequent rise in income.

In this situation it will make sense for some or all of the peasants to exchange their surplus food, not for other types of food, but for other goods which they need, such as clothing, footwear, better housing, etc. But of course this can only happen if there is some sort of (albeit small-scale) industry or manufacture of these things in existence. We can even go a little further here, and say that the development of agricultural productivity and thus of the agricultural surplus to a certain level is a necessary precondition for the emergence of specialist producers of non-agricultural commodities. For the emergence of such a surplus makes it possible for some people to give up subsistence agriculture entirely and trade non-agricultural products for food, and at the same time it enables an 'effective demand' for these goods to emerge, i.e. it creates a 'surplus' of food which can be exchanged for such goods (and indeed for non-material services such as are provided by priests or government officials). There have even been one or two attempts to quantify the level of agricultural productivity required to allow the emergence of non-agricultural production and trade. Using a measure of food output of 'kilogrammes of grain equivalent per person per year', De Vries for example calculated that the subsistence minimum for life stands at about 300 kg. Up to about 350 kg, he suggested, productivity improvements mainly go to improve diet, but at 400 kg and beyond sale of food and the emergence of full-time non-agricultural producers is possible (Clark and Haswell 1964, pp. 63–7). Certainly such numbers cannot be generalized across all history and all economies, but they do perhaps indicate the orders of magnitude involved. They also indicate, incidentally, that specialization and the beginnings of non-agricultural production start at only a short distance from the subsistence minimum. Nothing like an 'abundance' of food needs to be assumed.

However, if the inherent limitation on the human need for food suggests a necessary limitation on any economic development strategy focused purely on food production, this in itself tells us very little about the possibilities for a non-industrial development strategy for a particular economy in the real world. For, first, agricultural production is not restricted to food. Many industrial raw materials (such as sugar, vegetable fibres, oil and oil seeds, etc.) are agricultural products, and so even when non-agricultural production begins, it may produce an increased demand for agricultural products to replace or supplement the slowing demand for extra food. All over Europe and Japan from the sixteenth century onwards, the spread of the textile industry (using wool, flax and silk) increased the demand for plant and animal products, and when industrial production of cotton textiles began in Europe from the late eighteenth century onwards, that demand spread to the tropical and sub-tropical regions of the world where cotton could be grown.

However, whilst industrial demand for agricultural raw materials shows the practical limitations of the logical argument which we constructed earlier (based entirely on food production), it hardly counts as evidence for a non-industrial development strategy. This is because such a demand implies the presence of industry, or at least of non-agricultural manufacture (though this could be, and often was, on a small-scale or household basis).

There is, however, a second and more important weakness in the logical argument we presented above. For there we assumed that we were dealing with a 'closed economy', i.e. a closed system with no exports or imports. But of course in the real world there are a multitude of economies (mainly nation-states) with trade links between them. There is thus the possibility of having an agricultural economy or economies in which output and incomes grow as a result of the export of food and/or agricultural raw materials to other economies. If the exports are primarily food then we can assume that they will eventually meet the same natural limits as we specified above, and so a modified form of the original logic holds. If, however, the exports are agricultural raw materials for industry, then there may be continually rising output and incomes in the agricultural economy as a result of continually rising demand in the industrialized or industrializing economies. Something approximating this has certainly happened in the real world. The economic development of Denmark, New Zealand and Australia in the late nineteenth century was initially based on the export of meat and dairy products to the rapidly growing industrial economies of Europe, while in the period since the Second World War the economic development of the new states of Africa and South and South-East Asia has mainly been based on the export of food and agricultural raw materials to the industrialized economies of the west.

We have therefore to modify our original argument somewhat. Continually rising output and income (and therefore possibly continually rising per capita output and income) may occur in an agricultural economy provided that there are industrial (or at least non-agricultural) economies *somewhere* to provide continually expanding markets. The necessary blockage on 'pure' agricultural development of food crops, based on the structure of human needs, operates on a world scale (there must be non-agricultural economies somewhere) but not necessarily at the level of an individual national economy.

Once again, however, we are operating at the level of economic logic, and that may be a very poor guide to reality. In the real world, for example, we find that economies which at a certain stage in their development are dependent entirely or almost entirely on the production and export of food and raw materials very rarely stay that way, i.e. sooner or later an industrial structure emerges within these economies. There may be purely 'economic' reasons for such a development, to do with locally available raw material sources or the 'natural' protection afforded to local industrial producers by transport costs for competing imports. But very often the main impetus to such industrialization is political; governments of independent nation-states desire to have their 'own' industrial sector to decrease dependence on foreign suppliers, and to provide a base for an independent military capacity. They thus take steps to provide a favourable economic environment for local industrialization. It is such actions by governments which ensure that the agricultural surpluses of their economies are converted into demand for and investment in 'national' industries, rather than simply increasing local demand for already existing 'foreign' industries.

So then, summing up this section, we can say that whilst, under certain circumstances, there is nothing in economic logic to suggest that continually rising per capita incomes are impossible in particular economies devoted entirely or dominantly to agriculture, both economic logic and empirical evidence suggest that this would only be possible if such economies coexisted with dynamic non-agricultural economies elsewhere and traded with them. If one adds to this the political dimension implied in the fact that since the late eighteenth century most developing economies have been competing nation-states, both empirical evidence, and what may be termed 'economo-political' logic, tend to suggest that the rulers of agricultural economies will try hard to industrialize them once other industrialized nation-states have come into existence.

SCALE AND CONCENTRATION

So, then, both logic and empirical evidence seem to suggest that sustained economic development is not likely to come from agriculture alone. Or at least, such is the conventional wisdom. But the argument above fails to address some very important issues (which, as we shall see, were dear to the heart of the populists) because it is formulated in very broad and ahistorical terms. To begin with, I have spoken above as if all forms of non-agricultural production were identical and have used the terms 'industry' and 'manufacture' to cover them all. But the nineteenth-century political economists like Smith or Ricardo or Marx made a very clear distinction between 'manufacture' and 'industry', or what Marx called 'machinofacture' (Marx 1887, vol. I, pp. 336–427). In the one case – manufacture – what they mainly had in mind was small-scale house-hold production of non-agricultural commodities. Here the machinery was usually owned by its operators, and the labour involved was wholly or mainly family labour. In the case of 'machinofacture' however (what we would call industry), the machinery and the raw materials were owned by an owner/manager, a 'capitalist', they were installed in separate business premises, or factory, rather than in the homes of producers, and the labourers themselves were pure wage-labourers dependent on the wages paid by the capitalist for their entire livelihood.

The change from 'manufacture' to 'industry' (a change which has been so total that we now no longer make this distinction, but use 'manu-facturing' and 'industry' interchangeably) was thus a change of social structure, of ownership and economic power in society, as well as a change of scale. For industrial forms of non-agricultural commodity production involved much greater scale of production, the employment of much more labour and of fixed capital (buildings and machinery). It also meant much greater concentration of income and wealth in the hands of industrial capitalists, and the destruction of much of the earlier household production – especially in textiles to begin with, but then in other commodities – which was unable to compete with the new industrial capital. There was also a tendency for such industries to become spatially concentrated in new industrial towns and cities, and for peasants and former artisans (in the doomed handicraft or manufactur-ing industries) to migrate to such cities to seek work as propertyless 'proletarians' or workers.

It was this enlargement of scale and its concomitant social and spatial concentration of industry, income and power which many of the populist thinkers of the nineteenth century objected to, and to which they juxtaposed their ideal of a society of small-scale agricultural and non-agricultural producers living in villages or at most in small towns. Populism was not simply, therefore, a defence of the peasantry and of the merits of agricultural development against industry. It was just as much, or more, the defence of small-scale enterprise and of social and economic equality based upon it, against large-scale enterprise and inequality in both industry and agriculture.

For of course the use of the term 'agriculture' in the first part of this chapter was as loose as the use of the term 'industry'. And just as in non-agricultural production, so in agriculture, 'industrialization' has meant the enlargement of the scale of production in large farms, estates and plantations, the increased use of fixed capital (especially agricultural machinery) and the employment of wage labour by profit- and output-maximizing capitalist enterprises. It was to this transition too that populist thinkers objected from the early nineteenth century onwards, and to which modern, 'neo-populist', thinkers about contemporary development also object. We will consider the grounds of their objection in the next three chapters. For the moment we have to consider how conventional economic theory would explain and justify this expansion of scale and concentration of capital and enterprise in both industry and agriculture.

The primary concept used in explaining the tendency to expansion of scale in industry is that of 'economies of scale'. The basic idea here is that certain industrial processes require large amounts of fixed capital (plant and machinery). Up to a certain size of operation the volume of output from that fixed capital (we might think of an example such as the production of strip steel) grows proportionately with the size of the investment. But beyond a certain point, which varies with the technology being employed, the volume of output grows more than proportionately to the capital investment required to produce it − hence the cost in terms of fixed capital of each unit of output falls. Since highly 'capital-intensive' industrial technologies tend also to reduce the amount of labour employed per unit of output as the scale of production grows, then, all other things being equal, the enterprise using such techniques stands to reduce all costs per unit of output and thus to gain more profit per unit of output as output rises, and hence more profit overall.

These then are the so-called 'economies of scale' from mass production, and are clearly the product of the application of new technologies in certain types of industrial production. It is to be noted, however, that not all industrial processes lend themselves equally to such economies. If, for example, the industrial process involved is a very complex one in which it is technically difficult to design or utilize machinery to replace human labour, and if, in addition, there is for some reason an abundance of labour seeking employment and wages are low, then it may be more profitable for an enterprise to continue to operate in small units and to increase production by multiplying the units rather than by enlarging the scale of production in big plants. This has been the case in the production of electronic and optical equipment in Japan and other parts of South-East Asia (Broadbridge 1966). None the less, it cannot be denied that across a wide range of industries (and particularly heavy 'producer goods' industries like iron and steel, chemicals, cement manufacture, etc.) the world-wide tendency from the nineteenth century onwards has been towards a larger and larger scale of production.

It can also be argued that there are similar economies of scale in agriculture, though here the evidence is more ambiguous and its meaning more disputed. The major differences between agricultural and non-agricultural production are two-fold. First, the environment of agricultural production tends to be less controllable because of the variability of the weather and (to a lesser extent) of soils and pests. Second, a number of crucial operations in agriculture (particularly harvesting and weeding) tend to be technically difficult to mechanize effectively. As a result it is difficult to obtain the degree of 'capital intensity' of production in agriculture which can be obtained in a lot of industry. To be more precise, these constraints tend to mean that the degree to which economies of scale from large-scale production can be obtained in agriculture vary from crop to crop, and from one type of terrain and soil to another. Thus it is much more difficult to make general statements about the issue in agriculture. And the matter is further complicated by the fact that crops which had been thought to require large-scale production on plantations or estates in order to minimize costs and standardize quality have subsequently been grown on peasant smallholdings at lower cost and of comparable quality. The production of coffee, tea and pyrethrum by the peasant people of Kenya in the postwar period is a recent outstanding example of this (Heyer *et al.* 1976). Without going into details here (the matter will be considered in Chapter 3), it can be said that in general peasant producers seem to be able to compete with large-scale agriculture in the case of crops which are difficult to mechanize effectively and when they (the peasants) are willing to work very long hours on their plots for very low remuneration. Even then of course a technical innovation (like the invention of the combine harvester in the United States in the nineteenth century) may make such competition impossible in a particular crop by 'breaking through' the technical barrier. Thus, the introduction of the combine harvester in North America, along with other innovations in transportation, simply made a great deal of peasant wheat production in nineteenth-century Europe non-viable (Kautsky 1899).

Having considered the question of scale of production, we must now turn to the concentration of production. For not only has there been a persistent tendency for the scale of production to grow since the beginnings of industrialization but industry was also freed from the constraint of having to be located beside immovable sources of energy (such as water power), first through the utilization of steam power from coal, and then of electrical energy. As a result there has been a tendency for industries to cluster in urban areas rather than to be dispersed through town and countryside. Again, the conventional economic explanation refers to what are called 'external economies', i.e. savings in costs, or sales advantages accruing simply from factors external to the actions of policies of individual industrial enterprises themselves. Such external economies include access to better public facilities (roads, sewerage and waste disposal facilities, water supplies, energy supplies) that are available in better quality or greater abundance in urban areas. This may be partly because other industries are already established there. But none the less once they exist they will attract further industries which will calculate that the costs of establishing industries in such environments are much less than they might be in less developed areas, where these 'infrastructural' facilities may not exist, or may be less abundant.

In addition, however, to external economies of this sort, industries are likely to cluster in urban areas, because by definition towns and cities represent concentrations of potential consumers who are available close at hand (thus reducing transport and other costs involved in retailing goods). Obviously, these 'market' economies are likely to be especially attractive to industries producing consumer goods for individuals and families (rather than producer goods, i.e. goods manufactured for consumption by other industries). Though even in the latter case, the presence of industrial customers in urban areas may attract producer goods industries as well.

Of course not all industries will cluster in urban areas. Industries, for example, that use a raw material available only in certain locations, or which is expensive or difficult to transport, may choose to locate near that raw material source, even if such locations are quite remote (obvious examples are saw mills located in forest areas, and mining and quarrying industries). But none the less it is the external economies associated with urban areas which are conventionally used to explain and justify the spatial clustering of industry in towns and cities which has occurred frequently since the beginnings of industrialization.

It should, however, be noted that the external economies concept is rather weak as a political or social justification of the concentration of industry, mainly because the circumstances which give rise to such economies in the first place are to some degree politically alterable. Thus, for example, a government could choose to invest in public facilities in rural areas and to neglect urban infrastructure, thereby discouraging further industrial clustering in urban areas even where it had begun. Or again, governments could subsidize industries to set up in rural areas and/or tax those which set up in urban areas, and so offset some of the 'natural' cost advantages enjoyed by urban areas. Above all, perhaps, market economies in urban areas arise not just because of the spatial clustering of consumers but also because in many societies a large proportion of the better-off people are found living in towns and cities. Or, as economists say, a large part of the 'purchasing power' or 'effective demand' for goods is concentrated in urban areas. For a number of reasons, this is particularly so in the early stages of development when the better-off people may be relatively few and the poor relatively many, i.e. the distribution of income may be very unequal. Clearly in this situation, if a government either spreads the better-off people through-out the country or makes the distribution of income more equal (so that effective demand is spread more evenly both between people and between rural and urban areas), then again the tendency of industry to concentrate in urban areas might be reduced. As we shall see, this argu-ment is one which has been very much favoured by populist and neo-populist thinkers from the beginning.

THE MEANING OF DEVELOPMENT

So far in this chapter I have talked about 'developing' societies and economies and of 'development' as if these were concepts with an obvious or agreed meaning. In fact, however, this is not the case, and both now and in the nineteenth century there has been great debate about the meaning to be given to the idea of 'development' or, as nineteenth-century thinkers preferred, 'progress' in society. Indeed it is not too much to say that the debate between the populist thinkers of the nineteenth century and the economic orthodoxy of that century was primarily a debate about the meaning to be attached to the idea of 'progress', a debate which, as we shall see, has direct parallels in modern-day debates in development studies. Indeed, in mentioning income dis-tribution at the end of the above section, we are immediately at the heart of that debate, which was in fact about the distributional implications of capitalist industrialization.

To understand clearly the nature of this debate, we must understand the position of the orthodox 'classical' political economists of the late eighteenth and nineteenth centuries; men such as Adam Smith, David

Ricardo and indeed Karl Marx. For these thinkers, economic progress occurred in society if the volume and value of output or production in that society rose quickly and continuously. Each of them was obsessed with the question of how a society based on private property in land and in other goods (including factories and machines), and utilizing a 'free market' principle to distribute land, money, machinery and labour among the different types of production, could succeed in raising the volume and value of production continuously (or to 'grow' in modern economic parlance). Each of them gave different answers to this question, answers with very different political implications. But for all of them, this issue, the issue of production and its increase, was the primary one. They were interested in how production or 'output' was distributed among different individuals and social groups in society *only in so far as this 'distributional' issue impinged on production*, i.e. in so far as some aspect of distribution might threaten the capacity of a 'capitalist' economy (as Marx called it) to grow. Thus, for example, Adam Smith thought that the most important condition for continued growth was savings and investment, and he was anxious that a large part of the output and income produced should get into the hands of those who would save and invest as much of that income as possible (Smith 1776, Book 2, Ch. 3). Ricardo, on the other hand, thought that, for a number of rather complex reasons, there was a tendency for an increased proportion of the output in a growing economy to fall into the hands of the owners of land as rent, and that this tendency would starve both commercial farmers and manufacturers of capital and thus lower the incentive they needed to go on investing and producing (Ricardo 1817, Ch. 2). For Marx one 'contradiction' facing capitalism was the tendency of the workers in factories to become more and more impoverished and miserable at the same time as the capacity to produce was growing. He sometimes suggested that this might result in economic crises of 'over-production', i.e. the production of output for which there were no buyers (Marx 1887, vol. I, pp. 761–4).

For the populist thinkers, however, from Sismondi onwards (see Chapter 2) the issue of distribution was the primary one, and it was for them essentially an ethical and social issue. For them, the concentration of economic power and of income and wealth (stemming from the growth of scale and of industrial concentration discussed above) was simply and primarily unjust. They were appalled by the coexistence of great wealth and massive productive capacity, on the one hand, and mass poverty on the other. And they would not concede that any economic system which could produce such results could be called 'progressive' in any sense.

But though the question of distribution and the ethical and social issues it raised were for them primary, they did not rely solely on these kinds of ethical or social arguments. From time to time they also sought to show that such a system was also economically inefficient, or that it was not compatible with continued economic progress (in the pure 'growth' sense in which that term was understood by the classical political economists). From the mid-nineteenth century onwards, some populist thinkers borrowed arguments from Marx to supplement their demonstration of the 'contradictions' inherent in an economic progress based on growing inequality. Marx himself repudiated such borrowings, and his debate with Proudhon (a major populist thinker in mid-nineteenth-century France) is particularly illuminating in showing how different was his critique of capitalism from the populist critique, and how much he retained allegiance to the production-oriented economics of Ricardo and the other classical thinkers (Marx 1847).

I shall discuss these matters in detail in the next chapter, and shall also argue in later chapters that modern-day development studies is engaged in the same debate. In that debate modern-day 'neo-populist' critics are opposed to a 'growth orthodoxy', and their arguments manifest precisely the same ambiguity as those of their populist forbears. At times the critique is primarily an ethical or social one focused entirely or primarily on distribution, while at other times (as most notably in the cases of Michael Lipton and of the ILO) it takes the form of a critique of the economic efficiency of industrialization. The latter critique must thus attempt to confront directly the arguments about economies of scale and external economies, and indeed about the necessity for industrialization, which I have reviewed above.

CONCLUSIONS

To conclude this chapter I shall repeat again the arguments which have been adduced since the nineteenth century in favour of industrialization in general, and of large-scale, concentrated industrial production in particular, as the only road to development (where development is defined as high and continuous growth of output and incomes). These were:

1   The structure of human needs and the restricted 'income elasticity of demand' for agricultural products to which this structure leads. However, this argument is at its strongest only in a heavily qualified form which stresses the need for industrial economies to exist somewhere and for agricultural economies to be trading with them.

2   Economies of scale in mass production. These were, however, seen to operate only in some (albeit important) industrial sectors and, much more questionably, in agriculture.

3   External economies arising from the spatial concentration of industry in cities and towns. These, however, are seen to depend for their efficacy on political conditions, in that government action can to some extent undermine them or offset them.

In the next chapter we consider how populist thinkers attempted to combat these arguments, but we also document the way they treated them as secondary to the social and political issues raised by the inequalities produced by industrialization under capitalism.

2

Populism

My aim in this chapter is to outline a current of thought which, since the early nineteenth century, has been opposed to large, concentrated production and has argued instead for a pattern of development based on small-scale individual enterprise both in industry and in agriculture. Because I am primarily concerned here with a current or tradition of thought, and not with the connected political or social movements, I use the term 'populism' in a very wide sense to embrace all those thinkers who, since the beginnings of industrialization in the late eighteenth century, have offered an alternative of small-scale individual enterprise. This certainly broadens the term beyond what some contributors to the standard work on the subject (Ionescu and Gellner 1969) would accept, and includes thinkers like Owen and Proudhon, who have often been seen as pioneers of socialist or anarchist thought rather than as populists. Also, in speaking of 'neo-populism' in the next two chapters, I embrace contemporary thinking about development issues which also has very varied political implications and allegiances. However, these very broad concepts of populism and neo-populism can be justified by the broad similarity of the social and economic situations in which industrialization occurs. For, whether occurring through capitalist means or through state socialism, industrialization has generally encountered a pre-existent situation in which the major part of agricultural and non-agricultural production was carried out by households or families using 'means of production' (land and simple machines) owned or rented by those households and under their own managerial control. Conventionally those small-scale agricultural producers are known as 'peasants' and the non-agricultural producers as 'artisans'. I shall use these well-known terms, though both have difficulties (Wolf 1966, Redfield 1956, King 1977, Gerry 1979).

Given this pre-industrial world of peasants and artisans, it is obvious that the first generations of industrial wage workers will have to be recruited from among their ranks. This can only be done if either industrial work is made more attractive or remunerative than work as a peasant or artisan, or work as a peasant or artisan is made so un-remunerative or unattractive that even an awful industrial alternative seems better. There has been a fierce debate about which of these factors (the 'pull' factors making industry attractive or the 'push' factors making peasant and artisan life unbearable) was 'objectively' most important in the first Industrial Revolution in Britain (see Thompson 1963, and Currie and Hartwell 1965), but for our purposes we do not have to take sides in this debate. All we need to note is that if becoming an industrial wage labourer (the process of 'proletarianization', as it is often called) is experienced as a profoundly unpleasant or exploitative process, then it is likely that opposition to industrialization will be expressed through a desire either to defend or to recreate the world of small enterprise. Moreover, if industry is concentrated in cities and proletarianization is also, therefore, a process of migration from countryside to city, or from small town to large city, then that ideology of anti-industrialism is likely also to look back with nostalgia to the rural village or to the small country town, i.e. it may also be 'anti-urban'.

However, for late eighteenth- and nineteenth-century industrialization in Europe, including Russia, there is a problem. For in all these cases, the most complete, and certainly the best recorded, efforts to develop such ideologies of opposition to capitalist industrialization were made not by peasants or workers themselves but by urban intellectuals, very few of whom were of peasant or worker origin. And though some of these people (such as Proudhon or the English 'Ricardian socialists') were involved in political movements of skilled industrial workers and of artisans, it is difficult to know how far their views accurately reflect those of the people for whom they purported to speak. However, more recent work, certainly on the situation in Britain, suggests that some of these intellectuals may have been quite successful in getting their views circulated among skilled workers and artisans (E. P. Thompson 1963 and N. Thompson 1979). In the case of the later Russian intellectuals who were writing mainly about the peasantry, communication was a good deal more difficult, because nearly all Russian peasants were illiterate and suspicious of all outsiders, even (or perhaps especially) of urban intellectuals claiming to be their allies.

But again, for our purposes, this question of 'representativeness' is less important than simply recognizing the antiquity and ubiquity of certain populist ideas, and the frequency with which they recur. I shall argue that they recur so frequently because the situation which produces them (peasants and artisans confronted with certain pressures of industrialization) has itself recurred so frequently. Similarity of response betokens similarity of situation (Ionescu and Gellner 1969, p. 241).

Finally, by way of introduction to this chapter and Chapter 3, I must clarify the distinction between populism and neo-populism. In the usage which I employ, both populism and neo-populism are doctrines which oppose industrialization and large-scale production in the name of small-scale individual enterprise. As such they are both critiques of industrialization from the perspective of an implicit and explicit alternative. However they differ both in time and in the intellectual bases of their critiques. Populism emerged in Europe in the early nineteenth century and was essentially a critique of capitalist industrialization (i.e. industrialization in which the large-scale industrial units are privately owned and operated within a market economy), and based itself mainly on social and ethical grounds. Put in modern terms, nineteenth-century populism argued that the social and human costs of capitalist industrialization were unacceptable and outweighed such economic benefits as it might bring. Most nineteenth-century populists, being opposed to capitalism, thought of themselves as socialists of one form or another. Neo-populism, on the other hand, emerged in Russia and eastern Europe after the First World War, and was as much opposed to the pattern of state socialist industrialization which emerged in the USSR after 1917 as it was to capitalist industrialization. In addition, however, the neo-populists did not remain content with a social or human critique of industrialization, but attempted to call into question the conventional economic rationale for industrialization and large-scale enterprise, especially in agriculture. The major theorist of neo-populism was the Russian agronomist/economist A. V. Chayanov, whose thought remains very influential in present-day theories of the peasant economy and rural development.

Neo-populism is theoretically a much more ambitious critique of industrialization than nineteenth-century populism, in that it is not purely oppositional. Rather it attempts to argue that there is an alternative pattern or trajectory of economic development which can be just as effective or more effective than large-scale industrialization in eliminating mass poverty, and can also be less costly in social or human terms. In short neo-populism attempts to grapple directly, and on its own terms, with the conventional wisdom about economic growth which I outlined in the first chapter of this book.

For this reason, and since neo-populism is currently very influential and fashionable in contemporary writing and thinking about development, I shall obviously give more attention to neo-populism in this book.

But none the less it is important that the older populist tradition be understood, partly because if it were better known in the development studies field, certain ideas would be seen to be less than original, but also because the populist tradition very much influenced its neo-populist successor. It did so in two ways. First, the neo-populists took up and developed, with the help of economic theory, economic critiques which had been there 'in germ' and as a minor theme in the primarily social and ethical attacks of the populists on industrialization. Second, and more important, both populism and neo-populism have a common obsession at the root of their critique of industrialization and large-scale concentrated production – the theme of equality and inequality. For both populists and neo-populists, the prime failing of industrialization is that it massively exacerbates relative inequalities in society, inequalities between individuals and social groups, between town and countryside, between region and region, and between nation and nation. And, conversely, the prime appeal of their utopia – a world of individual small-scale enterprise located in small town and village – is that it is a world of approximately equal 'small men' and small enterprises, competing against each other to be sure, but in a way which is moderated and restrained by community and co-operative links, both formal and informal. It is a world of equality and community, but not of collectivism or state control.

THE INTELLECTUAL ORIGINS OF POPULISM

Some elements of populist thought, especially in respect to peasant agriculture, have precursors in the pre-industrial period, with the ideas of the Leveller and Digger radicals of mid-seventeenth-century England, for example (C. Hill 1972, pp. 107–50). Still, as a specifically anti-industrial doctrine the origins of populism should be situated in the early nineteenth century. And probably the first of the political economists of this period to take up theoretical positions which later came to be regarded as 'populist' was the Swiss, Simonde de Sismondi.

Sismondi

In his *Political Economy* of 1815 Sismondi defined political economy as 'the investigation of the means by which the greatest number of men in a given state may participate in the highest degree of physical happiness, so far as it depends on government' (1815, p. 110). He went on to argue that such a state could best be brought about by minimum government interference in the economy, combined with competition among small producers in both manufactures and agriculture. In the case of agriculture, however, Sismondi's argument was a subtle one. He was not against large-scale capitalist farming with wage labour (which he identified entirely with Britain) in a country 'where the supernumerary population may always be advantageously employed'. For

> Cultivation on the great scale spares much time which is lost in the other way; it causes a great mass of work to be performed in the same time by a given number of men; it tends, above all, to procure from the employment of great capitals the profit formerly procured from the employment of numerous workmen; it introduces the use of expensive instruments, which abridge and facilitate the labour of man. It invents machines in which the wind, the fall of water, the expansion of steam, are substituted for the power of limbs; it makes animals execute the work formerly executed by men. (p. 50)

But he made it clear that he thought these conditions restricted almost totally to Britain, and elsewhere

> Where population is already too abundant the dismissal of more than half the field-labourers is a serious misfortune, particularly at a time when a similar improvement in machinery causes the dismissal of more than half the manufacturing population of towns. The nation is nothing but the union of all the individuals who compose it, and the progress of its wealth is illusory, when obtained at the price of general wretchedness and mortality. (p. 50)

He pointed by contrast to France where 'the peasants are mostly proprietors: the number of those who cultivate their own lands prodigiously increased in the revolution; and to this cause must be attributed the rapid progress which agriculture is making in that country' (p. 50). And, in general, the kind of agricultural system desired by Sismondi was one which enabled the land to be worked by owner/cultivators, equipped with enough capital to cultivate well, and secure enough in their tenure and in enjoyment of the fruits of their labour and investment to undertake long-term improvements. It is clear that in general he preferred small but prosperous family farms as the optimal system. But recognizing that over most of Europe at this time most peasants were tenants of aristocratic landlords, he argued for a sharecropping system as against money rents (as being less onerous and more secure for the peasantry); he saved most of his ire for the system of land-mortgaging by aristocrats to contract loans, since he felt this generally resulted in increase of rents to pay the loans and thus to increased exactions on the peasantry with correspondingly less incentive to make improvements (pp. 35–56).

But Sismondi's preference for small-scale family farming on secure tenancies, and for small-scale manufacturing enterprises over large ones, did not derive primarily from the economics of production. His main argument in its defence was based on considerations of consumption not production. For he believed very strongly that the expansion of large-scale enterprise and the ruin of small producers tended to place a block in the expansion of markets. It is worth quoting his argument at length here, for it is an argument which reappears time and time again in populist theory.

The increase of population, and of national wealth, contributes to extend the market. Yet every conceivable increase of population and of wealth, does not, of necessity, extend the market; it is only such an increase as attends the increased comforts of the most numerous class. When cultivation on the great scale has succeeded cultivation on the small, more capital is perhaps absorbed by land, and re-produced by it; more wealth than formerly may be diffused among the whole mass of agriculturalists, but the consumption of one rich farmer's family, united to that of fifty families of miserable hinds, is not so valuable for the nation, as that of fifty families of peasants, no one of which was rich, but none deprived of an honest competence. So also in towns, the consumption of a manufacturer worth a million, under whose orders are employed a thousand workmen, reduced to the bare necessaries of life, is not so advantageous for the nation, as that of a hundred manufacturers far less rich, who employ each but ten workmen far less poor. It is very true, that ten thousand pounds of income, whether they belong to a single man or a hundred, are all equally destined for consumption, but this consumption is not of the same nature. A man, however rich, cannot employ for his use an infinitely greater number of articles than a poor man, but he employs articles infinitely better; he requires work far better finished, materials far more precious and brought from greater distance. It is he who especially encourages the perfection of certain workmen, that finish a small number of objects with extreme skill; it is he who pays them an exorbitant wage . . . [and thus] whilst the effect of increasing capital is generally to concentrate labour in very large manufactories, the effect of great opulence is almost entirely to exclude the produce of those large manufactories from the consumption of the opulent man. The diffusion of wealth, therefore, still more than its accumulation, truly constitutes national prosperity, because it keeps up the consumption most favourable for national re-production.   (pp. 62–3)

We have here an argument which, in modern economic parlance, rests on an 'income elasticity of demand' argument as outlined in the previous chapter. Beyond a certain point of income and wealth, says Sismondi, the demand for articles of the kind which can be mass-produced does not increase proportionately to income, and may even decline. Hence if 'the nation' wishes to have a buoyant demand for the 'manufactories' which produce such goods, it should also have forms of production which encourage a relatively equal distribution of income. 'No one rich but none deprived of an honest competence' was to become the central vision and slogan of populism.

It is important, however, to understand the historical situation in which Sismondi was writing, and thus not to be misled by some of his terminology. The 'manufactories' of which he speaks were not, in 1815 even in Britain, large-scale industrial factories in the modern sense. They were rather workshops of various sizes in which formerly independent artisans were gathered under the control of a master or employer. In most cases there had been little or no reorganization of the division of labour within the 'manufactory'; each workman essentially performed there all the tasks which he would have performed in his own home if he had been an independent artisan. In some cases he might even continue to own his own machine, and simply rent space and obtain raw materials from the master. In some of the larger 'manufactories' this was beginning to change by 1815, and some (especially in the cotton industry) had effectively reduced their workers to simple wage labourers, and had reorganized the labour process within the factory to make the individual operator much more a 'detail worker' undertaking one simple, repetitive task in a division of labour which embraced the whole factory. But this was still a minority phenomenon in 1815, and so it was possible for Sismondi to envisage a world of 'mass production', by early nineteenth-century standards, which was none the less based on small units (he mentions ten employees). Individual workers would still enjoy a real degree of independence and prosperity within their workshops and would support each other's employment through a relatively equal distribution of what, in modern terminology, would be called 'purchasing power'. Conversely he was against extremes of opulence, because the luxury consumption which they generated gave employment only to a very narrow stratum of elite artisans, many of whom, in the early nineteenth century, were often the personal retainers of aristocrats and others (pp. 62–3).

However, Sismondi was no socialist. As we see above, he had no objection to wage labour as such, and he was a firm believer in *laissez faire* and in the merits of competition between both agriculturalists and manufacturers. He was also an ardent advocate of international free trade (pp. 67–78). He speaks, as can be seen, for the small employer in manufacturing and for the sturdy independent peasant or yeoman farmer in agriculture. He is strongly against the inequality and poverty produced by proletarianization in English agriculture and in large-scale manufacturing, but his solution is to institute as far as possible a world of small property. He calls in England, for example, for the division of the common land to provide holdings for the landless labourers in agriculture, a solution he thought infinitely preferable to the system of poor relief which supported the English rural poor at this time (on this see also Hammond and Hammond 1911, pp. 116–48).

However, the very first generation of specifically socialist thinkers was emerging in England in this same period (the twenty years after 1815) and making use of ideas then dominant in political economy, especially in the work of David Ricardo. These 'Ricardian socialists' utilized the 'labour theory of value' first set out, as an economic theory, by Adam Smith, but purged of some of Smith's more glaring inconsistencies and brought to new levels of comprehensiveness and sophistication by Ricardo. The Ricardian socialists used the labour theory of value to argue for forms of economic and social organization which would ensure that the whole product of labour accrued to the labourers. They were particularly fond, as we shall see, of co-operative schemes of various sorts and of the idea of 'labour money'. The particular targets of their criticism were the merchants, middlemen and bankers who, through manipulation of credit and debt, 'stole' a part of the labourer's product. The aim of all their schemes was to cut out these middlemen exploiters. As well as influencing these first English socialists, however, the labour theory of value also profoundly influenced the first generation of French socialist thinkers, and especially Pierre Joseph Proudhon, who 'independently' devised a very similar 'labour exchange' scheme and actually tried to initiate it as a 'People's Bank'. Proudhon in turn, along with Sismondi, influenced several generations of Russian intellectuals (the primary foreign language of the nineteenth-century Russian intelligentsia was French), and he was thus one of the intellectual forerunners of Russian populism, with which we shall be concerned in the third section of this chapter.

The Ricardian socialists

Conventionally, four theorists are regarded as the 'Ricardian socialists' of 1820s and 1830s England. They are Thomas Hodgkin (1787–1869), John Gray (1799–1883), William Thompson (1775–1833) and John

Francis Bray (1809–97). They are called Ricardian because it was thought by some of their contemporaries that the political economy of David Ricardo was the single most powerful theoretical influence on their thinking, and this opinion has been echoed by a number of historians of English socialism (see, for example, Beer 1919). More recently, however, it has been cogently argued that the Ricardian socialists in fact owed far more to the labour theory of value as expounded by Adam Smith than they did to Ricardo (N. Thompson 1979). But whether this is so or not is of little importance here. It is only necessary for us to grasp the essentials of their thought, and that of Proudhon, and the influence it had on subsequent populist thought.

All the Ricardian socialists and indeed virtually all the socialists and radicals of post-1815 England began from the same premise, which was that 'labour is the source of all wealth'. As an economic doctrine this has been traced back to the seventeenth century, to such thinkers as William Petty, John Locke and John Bellers (Beer 1919, pp. 174, 190–2), but it undoubtedly enjoyed its widest popularity from the late eighteenth century with its systematization in Smith's *Wealth of Nations*. But we can find it not only in Smith and Ricardo, and in the Ricardian socialists, but in Sismondi, in Robert Owen (the founder of the co-operative movement), William Cobbett (an English radical of this same period) and a host of other minor thinkers.

The Ricardian socialists argued that if labour was the source of all wealth, if labour created all the useful products in the world, both in agriculture and manufacture, then it followed that labour should receive the full reward of its efforts. How was this to be assured? – very simply. If a particular commodity took a labourer three hours of labour to produce, then a fair and equal 'reward' for that product could be obtained if it were exchanged for another commodity which had also taken three hours to produce. Indeed were labourers allowed to exchange directly one with another, this is clearly what would happen. However, in the real world, argued the Ricardian socialists, such direct exchange did not occur. Rather, exchange had to occur through money. But money, or at least currency based on gold and silver, tended to oscillate in value, and as a result exchanges of products could often become unequal, so that the labourer did not gain the full reward of his labour. The need therefore was to have a form of money which was not subject to such fluctuations, and the obvious solution, particularly advocated by John Bray, was a form of 'labour money' issued interest free by a single central bank which would control all exchanges and ensure that equality of labour exchange occurred. Although the other Ricardian socialists did not carry their schemes for currency reform as far as Bray (whose scheme was reproduced 'independently' by Proudhon in France), they were all, to one extent or another, advocates of direct exchanges of the products of labour valued purely in labour terms. Indeed a number of such 'labour exchanges' mainly trading the products of small artisans and craftsmen were set up in London, Birmingham and a number of other English towns and cities in the early 1830s. Robert Owen was the pioneer of this type of currency reform, first outlining it in his *Report to the County of Lanark* (1820) (Beer 1919, pp. 174–81, E. P. Thompson 1963, pp. 869–71).

However, the Ricardian socialists did not believe that the instability of money was the only obstacle to the equal and fair exchange of labour. For in the England of the 1820s and 1830s, many small artisans and craftsmen did not work in independent enterprises, but were dependent in one way or another on large merchants and middlemen who supplied them with raw materials, often on credit, and sold their product when it was complete. Moreover, most agricultural labourers in England by this date were landless and worked for capitalist farmers or, if they did retain a small plot of land, had to pay rent to a landlord.

Both these circumstances were also severe impediments to a true or just reward to labour because they interposed between labourers – as producers and consumers – a host of middlemen who used their power to deduct a proportion of the product of labour for their own use. In the case of the merchant capitalists who controlled the small-scale artisans through the 'putting out' system, this deduction occurred purely and simply through fraud and theft – the manipulation of money and prices – i.e. the charging of usurious interest rates to producers and of arbitrarily inflated prices to consumers. Through these fraudulent practices, which in the eyes of the Ricardian socialists were little more than legalized theft, merchants appropriated a large part of the labourers' product and became rich while the labourers became poorer. The thing therefore was to eliminate these fraudulent middlemen, and all the Ricardian socialists were keen advocates of co-operative organizations among producers. These organizations would bring producers together to supply their own raw materials and to market their own produce directly, thus ensuring that the full product of their labour returned to the labourers.

In the case of the landlords and capitalist farmers, the matter was simpler. They were able to deduct a proportion of the labour product for their own profit and rent because they owned or controlled the land privately and in large holdings and estates. The aim therefore should be to nationalize the land, and then either to have all the labourers work the land co-operatively or to divide it into small independent holdings which could then have the same co-operative supply and marketing arrangements as the urban artisans.

We see then three strong themes in Ricardian socialism, and indeed in the co-operative ideas and schemes of Robert Owen. These are:

1 A strong distrust of money, and of all financial and credit transactions and transactors, who are seen as 'unproductive' and merely predatory on the labour of others. This analysis of the role of money, finance and credit (as so much legalized theft) leads on to schemes for currency reform, and for labour exchanges and cooperative supply and marketing (but not, generally, for collective production).

2 A particular understanding of the labour theory of value, which moves directly from the initial proposition that labour is the source of all wealth, to the implication that labourers or direct producers should receive the total product of labour, and that anything else is unjust.

3 A 'deduction' theory of profit and, in the agricultural sphere, of rent from land, which sees the power to make such deductions as springing from the ownership of means of production (land, money, raw materials), which ownership, however, has only come about through force and fraud.

However, whilst the Owenite and Ricardian socialists saw that part of the problem of inequality, of opulence and poverty, stemmed from the ownership of property, they tended to echo Sismondi's belief that the major problem to be solved was one of distribution and consumption. The main problem, as they saw it, was that a system of 'unequal exchanges' (stemming to be sure from abuse of power and property) prevented labour from receiving its full product. The essential problem therefore was to reform the system of distribution and consumption to make it fairer and more equal. Hence their obsession with labour exchanges and other co-operative ventures, and with currency reform.

As we shall see, distrust of money and credit and of all institutions and individuals concerned with them was to be a staple feature of nineteenth- and twentieth-century populist movements, as indeed were co-operative schemes designed to eliminate the 'middlemen' between producer and consumer. By the late nineteenth century such schemes were largely shorn of their original basis in a labour theory of value and, more importantly, were restricted almost entirely to the agricultural/peasant context. The reason for this of course was that with the spread of proletarianization in Europe the class of independent artisans and small manufacturers, who were the target of Ricardian socialist schemes, gradually disappeared, being totally marginalized or proletarianized and drawn much more into collective class struggles for trade union rights, etc. In short, Ricardian socialism and indeed the Owenite co-operative movement with which it was closely connected were ideologies of a declining class of independent artisans and 'small masters' struggling against domination by merchant capitalists, a domination which was to end, for many of them, in pauperization and enforced inclusion in the new propertyless proletariat working in large industrial enterprises. In England this process was essentially completed by the 1850s, and in fact the Chartist movement of the 1840s can be seen as the last radical political movement in England whose primary support lay in this declining social group (Gammage 1854).

But even in the 1820s and 1830s the process of proletarianization was proceeding apace, and both the Ricardian socialists and the co-operative movement found it hard to embrace this process (either theoretically or practically). Proletarianization necessarily posed problems for an alliance consisting, on the one hand, of a large number of small independent artisans trying desperately to maintain that independence against merchant capitalists and growing industrial competition and, on the other, a rapidly increasing group of workers, already proletarianized, who were less interested in the re-creation and protection of a world of small property, than in securing trade union and other collective rights against employers (see for example E. P. Thompson 1963, pp. 870–1, for the greater appeal of labour exchanges to artisans than to textile workers).

This problem is reflected theoretically in the writings of the Ricardian socialists themselves. William Thompson, for example, moved from arguing with Thomas Hodgkin for a world of independent small producers exchanging the products of their labour 'equally' at their value, to arguing that this could only be brought about by the creation of a general or 'universal' system of co-operation which would have included large enterprises owned collectively by their workers through joint stock companies (Beer 1919, pp. 218–28). Thus, whilst the predominant strain in the English socialism of the 1820s and 1830s (the word 'socialism' in fact originates from this period) can be regarded with hindsight as romantic or nostalgic, desiring to protect and re-create a world which was already going out of existence, the transitional nature of the period produced considerable shifts and ambiguities in the ideology. The Owenite and Ricardian socialists of this period are only partially the theoretical ancestors of populism; in part, too, they look forward to later trade union and industrial socialist movements.

But another reason for their theoretical ambiguity was that the

Ricardian socialists were overwhelmingly concerned with the situation of non-agricultural producers. They talk frequently of the need to nationalize land and to abolish rent on land, but they have little to say beyond that. And the reason for this of course was that, long before this period in England, an 'independent' peasantry on the European model had largely disappeared. English agricultural production was, even at this period, carried on predominantly by large-scale capitalist farmers using hired labour. Thus whilst small artisans and workshop proprietors were still abundant and one could hope to restore them to independence and prosperity through co-operative schemes, in agriculture there was little small property left to protect.

Small wonder then that as soon as we move outside England to the France of Pierre Joseph Proudhon, the ambiguities of the Ricardian socialists disappear. For, living in a country where the peasantry still formed the mass of the population and where industrialization was much less advanced, it was possible to sustain a critique of capitalism based on a consistent and much more agrarian populist alternative.

Proudhon

After a lengthy discussion of the Ricardian socialists, it is possible to deal with Proudhon much more briefly because, theoretically at least and against the background of the Ricardian socialists, he is totally unoriginal. He became famous through his polemicial tract *What is Property?* (1840) in which he averred that 'property is theft', a statement which made him forever one of the great *bêtes noires* of European conservatives. But, as he makes clear in the tract and as he was at pains to stress frequently in later writings, he was opposed only to forms of property or wealth which did not rest on direct possession. And in *What is Property?*, which significantly is concerned overwhelmingly with landed property, Proudhon is essentially concerned to deny the right of landlords to large-scale rental property, in favour of the rights of possession of the peasant farmer, whose claim to the land is valid in Proudhon's eyes because it is a claim based on use. The peasant labours on the land and his labour brings forth a product from which the landlord deducts rent, a deduction made possible only because the landlords or their ancestors stole the land through force and fraud. In subsequent writings Proudhon went on to generalize this argument against property not based on use and possession, relying on the same interpretation of the labour theory of value as the Ricardian socialists, and directing his attacks particularly against what he termed '*aubaine*', income and wealth derived from rent (of land, houses and moveable property), dividends (from monetary investments), interest (from loans) and 'return, gain or profit (none of which must be confused with wages or the legitimate price of labour)' (Proudhon 1840, p. 20). Predictably enough, this critique of wealth gained in monetary forms, led on, as we have already noted, to a scheme for a 'People's Bank' using a form of labour money and providing interest-free loans to small traders and artisans. Proudhon actually incorporated this bank in Paris in 1849, but in fact never managed to raise the minimum capital to allow it to function.

It will be seen then that Proudhon's economic theory and his schemes for reform of monetary and exchange relations echoed those of the Ricardian socialists almost exactly, something which Marx pointed out in his famous polemic against Proudhon (Marx 1847). Unlike the Ricardian socialists, however, Proudhon consistently held through his life to a conception of a reformed France made up of competing small producers in industry and agriculture (he believed firmly in the economic advantages of competition), but with this competition 'regulated' by 'mutualist associations' of producers, organized into a federation of communes, which would ensure by their internal arrangements that all exchanges between producers were based on equal quantities of labour. Marx's critique of Proudhon was many-sided, calling attention to the essentially derivative nature of Proudhon's schemes, and also criticizing Proudhon's use of Ricardo's labour theory of value. In Marx's view Proudhon, like the Ricardian socialists, had seriously misunderstood Ricardo (Marx 1847, pp. 43–102).

But for our purposes, we should note only one aspect of Marx's critique of Proudhon, expressed succinctly in his letter to Annenkov.

> He [Proudhon] does what all the good bourgeois do. They all tell you that in principle, that is, considered as abstract ideas, competition, monopoly etc. are the only basis of life but that in practice they leave much to be desired. They all want competition without the lethal effects of competition. They all want the impossible, namely the conditions of bourgeois existence without the necessary consequences of those conditions.   (Marx 1846, p. 15)

'They all want competition without the lethal effects of competition.' We shall have cause to return to this observation as we proceed with this examination of populist and neo-populist thought. For the moment, however, we must briefly consider one other major theme in these first socialist/populist critics of industrialization before going on to the Russian populism of the later nineteenth century.

Industrialization and the fragmentation of labour

'The understandings of the greater part of men', said Adam Smith, 'are necessarily formed by their ordinary employments. The man whose whole life is spent in performing a few simple operations has no occasion to exert his understanding. He generally becomes as stupid and ignorant as it is possible for a human creature to become' (Smith 1776, Book 5, Ch. 1, p. 782).

It is by the variety of its operations that our soul is unfolded. It is to procure citizens that a nation wishes to have men, not to procure machines fit for operations a little more complicated than those performed by fire or water. The division of labour has conferred a value on operations so simple, that children, from the tenderest age, are capable of executing them; and children, before having developed any of their faculties, before having experienced any enjoyment of life, are accordingly condemned to put a wheel in motion, to turn a spindle, to empty a bobbin. More lace, more pins, more threads, and cloth of cotton or silk, are the fruit of this great division of labour; but how dearly have we purchased them; if it is by this moral sacrifice of so many millions of human beings!   (Sismondi 1815, p. 65)

The sympathies are very different, but the observations are essentially the same, the damage done to human beings by a highly developed division of labour in factory and workshop. With the restriction of men, women and children to simple repetitive tasks comes, it is argued, a stunting of intellectual development, a narrowing and warping not only of the body but of the mind and spirit, a degradation and fragmentation of the whole personality. Such observations can be found in virtually every major social critic writing in England during the initial period of industrialization. Observations of this sort are found in Robert Owen, in all the Ricardian socialists, in William Cobbett as well as in such socially conservative critics of industrialism as Coleridge and Southey (E. P. Thompson 1963, pp. 781–915). In classical political economy, the damaging effect of the division of labour seems to have first been mooted by Adam Ferguson, but was taken up by Adam Smith, Sismondi and by a host of others, including Proudhon and Marx. Marx did not locate the problem in the division of labour as such, but in the specific forms of the division of labour introduced with capitalist control of manufacture. In short, this contrast – between the wealth and productivity of industry and the apparently growing intellectual, moral and physical impoverishment of the industrial labourer – assumes the status of a conventional wisdom of the period.

In some writers (of whom Cobbett and Proudhon were outstanding examples, along with the poet and artist, William Blake) this material and spiritual impoverishment of the industrial labourer was expressly contrasted with the much more desirable situation of both the artisan and the peasant. The peasant and artisan were seen to embody a 'wholeness' of personality and spirit which precisely reflected the much more integrated and varied nature of their productive activity. The peasant and artisan both undertook a whole process of production, not simply some minute fragment of it. Moreover, their rhythm of work was much more under their own control, and they could combine leisure with intense activity in a manner dictated by the task they had to perform. More recently it has even been suggested that the totally different organization of the work process among pre-industrial artisans and peasants, as compared with industrial proletarians, gave them a completely different sense of time (E. P. Thompson 1967).

The wholeness, the organic integration of productive activity among peasants and artisans in contrast to the wretched fragmented existence of the urban proletariat was often given as a reason for the contentment and stability of the peasantry, a line of thought which then led to conservative opposition to industrialization as a threat to established authority. But among the more radical writers whom we are considering here, it was only one more argument for the defence/reconstitution of a world of small-scale enterprise in which labour was not 'alienated' and fragmented, but multi-dimensional and purposive. As we shall see, the merits of the peasant way of life in contrast to that of the urban proletarian was a central theme in Russian populism, the central issue for Russian writers being how the peasantry could best be protected from the ravages of capitalism and industrialization with its apparently necessary concomitants of proletarianization and urbanization.

This concentration on protecting the peasant way of life reflects the major shift in populist thought as we move from early and mid-nineteenth-century England and France to mid- and late nineteenth-century Russia. For much more even than France in 1840 (when Proudhon wrote *What is Property?*) Russia in the 1850s, and indeed until the 1890s, was for all intents and purposes an entirely pre-industrial economy and society. Over 90 per cent of its population were peasants, and nearly all the rest were pre-industrial artisans and traders, the whole edifice being capped by a very narrow stratum of aristocrats and gentry from which was drawn the entire government bureaucracy and intelligentsia. And therefore, just as the transition from England to France produces in Proudhon a much more consistently populist (or what Marx called petty-bourgeois) alternative to capitalism to that advanced by the Ricardian socialists, so in the movement east from France to Russia, the 'peasant question' was even more central. In fact it was out of the application of populist/socialist ideas developed in the west to the particular agrarian conditions of Tsarist Russia (and of eastern Europe in general) that classical Russian populism and its neo-populist offspring were developed.

RUSSIAN POPULISM

The movement known to history as Russian populism had many and varied intellectual antecedents and many dimensions, including those which overlap with the history of the European socialist movement in general, and with the political struggle in Russia, from the 1820s onwards, to overthrow or reform the Tsarist state. However, we are only examining populist concerns with patterns and possibilities of economic development prior to 1869 (the period which has been identified by a major authority on the subject – Walicki 1969 – as the onset of 'classical' populism). Two individuals are of major importance here, Alexander Herzen and N. G. Chernyshevsky.

It was Herzen who, in the wake of the defeats suffered by western revolutionary and reformist movements in 1848, postulated what became for the next fifty years the central theme of Russian populism. This was that Russia might not have to pass through a process of capitalist industrialization in order to achieve socialism, but could leap directly from feudalism (for serfdom existed in Russia until 1861) and absolutism to socialism. Whilst it might appear, said Herzen, that Russia's comparative economic backwardness was a disadvantage, in fact it might prove a great advantage for Russian socialists because the almost total lack of capitalist penetration meant that both pre-capitalist values and pre-capitalist economic and social institutions were still untouched, especially among the peasantry. Herzen pointed particularly to the Russian village commune or *obshchina* which might provide a spring-board direct to socialism (Venturi 1966, pp. 20–1, 31–5). Since the *obshchina* remained the central obsession of populist economic and social theories from this time forward, it is necessary to explain a little about it. The *obshchina* was, prior to the abolition of serfdom in Russia, the unit responsible to the landlord for peasant rent payments and/or for the organization of peasant work on the lord's land. These responsibilities were exercised by a council of elders. This council was known as the *mir*, and it acted in the name of the *obshchina* for most purposes. This led to the two terms (*mir* and *obshchina*) being used interchangeably in much discussion, though strictly they are distinct.

The *mir* exercised the power of allocation and redivision of land tilled by peasant households for their own subsistence. These powers were supposed broadly to keep land holdings in accord with family needs. Within the larger village community of the *obshchina*, smaller family units (known as *dvor*) – sometimes nuclear, sometimes extended – cultivated the land in common. The heads of individual *dvor* made up the *mir*.

When Tsar Alexander II abolished serfdom in Russia in 1861 the *obshchinas* retained their collective obligation to ensure the payment of rent for land farmed by peasants which remained in the lord's possession. In addition they obtained collective legal title to the land which had traditionally been allocated to them in return for their members' *corvée* (unfree) labour.

What so excited Herzen and many other populist intellectuals in Tsarist Russia about the *obshchina* was its apparently collectivist or proto-socialist nature. It seemed to embody values of communal control over individual greed and competition (through the *mir*'s allocation and redivision powers), and to operate the socialist principle of land as a social utility – a source of general welfare – rather than as an exploitable commodity. From 1849 onwards, when Herzen first called attention to its socialist potential, the 'health' of the *obshchina* became a constant pre-occupation of Russian intellectuals. They were continually on the lookout for signs of capitalist penetration into the *obshchina*, signs that communal controls were breaking down, through the gradual ossification of redivision powers, or that commercial opportunities were individualizing household land use and control. In addition, however, there was constant debate about whether the *obshchina*, if left to itself, could become the kernel of socialism in Russia, or whether active state intervention would be required to modernize it whilst maintaining its basic socialist form.

N. G. Chernyshevsky was the first major proponent of the latter view, arguing that it was not enough to keep the ancient *obshchina* intact and the baleful influences of westernization and capitalism at bay. His solution was to set the *obshchina* within a nationwide system of agricultural and industrial co-operatives operating on the basis of labour-based exchange values but also acting to modernize and improve peasant agriculture (Venturi 1966, pp. 147–52, 160, 165–7). In the non-agricultural sector, Chernyshevsy's vision is also familiar: he advocates the protection of small-scale domestic industries against large-scale factory production, principally by their association in co-operatives. In the case of agriculture, however, Chernyshevsky was more ambiguous, tending to argue that mechanization of agriculture could occur, without damage to peasant welfare, within some reformed *obshchina* structure.

From the early 1860s to the 1880s, the specifically economic elements in Russian populist thinking remained largely unchanged, very much taking second place to political activity, notably anti-Tsarist terrorism and attempts at peasant mobilization (through going 'to the people') associated with the revolutionary 'Land and People' and 'People's Will' organizations. However, by the 1880s the process of industrialization in Russia was beginning to make real advances, and made even more rapid progress under the modernizing Tsarist regime of Count Witte (1892–1903). Chernyshevsky himself had noted that heavy state taxation on the peasantry, used in part to pay for state railway development and the beginnings of industrialization in Russia, threatened the integrity of the *obshchina*. This point was taken up by N. Flerovsky in his *The Situation of the Working Class in Russia* (1869), in which he also noted that the abuse of their taxation powers by certain leaders in the *obshchina* was providing the basis for individual capital accumulation by rich peasants, who were also beginning to move into trade and merchant roles (Venturi 1966, p. 491). He called these rich peasants *kulaks* and *miroeds*.

But these tendencies were just beginning in the 1860s and 1870s, and it was possible to argue then, as many populists did, that it might still be possible for Russia to avoid the pains and horrors of capitalist industrialization and pass directly to socialism. By the 1880s, however, the railway network was much more advanced, and large-scale factories were being established in St Petersburg, Moscow and elsewhere (Pushkarev 1963, pp. 223–9). Populist arguments therefore were adapted to reflect this trend, but only in a manner which was consistent with earlier formulations. Thus the major economic theorists of Russian populism in the 1880s and 1890s, V. P. Vorontsov and N. Danielson, both argued that though capitalist industrialization had commenced in Russia, it was incapable of progressing very far or of transforming the whole society and economy as it had done in the west, because it was trapped in a contradiction. Capitalist industrialization in Russia, argued these two thinkers, had occurred under the auspices of the state and under the strong control of the banks. Both these factors, along with the direct importation of the most advanced technology from the west, meant that plants were large scale and capital intensive. Thus they employed very few workers in comparison to the total population. Moreover, the tendency was for production to become ever more capital intensive, and for factories to concentrate on raising the amount of output per worker. Danielson in particular held that this tendency implied that, as the volume of output grew, the number of workers employed would proportionately decrease, and as a result the share of wages in total income would fall. In the meantime the very process of industrialization was destroying the indigenous handicraft activities of the peasants, and (continuing an earlier theme) the crushing taxation upon the peasantry necessary to pay for the railways and to provide capital for industrialization was ruining all but a small minority. Hence, and this was the centre of the argument of both Danielson and Vorontsov, the particular form of capitalist industrialization in Russia meant that it was bound to encounter an early and impassable blockage in the destruction of the domestic market (Walicki 1969, pp. 115–26, Danielson 1902, pp. 471–99). The Russian bourgeoisie would soon find that nobody, or at least an inadequate number of people, was capable of buying the products which their factories were producing. At the same time, precisely because Russia was a comparative latecomer in capitalist development, she could not industrialize through exporting to external markets, since they were already monopolized by the more advanced western nations. Vorontsov therefore was able to restate in a much more sophisticated form the old populist thesis of the advantage of a late start in capitalist development. This did not lie only in the continued existence of precapitalist but proto-socialist institutions such as the *obshchina*, but in the fact that, to state the matter somewhat paradoxically, late starting in capitalist industrialization made specifically *capitalist* industrialization actually impossible. For Danielson (but not for Vorontsov) the only way for Russia to industrialize on the basis of indigenous resources was to proceed immediately to a socialist revolution, a revolution which would protect the peasant and artisan from ruin by capitalist competition and would at the same time adopt a form of industrialization which would ensure a higher share for workers in the income generated. These two measures together would in turn ensure a healthy domestic market for Russian industry. Such a revolution was also necessary to arrest the processes of pauperization and growing differentiation within the peasantry (though neither Danielson nor Vorontsov thought the latter tendency had advanced very far) which threatened the *obshchina*.

Vorontsov, however, as a 'legal populist' differed from Danielson in believing that a socialist revolution was unnecessary and that a reforming Tsarist state could arrest the damaging economic tendencies inherent in the necessarily abortive attempt at capitalist development in Russia. He therefore advocated changes in state policy to include cheap credit for artisans and other small non-agricultural producers, lower taxes and rents for the peasantry, and free agricultural advice to the peasants to enable them to increase their productivity.

In fact Vorontsov's writings of the 1880s and 1890s outline what today would be regarded as a rural development programme for Russia, and

Mendel (1961, pp. 64–76) quite rightly points out the similarity of Vorontsov's ideas to those put forward by a number of modern writers on rural development. Later, however, Vorontsov was to place much less stress on the possibility of slowly modernizing peasant agriculture and artisan activity by these piecemeal methods, and was to endorse Danielson's view that industrialization was necessary for Russian development, but a form of industrialization which would be less destructive to the peasantry (Mendel 1961, pp. 57–64).

The Russian populists also demonstrate the anti-urbanism and the suspicion of money and credit which we have already seen in the case of the Owenite and Ricardian socialists and Proudhon. But in the Russian case the two trends are combined in interesting ways. In Danielson, for example (1902, pp. 446–50), Moscow and St Petersburg are seen as the twin exploiters of the peasantry. From the St Petersburg banks come the credit and 'paper money' which the merchants use to obtain the peasants' corn at low harvest prices. From St Petersburg too were issued the tax demands which crippled the peasantry and forced them to sell their grain. From Moscow, however, or from Moscow's factories came the manufactured commodities (especially textiles) which destroyed the peasants' handicrafts by undercutting them and stealing their market. This process rendered the peasants more dependent on money to buy their means of subsistence (which previously they had produced for themselves), and placed them even more firmly in the hands of the corn merchants and money lenders. These latter of course were working with St Petersburg credit and paper money. Very similar arguments are also found in Stepniak's writings, in which the hostility to credit and 'paper money' is very marked (Stepniak 1888, pp. 11–71)

These populist theorists of the 1880s and 1890s were fiercely opposed by other Russian radicals and particularly by more orthodox Marxists (Danielson considered himself a Marxist, and in fact produced the first Russian edition of Volume 1 of Marx's *Capital*). These argued that the populists were flying in the face of the facts. Capitalist industrialization was advancing rapidly, they argued, stoutly aided by the very state to which Vorontsov was appealing to alter the whole process. Moreover, such a development was historically necessary (as the essential prerequisite of the formation of a revolutionary industrial proletariat) and had to advance much further before socialism could be contemplated. Both the 'father of Russian Marxism', George Plekhanov, and Lenin himself in his *The Development of Capitalism in Russia* (1899) argued along these lines, though with important differences of emphasis. The latter work in particular was designed to refute Vorontsov's and Danielson's arguments concerning the necessary collapse of the internal market as a result of 'late' capitalist development, and argued that, on the contrary, the very ruin of peasant handicrafts and the growth of proletarianization extended the internal market.

Since we are concerned here with the Russian populists and not with their opponents, we cannot consider the details of this more orthodox Marxist critique of the populists. Instead we must turn to the final period of pre-revolutionary populist thought from the 1890s until 1917, when in fact there was very little substantial change. Though organized into their own revolutionary party (the Social Revolutionary Party or 'SRs', formed in 1901), the populists continued to seek a socialism based on the peasantry, and to offer as their essential vision a society of *obshchina* bound together in co-operatives and in federal or regional associations, assisted by state-backed programmes of agricultural education and improvement. The ever increasing pace of capitalist industrialization in Russia did not alter this essential vision, and in general the populist theorists continued to minimize the significance of this development both economically and politically. And there was some justification for doing this – after all, even in 1917 there were still only some 5 million industrial workers in Russia, out of a total population of 180 million.

One important change did come over rural Russia after 1905 in the agrarian reforms carried out by Count Stolypin.

> Stolypin's reforms of 1906 and 1910 made it possible for the peasants to sever their connections with the *obshchina* through a simple and advantageous procedure, permitting them to acquire personal ownership of the land and in the process often to swap the numerous strips of their former allotment for a single consolidated holding.
>
> (Gershenkron 1962, p. 134)

The particularly significant aspect of the Stolypin reforms was that, investing ownership of the land in the head of the cultivating household and not in the *obshchina*, nor even in the small family units or *dvor*, they effectively severed the claims of other *dvor* members on household land, and abolished the powers of land redivision and allocation of the *mir*. In addition tax obligations were transferred from the *mir* to the individual household heads. In theory, then, more enterprising peasants could buy the lands of their neighbours and ascend to the status of large-scale commercial farmers (and in fact the reforms were explicitly designed to encourage this). At the same time less successful peasant farmers, as well as younger sons and others cut out from the landed patrimony of the *dvor*, would have to join the ranks of the rapidly growing industrial proletariat or become labourers on the land of the more successful peasants.

The legal situation was very clear, as were the aims of the reform. Fierce debate ensued, right up to 1917, about the extent to which legally available opportunities were actually acted upon by the peasants. Generally speaking the SRs argued that, except in a few untypical and highly commercialized areas near towns and cities, most *obshchina* remained untouched by these changes, in the sense that there were few or no land purchases or sales, and that very few peasants became proletarianized either in the countryside or in urban industry. Conversely those areas which were affected by the reform were those which had been most commercialized in any case, and where the *mir* had in fact already lost many of its functions of land control long before it had lost them in law. Both Bolshevik and Menshevik theorists of the more orthodox Marxist party (the Russian Social Democrat Party formed in 1903) argued that on the contrary the Stolypin reforms marked an effective *coup de grâce* for the *obshchina*, and that any schemes for socialist construction based upon it were by now clearly utopian. They argued, moreover, that stratification of the peasantry was proceeding apace. On the one hand, there was a small stratum of rich peasants or *kulaks*, buying land, engaging in trade, hiring labour and using more advanced agricultural technology. On the other hand, there were a growing number of poor peasants, unable to subsist on the land they held, and having to migrate to cities or to work part time or full time for other peasants. Predictably enough, the SRs minimized this trend, saying that despite some small-scale movement towards increased inequality, the vast majority of Russian peasants in 1917 remained of a 'middle peasant' status. They worked their own land with their own family labour, produced mainly for their own subsistence (rather than for the market), and did not hire labour or use anything other than the very basic hand tools and simple ploughs which their forefathers had used. And whatever the legal situation might be, said the SRs, the vast majority of Russian peasants were still in reality set firmly within the community controls of the *obshchina*. They were not capitalists or even proto-capitalists.

These debates continued after the Revolution, though set in a somewhat different context, and argued with increasing theoretical and empirical sophistication. In fact, it is in the work of the Russian economist/agronomist, A. V. Chayanov, in the 1920s that the populist defence of the peasantry (continuing many of the themes first enunciated by the SRs after 1905) reaches its highest point of theoretical sophistication and marks the starting point of what I term 'neo-populism'.

'Neo-populism' is distinguished from populism in that it is not a purely anti-capitalist doctrine, but rather opposes all forms of large-scale industrialization including state socialism. It is also distinguished from populism in the far greater sophistication of its economic arguments, and its willingness to challenge industrialization strategies directly, on the basis of their own economic rationale. In Chayanov, for example, we encounter the first really coherent economic argument that small-scale peasant production may have certain advantages over large-scale capital-intensive production in agriculture, i.e. that reliance on the slow improvement of peasant agriculture may actually be more economically efficient, in certain circumstances, than large capitalist or state farms.

It is the absence of such an economic logic that characterizes the classical Russian populism of the nineteenth century. Because of the main concerns of this book, I have concentrated this brief account on thinkers like Chernyshevsky, Flerovsky, Vorontsov and Danielson, populists who had strong economic interests or thought of themselves as economists. But they were in fact not typical of the movement as a whole. The vast majority of the Russian intellectuals who took up the populist cause were much more interested in philosophy, theology, art and literature than they were in the economics of industry or of the peasant farm (this was particularly true up to the 1880s). As a result their critique of capitalism and indeed their allegiance to populism owed a lot more to moral and social considerations than to economics. Most populists opposed capitalism because of the horrors and suffering which they thought that it must bring to Russia, horrors which it had brought to the west already. Virtually all Russian intellectuals of every persuasion accepted Marx's terrible picture of the costs of 'primitive accumulation' in western Europe. They wished therefore to find some form of development for Russia which would avoid the social and human costs of proletarianization, and the ever worsening extremes of riches and poverty which they thought capitalism implied. They opposed capitalism for another reason as well, because they equated it with 'westernization', and thus with the increasing domination of Russia by western ideas and values. Populism thus had a very strong nationalist dimension from the very beginning, and we shall return to this dimension in Chapter 6.

For the moment, however, I simply wish to stress the strongly philosophical and moral nature of much of Russian populism, and to do so by quoting two typical populist thinkers whose writings had great influence on their contemporaries. The first of these thinkers and activists is P. L. Lavrov, whose *Historical Letters*, published in 1869, was a major influence on the populist movements of the 1870s. In Chapter 1, on 'The Cost of Progress', Lavrov stressed the terrible cost in suffering and exploitation involved in the creation of a cultivated minority in a generally poor society. 'Each thought, each idea', he said, 'has been bought with the blood, sufferings, or toil of millions,' and thus a civilized minority can only justify its existence if it works for good. 'I shall relieve myself of responsibility for the bloody cost of my own development if I utilize this same development to diminish evil in the present and in the future' (Lavrov, quoted in Edie et al. 1965, vol. 2, p. 138).

The second of these more typical populist thinkers is Mikhailovsky, who published his *What is Progress?* also in 1869. In it he answers the question of the title:

> Progress is the gradual approach to the integral individual, to the fullest possible and the most diversified division of labour among man's organs and the least possible division of labour among men. Everything that impedes this advance is immoral, unjust, pernicious and unreasonable. Everything that diminishes the heterogeneity of society and thereby increases the heterogeneity of its members is moral, just, reasonable and beneficial.
>
> (Mikhailovsky, quoted in Edie et al. 1965, vol. 2, p. 187).

Given this definition, it is but a short step to advocating the peasant *obshchina* as the basis for a progressive Russian society.

> The Russian peasant, like primitive man, lives a life which is poor but full; being economically self-sufficient he is, therefore, an independent 'all round' and 'total' man. He satisfies his needs by his own work, making use of all his capacities. He is a tiller and an artisan, a shepherd and an artist in one person. The peasant community is egalitarian, homogeneous, but its members have differentiated, many-sided individualities. The lack or weak development of complex co-operation enables them to preserve their independence and simple co-operation unites them in sympathy and understanding. This moral unity underlies the common ownership of land and the self-government of the Russian *mir*. (Walicki 1969, p. 53).

Eight years later (in 1877) Mikhailovsky was engaged in furious intellectual and political battles with orthodox Russian Marxists who argued that Russia had to pass through a process of capitalist industrialization if socialism was to be attained. In his article 'Karl Marx before the Tribunal of Mr Zhukovskii', Mikhailovsky drew out the logic of a strict application of Marxist doctrine to Russia, and the moral dilemma to which it led:

> All this 'maiming of women and children' we still have before us, and,

from the point of view of Marx's historical theory, we should not protest against them because it would mean acting to our own detriment; on the contrary, we should welcome them as the steep but necessary steps to the temple of happiness. It would be, indeed, very difficult to bear this inner contradiction, this conflict between theory and values which in many concrete situations would inevitably tear the soul of a Russian disciple of Marx. He must reduce himself to the role of an onlooker, who . . . writes in the annals of the two-edged process. He cannot, however, take an active part in this process. He is morally unable to push forward the wicked side of the process and, on the other, he believes that activity motivated by his moral feelings would only contribute to make the whole process longer and slower. His ideal, if he is really a disciple of Marx, consists among other things, in making property inseparable from labour, so that the land, tools and all the means of production belong to the workers. On the other hand, if he really shares Marx's historico-philosophical views, he should be pleased to see the producers being divorced from the means of production, he should treat this divorce as the first phase of the inevitable and, in the final result, beneficial process. He must, in a word, accept the overthrow of the principles inherent in his ideal. This collision between moral feeling and historical inevitability should be resolved, of course, in favour of the latter.

(Mikhailovsky, quoted in Walicki 1969, p. 146).

I have quoted Lavrov and Mikhailovsky at length, partly to provide a flavour of Russian populist thought but also because the issues raised in these passages recur in the dilemmas faced by present-day developing countries. In particular, as we shall see, the evocation of elite guilt as the basis of an ethic of service to the poor, seen here in Lavrov, is reproduced almost verbatim in Nyerere's writings. Both the romantic notions of peasant culture and personality and the cruel dilemma of entering consciously upon a process whose social and human costs are not unknown are still, as we shall see, live issues.

However, it would be a gross injustice to Russian populism if I were to suggest that it was primarily a philosophical and moral doctrine or a vision of Russian intellectuals (usually of noble birth). This strand remained strong, but after 1880 in particular it became mixed with a much more practical and economistic 'populism' whose history is still largely unwritten. For when the Russian Tsar Alexander II instituted a limited form of quasi-democratic regional government (the *zemstvos*) in 1864, a large number of Russian intellectuals, who had either never shared or had lost faith in the revolutionary beliefs of the 'Land and

People' organization, entered the *zemstvos* organizations as civil servants. This trend accelerated in the 1880s with the widespread repression of revolutionary populism following the assassination of Alexander II. As a result of this massive but relatively unstudied movement of intellectuals with populist sympathies into Tsarist regional government, there began a whole series of large-scale statistical surveys of peasant agriculture conducted under *zemstvos* auspices. The result of this silent but massive and conscientious work was that Russia, which in 1917 was still one of the poorest countries in Europe, possessed probably the best official statistics on peasant agriculture existing in the world at that time.

Consequently, from the 1880s onwards populist thought about the Russian peasantry, and populist debates with Marxists and other opponents about trends in the Russian countryside, became much more empirically informed and sophisticated (as is evident to anyone who reads Lenin's massive work on *The Development of Capitalism in Russia*). Moreover it was the experience of designing and carrying out such surveys and of analysing their results which informed Chayanov's theory of the peasant economy, a theory which is still a strong influence in present-day thinking about development.

3

Neo-populism

At the beginning of this century the radical group known as 'Neo-Populists' no longer maintained that capitalism was impossible in Russia; the growth of industry had gone too far for that. But they could shut it out of agriculture. Their immediate aim was socialization, not socialism: 'a free *obshchina* in a free State', which apparently meant the communal holding of land but with a prohibition on employing paid labour or on leasing land within the *mir*. Nor did they any longer look upon the *mir* as 'an offspring of natural law, a negation of evolution'. On the contrary they only saw in it 'a form of transition' towards one of two possible ends. It might either develop into a (village) guild of production, which they would have preferred; or, if it were true that the *mir* was by way of falling to pieces, then the end could only be the nationalization of the land and its leasing by the State to individual small peasants, who would be forbidden to employ paid labour. A comprehensive co-operative system would enable the peasants to keep out the capitalist. The Neo-Populists also believed in technical progress. They spoke of the 'increased purchasing power' which their programme would give the peasants, admitting thereby that large industry had come to stay, whereas their original forerunners wanted 'a general division of labour between human organs' to correspond to the least possible division of labour between individuals. The theoretical evolution had thus been considerable. (Mitrany 1951, p. 67).

Mitrany perhaps overdraws the distinction between the populism of the nineteenth century and the neo-populism of the early twentieth century. As we have seen, from Chernyshevsky onward there had always been a more progressive, improvement-oriented strand in populist thinking. But it is certainly true that, by the time Chayanov published his *Theory of Peasant Economy* in 1925, the 'theoretical evolution' begun after 1905 had gone even further. Most crucially, the Stolypin reforms and then the nationalization and peasant sub-division of landlord estates after the Bolshevik Revolution of October 1917 had partially undermined the *obshchina*. Russia had become increasingly a country of individual peasant holdings, and the concern of the Bolshevik regime in the period of the New Economic Policy (NEP, 1923–9) was how to improve the productivity of these holdings and, above all, to secure the food supply to the cities, which periodically from 1917 had been ravaged by famine. The essential problem facing the regime was that after nine years of war and civil war (1914–23) Russian industry had almost completely collapsed. This meant there were simply no consumer goods for which the peasant could exchange his grain. As a result peasants in general cut down the area of land which they sowed, and simply ate more of what they produced, thus starving the towns of grain. The aim of the New Economic Policy was to restore the grain supply by allowing a free market, while at the same time trying to expand the production of the consumer goods which the peasants wanted.

However, this policy was fiercely disputed inside the Communist Party of the Soviet Union (CPSU) – as the Bolsheviks had now become – and in particular a 'Left Opposition' led by Trotsky challenged the economic and political assumptions behind the policy. They argued that it would simply strengthen the hand of the rich peasants or *kulaks* who provided most of the marketed surplus of grain, and whose aim was to turn themselves into capitalist farmers. As such they would form a basis for counter-revolution against the still very fragile communist regime. The 'Left Opposition' also argued that if these dangers were to be avoided, peasant agriculture would have to be collectivized and then mechanized. At the same time priority should be given to producer rather than consumer goods, for this was the only way to ensure long-run industrial growth and to provide the crucial inputs (fertilizer, tractors) needed to modernize agriculture and ensure a rapidly rising food supply for the cities and the industrial workers. E. Preobrazhensky's *The New Economics* (1926) was the most complete theoretical statement of the Left Opposition's position.

In this situation Chayanov's book (1925) represented a defence of the peasantry and a (mainly implicit) rejection of the Left Opposition view. The central plank in this defence was a very sophisticated argument that peasants were not capitalists or even proto-capitalists because they operated on the basis of a completely different economic rationale.

Chayanov argued as follows. On a capitalist farm the aim of the farmer is to maximize output or, more exactly, to maximize profit, which means both maximizing output and minimizing the cost of that output. In order to do this the capitalist hires workers for a wage. He will continue to pay that wage so long as the workers continue to produce an output which is in excess of or at least equal to their wages (and his other costs) plus the average rate of profit. When they cease to do so he will sack some or all of them and cut production.

For the capitalist farmer, therefore, labour is a 'variable cost'. He can hire and fire labourers as he wishes in order to maximize or protect his profits. For the peasant, however, labour is not a variable cost; it is rather a fixed cost, for the labour of the peasant farm, in the overwhelming majority of cases, consists mainly of the peasant family (Millar 1970). In short, agriculture is not a business for the peasant; it is first and foremost a source of subsistence. Moreover, in any peasant society at any moment of time there will be a customary or socially accepted level of subsistence which is the minimum which the peasants will accept. Since they generally operate only with the simplest type of technology, the main resources which a peasant family have to achieve this level are of course their land and, above all, their labour or capacity to labour (their labour power).

Having outlined the situation of the typical peasant family farm in Russia in this way, Chayanov draws from it his central principle. This is that the peasant family will work for as long and as hard as is required to obtain their minimum subsistence but that, having once attained it, their labour input will start to drop sharply. The reason for this is that work on the land with only a primitive technology is a physically laborious and tiring business (Chayanov terms it 'drudgery', *tyagostnost truda*), and peasants will not want to continue doing it a moment longer than they have to. But conversely, they will continue doing it (up to the physical limits of human endurance) for as long as they have to, even if at the margin the return to their labour is actually negative.

Again, the best way to make clear what is meant here is to contrast the peasant's situation with that of the capitalist farmer. The capitalist will pay his labourers to work an extra hour or day on the farm only if the product of that hour or day (in terms of extra output) is at least equal to the extra wages he has to pay. Otherwise the extra labour he has paid for will be a loss-making proposition for him. But for the peasant the central concern is not the extra output which he obtains from working another hour, but the total output which gives him and his family their minimum subsistence. He and they will therefore continue working extra hours and days to achieve this minimum target even if the marginal product of their extra labour is negative. To put the matter in modern economic parlance, the peasant does not respond to diminishing marginal returns to labour in the way that the capitalist does.

What is true of labour is also true of land. For the capitalist the rent or purchase price which he is willing to pay for extra land must be related to its marginal product. If the extra land will not yield him an extra amount which is at least equal to the rent he has to pay for it, or which will enable him to recoup its purchase price in some minimum period of time, then he will lose (either in the short or medium term) by acquiring it. For the peasant, however, the only consideration is to have enough land to provide the minimum family subsistence given the (family) labour resources he has at his disposal. If his land resources fall short of this minimum then he must acquire more, whatever the cost in rent or purchase. Hence in a densely populated area of peasant farming, argued Chayanov, the rent of land will always be well in excess of its marginal product, as will be its sale price. And for precisely the same reason, peasants living in such areas who have land in excess of their minimum subsistence needs will always find it in their interests to rent out or sell that land rather than work it themselves.

If the basic assets of a peasant family are its land and labour power, then clearly their prosperity will depend crucially on the amount of both which they possess. If their land resources are inadequate they can to some extent make up for this by using their labour more, i.e. by working harder and cultivating their land more intensively. But in general both the amount of land which a peasant family holds and the intensity with which they work it will be determined by their labour resources. And since most peasants rely overwhelmingly on their own families for labour, Chayanov concluded that the size and intensity of use of peasant land holdings will be determined by the size and constitution of the peasant family. And the particularly important variable here is family constitution, for this determines the peasant 'labour/consumer balance'. When a peasant family is made up of few adults and a lot of small children, its 'labour/consumer balance' is adverse, i.e. it has a large number of dependents whose consumption needs are not balanced by their capacity to produce. The result is that the amount of drudgery required from the working adults in the family is likely to be large. When, however, the children grow up and can contribute much more to the production of the food and other essentials they consume, then the family labour/consumer balance becomes positive and the amount of drudgery per family member required to obtain the total family subsistence is likely to fall. Moreover, with a family of young healthy adults and growing children it may be possible to raise the total family subsistence absolutely (to raise the family income) with comparatively little extra drudgery per family member.

However, children grow up, marry and set up their own farms, so both the amount of labour input required for the subsistence of aging parents left on their own and their capacity to undertake drudgery fall, and with it the farm income. Meanwhile on the new farms created by the splitting of the family, the demographic cycle – and with it the cycle of peasant family prosperity – is starting again.

Chayanov implies and those who have been influenced by him (Shanin 1972, Lewin 1966) now state outright that the demographic determinants of peasant farm income suggest that Lenin's theory, taken over by the Left Opposition, of growing class differentiation among the peasantry was fundamentally mistaken. For the demographic cycle ensured that no peasant family could obtain a permanent position of superiority over others, though it might do so temporarily. This aspect of Chayanov's theory has been much disputed, both at the time and since (Harrison 1975), but that is not our central concern here.

The important point from our perspective is that Chayanov's theory provides the basis for an account of why under certain circumstances peasant farmers may be able to compete with large-scale capitalist enterprises and be successful. The fundamental element was the peasant's willingness to work long hours at very low rates of marginal remuneration in order to ensure his basis subsistence. Together with the need, in a situation of land scarcity, to substitute labour for land, i.e. to work the land more intensively, this factor implied that output per unit of land on the peasant farm was frequently higher than on the large mechanized farm. Thus though the output per labourer might be lower (since peasant farms were not capital intensive, i.e. did not add significantly to human labour with advanced machinery), none the less the marginal cost of peasant-produced crops, particularly those which required a lot of labour input and were difficult to mechanize, might be lower than on the capitalist farm. Perhaps the best way of thinking of this is to say that when the peasant sells his crops he does not value his own labour, and therefore does not deduct his 'wages' from the price he receives. His only concern is that the total sum of what he sells and what he eats should give him at least his basic desired subsistence. Hence for the peasant any unit price he gets for his crop which is

1   in excess of his (usually very small) money costs of production and
2   when multiplied by his marketed output gets him above his minimum subsistence target

is acceptable to him. Very frequently and particularly where either

1   pressure on land is severe and so minimum subsistence targets are lowered or
2   the crops involved are very labour intensive and difficult to

mechanize (so that the capitalist farmer finds it difficult to compete by substituting machinery for paid labour)

peasant crop prices may be below those which the capitalist farm has to charge. Of course this is only possible because, as Chayanov pointed out, the peasant is effectively 'exploiting' himself and his family severely, working very long hours for very low marginal rates of return. None the less it is possible and does occur.

Chayanov himself cited as examples crops like flax, hemp, sunflower and tobacco grown in 'overpopulated areas' of Russia

> in which the labour intensity and high gross income so attract peasant farms that they agree to very low payment per labour unit for these crops. As a result, such a low-price market situation is created for this produce that it becomes completely disadvantageous for the capitalist farm and disappears from its organizational plan. Fiber flax cultivation is particularly characteristic in this respect; before the war [the First World War] more than 90 per cent was sown on peasant fields. (Chayanov 1925, p. 239)

But this was not all. Because for peasants the economic rent of land (and its price) is not related to its marginal productivity, in areas of high population density peasants may be willing to pay rents and prices well in excess of those which are economic for the capitalist farmer. And conversely large landowners (such as there had been in Russia before 1917) who hold land in areas of high population density will often find that it pays them better to rent it to peasants than to retain it in their own hands for large-scale cultivation. Chayanov gave as an example of this phenomenon

> the sale of private landowners' holdings to peasants in Russia at the end of the nineteenth and start of the twentieth centuries. . . . Of the lands retained by private owners in 1861, in 1877 they owned 87 per cent; in 1887, 76 per cent; in 1897, 65 per cent; in 1905, 52 per cent; and in 1916, 41 per cent. Moreover, of this amount two-thirds was rented by peasants. (Chayanov 1925, p. 237)

None of this was entirely new. Over twenty years prior to Chayanov's work, the Austrian Marxist, Karl Kautsky (1899), had considered the 'failure' of the peasantry in central Europe to disappear at the rate which Marx had predicted and had explained the phenomenon in general terms very similar to Chayanov's. And as early as 1831, from the experience of colonial India, Richard Jones had questioned whether the Ricardian theory of rent was applicable to peasant agriculture (Stokes 1978, pp. 94–5). What is new in Chayanov is that these general ideas about the peculiarities of peasant economies as a whole are derived, in a fairly rigorous way, from a complete theory of the workings of the individual peasant or 'labour' farm (as Chayanov called it). And although Chayanov's theory of the peasant farm owed a lot, as he makes clear, to the *zemstvos* statisticians and analysts who had preceded him and who had provided the economic data which he used, he was the first to provide a complete theory to explain the particular or discrete observations which they had made. Once formulated, Chayanov's theory of the peasant farm was to exert a profound influence on all subsequent work on peasant agriculture, including present-day studies of the Third World (see, for example, Shanin 1971, Thorner 1971, Stirling 1965, P. Hill 1972, Wolf 1966).

For precisely the same reason − their foundation in a rigorous and sophisticated understanding of the peasant farm − Chayanov's ideas on the mode of capitalist penetration of peasant agriculture, and on the possible forms of socialist organization of that agriculture, were a lot more precise and insightful than anything which had gone before. Certainly they were much more exact than anything provided by the nineteenth-century Russian populists.

The starting point of Chayanov's analysis of capitalist penetration in peasant agriculture was the assertion that the Russian Marxists (and, by implication, Marx himself) had been wrong to look for this penetration purely or primarily in the growth of large-scale production. For Chayanov, the much more typical and important form of capitalist penetration of peasant agriculture was through the circulation process rather than through production directly. That is, the first stage of such penetration consists typically in peasants being drawn into a market mechanism, first simply as sellers of a part of their output and then, through the aegis of merchant and trading capital, as buyers of part of their inputs (often on credit).

The latest studies on the development of capitalism in agriculture indicate that bringing agriculture into the general capitalist system need by no means involve the creation of very large capitalistically organized production units based on hired labour. Repeating the stages in the development of industrial capitalism, agriculture comes out of a semi-natural existence and becomes subject to trading capitalism that sometimes in the form of very large-scale trading undertakings draws masses of scattered peasant farms into its sphere of influence and, having bound these small-scale commodity producers to the market, economically subordinates them to its influence. By developing oppressive credit institutions, it converts the organization of agricultural production almost into a special form of distributive office based on a 'sweatshop system'. (Chayanov 1925, p. 257)

Nor was this all. Once peasants are partially subordinated through control of their output and perhaps of part of their inputs (credit, fertilizer, etc.), it then becomes possible for merchant or trading capital to begin to interfere directly in the production process, often by laying down quality standards which the peasants have to meet in order to get their product marketed. With the quality standards, however, comes a whole package of controlled seed distribution, fertilizer applications, forms of crop rotation, etc.

A characteristic example of this sort of thing was the plantation sowings of sugar beet on peasant fields by contract with the sugar factories or contractors. After selling channels were acquired and its raw material base created, capitalism in the countryside began to penetrate into the production process itself. It split off from the peasant farm individual sectors, predominantly those in the primary processing of agricultural raw material and, in general, those connected with mechanical processes. (Chayanov 1925, p. 262)

Chayanov called this process the 'vertical concentration' of peasant agriculture, its integration into a total process of production, processing and distribution controlled by large capitalist organizations. He noted how far such processes had advanced all over Europe, but especially in the USA.

These ways convert the farmers into a labour force working with other people's means of production. They convert agriculture, despite the evident scattered and independent nature of the small commodity producers, into an economic system concentrated in a series of the largest undertakings and, through them, entering into the sphere controlled by the most advanced forms of finance capitalism. Compared with this vertical capitalist concentration, the transfer of farms from 10 to 100 or 500 hectares, with the corresponding transfer of a considerable number of farmers from a semi-proletarian to a clearly proletarian position, would be a small detail.

(Chayanov 1925, p. 262)

However, Chayanov noted, this particular form of capitalist penetration of agriculture, this vertical concentration of peasant production through market and financial controls, though begun in Russia before the Revolution, had not advanced very far. The majority of peasants were still untouched by it. Moreover, with the Revolution of 1917, there was now (1925) no possibility of it advancing any further. None the less, it did suggest what should be the strategy of 'state capitalism' in Russia (this was the official term used to describe the NEP) in order to modernize peasant agriculture. It should use co-operative forms to start or continue a process of *state-controlled* vertical concentration of the peasantry. He noted that there were precedents for such a policy elsewhere in Europe and especially in Denmark. But again, unlike so many of his populist predecessors, Chayanov is very precise about the role of the state co-operatives and even about the broad sequence or stages of their development. These stages (modelled, as he says, on the stages of capitalist penetration) are:

1 Formation of small co-operative groups of peasants to purchase certain inputs or 'means of production'.

2 Organization of the sale of produce on a co-operative basis. This is to go along with the formation of 'gigantic' co-operative unions, embracing hundreds of thousands of producers. This enables a 'primary accumulation of co-operative capital', which itself allows

3 The co-operative organization of primary processing, '(cooperatives in dairying, potato pulling, canning, flax scutching, and so on) in conjunction with its selling operations. It separates out the corresponding sectors from the peasant farm, industrializes the countryside, and thus takes over all commanding positions in the economy.' State assistance and state credit speeds up this process even compared with its capitalist equivalent and leads on to

4 Use of co-operatives to 'concentrate and organize agricultural production in new and higher forms'. The producer (i.e. the peasant), now firmly controlled, is 'obliged' to change 'his farm's organizational plan according to co-operative selling and processing policy, to improve his techniques, and to transfer to improved methods of tillage and livestock farming, insuring a fully standard product, subject to careful sorting, processing, packing and canning according to world market demand'. (Chayanov 1925, p. 268).

From then on, the state co-operatives penetrate ever further into the production process (he mentions the setting up of machine partnerships, stud farms, control and pedigree unions, joint working irrigation schemes), whilst at the same time the state is using profits from such enterprises and other resources to build up what is today termed 'infrastructure' in the countryside: 'electrification, technical installations of all kinds, systems of warehouses and public buildings, network of improved roads, and cooperative credit'. In short,

The elements of social capital and the social economy increase quantitatively so much that the whole system changes qualitatively. It is converted from one of peasant farms that have formed cooperatives for some sectors of their economy to one of a social cooperative economy, founded on socialized capital, that leaves in the private farms of its members the technical fulfilment of certain processes almost on the basis of a technical commission. Such is the origin of the new forms of agriculture based on the principle of vertical concentration. (Chayanov 1925, p. 269)

Of course the idea of moving gradually from a system of small-scale co-operatives to 'universal' co-operation and thus, by stealth as it were, to a totally socialized economy is an old one. It goes back, as we have seen, to Robert Owen and the Ricardian socialists, and recurs frequently in Russian populism, which is why it is proper to see Chayanov as a legitimate heir of this tradition. But unlike so many of his predecessors, Chayanov is able to infuse the general idea with a much more specific and detailed grasp of agriculture and economics, and thus make it sound much more like a policy statement and much less like a dream or vision. We should also stress the prescience of his analysis and his prescriptions. More recent analyses of India in the 1960s (Epstein 1962) and of Kenya in the 1970s (Cowen 1972, 1975) have demonstrated that these 'indirect' mechanisms of capitalist penetration of peasant agriculture, outlined by Chayanov, are still powerful ones, and can occur alongside, or even in place of, the expansion of large-scale estates and plantations. Moreover, his stages of co-operative development sound at times like a schematic description of what has happened, or at least been attempted, in India and sub-Saharan Africa since independence. However, in these areas co-operatives have encountered problems which Chayanov did not foresee, and thus their development has been halted or even reversed (see Thorner 1962 and Widstrand 1970).

But for all their sophistication and prescience, his ideas availed Chayanov and the USSR little. In 1929 Stalin put an end to the free market policies of the NEP, and commenced the crash collectivization of peasant agriculture. With this step, the official indulgence of neo-populist and non-collectivist approaches to peasant agriculture which had been displayed in the mid-1920s, as a result of the political and theoretical dominance of Nikolai Bukharin (see Cohen 1973 and Lewin 1968), came to an abrupt end. Chayanov lost his job as Director of the Moscow Institute of Agricultural Economy in 1930 and died, in somewhat mysterious circumstances, in 1939.

Whilst his ideas had little influence on agricultural policy in the

Soviet Union, they were influential, along with populist thought generally, in the politics and policies of the peasant parties which were extremely powerful in eastern and south-eastern Europe in the inter-war period. These parties and the 'Green International' which they attempted to found represent the high point of populist political influence before the Second World War, and we must therefore examine them briefly, before considering the demise and subsequent 'renaissance' of populist ideas in the west and in the Third World in the 1960s and 1970s.

THE PEASANT PARTIES OF EAST AND SOUTH-EAST EUROPE, 1918–45

The end of the First World War saw the collapse of the Austro–Hungarian Empire and of the Turkish (Ottoman) Empire in eastern Europe and the Balkans. New states were created out of this collapse (Yugoslavia, Romania, Czechoslovakia, Bulgaria), whilst at the same time the hold of the old landed ruling classes was weakened in Hungary and Poland. In the countries where large landed estates had belonged to representatives of the old Imperial powers, i.e. Austrians, Turks and Magyars, these estates were confiscated and divided up among the native peasants who had previously worked them. In some cases the land reforms involved were extremely radical. In Romania, for example, 15 million acres were taken from landlords at very low rates of compensation, and the areas covered by peasant holdings rose from 55 to 88 per cent of all arable land (Mitrany 1951, p. 108). In Bulgaria, where large estates were much rarer, the postwar reform took all land above 75 acres from all owner-cultivators, and all land above 25 acres from owners who did not cultivate. As a result by 1926, 80.6 per cent of all peasants owned their own holdings. In Hungary and Poland the reforms were less far reaching because pro-landlord regimes regained power very soon after 1918, but even here there was some expansion of the smallholding peasantry. In Poland, for example, between 1921 and 1937 some 6 million acres were divided up (Mitrany 1951, p. 109).

The net effect of these reforms was to strengthen the grip of a smallholding peasantry on the land, but in general, after a postwar fever of nationalistic revolution, most of the regimes in east and south-east Europe lost interest in agriculture and the peasants. Thus throughout the area, the large estates having been divided, little was done by governments to supply the peasants with the inputs, technical knowledge or marketing facilities which would have allowed them to increase production. As a result, in a pattern which was to become familiar in many parts of the Third World, the marketed output from the land fell (i.e. the peasants sold less and ate more of what they produced). In addition, nearly all the governments involved opted not for policies of agricultural development but for industrialization; and, just as in Russia, precedence was given to capital-intensive producer goods, heavily protected by state tariffs and duties, and often financed by foreign loans.

The dispossessed landed class had to seek refuge in civil and military positions, and in industry, trade and banking, which were pushed artificially beyond the means and needs of those countries. This could only be done with help from the State which made agriculture in general and peasants in particular pay for these costly undertakings. At a time when the peasants needed help to organize their new holdings their meagre cash resources were instead being drained by protective import duties and by taxes. Taxes being difficult to raise, the weight was thrown on indirect taxation; in the thirties this brought in 64 per cent in Bulgaria, in Yugoslavia 65.6 per cent and in Rumania 72.5 per cent of the total tax receipts. (Mitrany 1951, pp. 121–2)

Moreover, all this was occurring in countries which, certainly by western European standards, had a high population density on the land, and which did not have the alternative (open to the peasants of east and western Europe in the late nineteenth century) of massive migration to the United States. The net result was that, all over east and south-east Europe in the years after 1918, mass-based political parties sprang into being to try and protect the interests of the peasants who had been politically awakened by nationalist revolution and land reform but then 'betrayed'. The pronouncements and policies of all these parties were classically populist, or rather neo-populist.

Thus, for example, the Polish People's Party demanded in their programme of December 1933 that new industries, instead of being capital intensive and concentrated in urban areas, should be small scale, labour intensive and spread across the land (Mitrany 1951, p. 262). With little government support for such schemes, the peasant parties attempted to implement them themselves through co-operation. In Poland co-operative slaughtering and meat-canning factories were set up, and in Bulgaria there were co-operative fruit pulp and canning factories and co-operative export agencies. The most highly developed of all these schemes was probably that in Croatia (Yugoslavia), where the Croat Peasant Party set up two separate co-operative organizations the 'Gospodarska Sloga' (Economic Concord) and the 'Seljacka Sloga' (Peasant Concord). The former was broadly concerned with economic matters, the latter with cultural affairs. At the high point of its development the 'Gospodarska Sloga' had 5000 village branches and 230,000 members. It organized such activities as collective road building and irrigation construction and repair, rural electrification, food marketing and price regulation including fixing minimum crop prices. The 'Seljacka Sloga' organized schools, libraries and adult literacy programmes and even published textbooks. There were also very active co-operative movements in Czechoslovakia (where co-operative dairying was particularly important), in Romania and in Serbia (Mitrany 1930, pp. 373–414, and 1951, pp. 265–6).

As well as organizing co-operatively against policies of urban-based heavy industrialization, the peasant parties also carried on a consistent ideological battle for populist ideas, both against their own governments and among the peasantry. The themes which emerge in that ideology are predictable enough. Dr Macek, leader of the Croat Peasant Party, stated:

> Forty years ago we wanted to preserve and defend the *zadruga* [the Croatian version of the *obshchina*] as a unit of production and consumption. The crisis has taught us that this is no longer possible. But it is possible to turn the village into an economic unit. Every peasant holding produces partly for the needs of the peasant family and partly for the market. The part produced for the needs of the family and which never reaches the market should remain the business of the peasant family also in the future. As to the other part, production for the market, the trend of evolution leads towards co-operative production as a common concern of the village as a whole. Where there is lack of land new possibilities of earning a livelihood must be created within the village, ranging from home industries to village factories. But the peasant's connection with the land must not be severed, he must not be driven from the soil.
>
> (Mitrany 1951, pp. 135–6)

We have already noted the demand of the peasant parties for the de-concentration of industry, and its distribution through the countryside to provide employment both for the surplus rural population and for all peasants in the slack periods of agricultural work (Mitrany 1951, p. 124). Virgil Madgaaru, a leader of the Romanian Peasant Party, insisted, however, that unlike the old Populists his party was not against industry as such. But 'If there is not in Peasantism an inherent tendency against industrial development, it is on the other hand against protectionism, the breeder of hothouse industries, of trusts and cartels' (Mitrany 1951, p. 124).

Moreover, because the crash industrialization policies favoured by all the new states of east and south-east Europe tended to favour the major towns and cities, most of the peasant parties manifested a pronounced anti-urbanism. Professor Dragoljub Jovanovic, leader of the Serbian Agrarian Party, thought that

A village property owner is not identical with an urban capitalist nor is a village labourer identical with an urban proletarian. If in our present system the worker is oppressed by the capitalist, the village as a whole is oppressed and wronged by the town.

(Mitrany 1951, p. 156)

Thus the peasant parties of inter-war eastern Europe manifested all the essential features of neo-populism: a belief in the virtues of agrarian life and of small-scale enterprise and a conviction that large-scale industry in and of itself could never provide employment for the 100 million or so peasants in these countries, and must be supplemented by co-operative rural industrialization. However, unlike many populists, they also favoured rural improvement and development schemes of all types under co-operative auspices, to give the small producer the kind of collective strength (in processing, but above all in selling and buying) which he could never have alone. All this went along with a hostility to the town and city, to 'middlemen' – bankers, traders, etc. – but also to any form of state collectivization and industrialization of agricultural production. In so far as socialist parties either in east or western Europe were thought to favour this, then the peasant parties tended to be opposed to them as well (Mitrany 1951, pp. 162–3).

But what made the peasant parties of eastern Europe significant was not their ideologies or programmes but their political success. For they were the first populist parties in Europe to succeed in organizing hundreds of thousands of peasants in their co-operative and other activities. In Bulgaria and Czechoslovakia peasant parties actually held or shared government power for limited periods of time. In all the countries of eastern Europe, for as long as free elections were allowed (i.e. generally up to the time of the Depression, after which ultra-conservative or even fascist regimes generally took over), they were nearly everywhere an electoral force to be reckoned with. At the high point of their influence (the mid-1920s), they even tried to found a 'Green International', to rival the Socialist and Communist Internationals and to bring together all the peasant-based parties of east and western Europe (Mitrany 1951, p. 158).

Yet despite all this they were to leave little lasting trace on the politics of Europe or on the corpus of thought about development. With the end of the Second World War, and the installation of Communist regimes in all the countries of eastern Europe in which the peasant parties had been important, they ceased open political activity and their ideas found no public expression. In the west, despite or perhaps because of the cold war, little was known about them, and what had been known was forgotten by all but a handful of scholars. This loss of a tradition of thought and activity also extended in large part to the Russian neo-populists, finally suppressed after 1929, and to their nineteenth-century predecessors (most of whose work was and is untranslated and is difficult even to obtain in the west). Therefore when neo-populism emerged again in the Third World and in western development theory in the 1960s as a result of the 'failure', as it was seen, of postwar growth strategies, the thinkers and theorists involved tended to be unaware of the intellectual and political antecedents of their own ideas, as indeed were most of their audience. Hence theories and sentiments that any eastern European populist or neo-populist would have found familiar enough have often claimed an originality that even the most sympathetic historian must regard as spurious.

This is not to say that modern neo-populist theory is identical to its prewar predecessor. I shall argue in fact that it is distinguished by the partial, but not total, loss of the utopian and moral elements in the earlier neo-populism, and is more economistic and instrumental than its ancestor. That is, modern neo-populism places much greater emphasis on the economic necessity of its strategy, as the only 'practicable' alternative to a more conventional strategy which is deemed to have failed or to be incapable of success in Third World conditions. In a sense this too simply represents a continuation of an older process. For as we have seen, neo-populism in Europe was both more economically sophisticated and somewhat more instrumentalist than its populist predecessor. But whereas in the work of Chayanov there is only an economic/theoretical critique of large-scale production in agriculture (a position taken up by all the peasant parties between 1918 and 1939), in the neo-populism of the 1960s and 1970s that critique is extended to large-scale industrial production as well. This critique bases itself primarily upon the 'employment problem' in Third World countries, and the alleged inability of large-scale capital-intensive industry to solve that problem. As we have seen, from Chernyshevsky and Vorontsov onwards this was a sub-theme in the populist critique of industrialization and, if anything, it grew in importance after 1918. It seems to manifest itself in any situation in which peasants are both absolutely numerous and relatively dominant in an economy, and in which the rate of growth of industrial employment is low. But in postwar neo-populism that sub-theme has become the main strand of criticism, linking together such apparently diverse thinkers as the theorists of the ILO's World Employment Programme and of the World Bank's *Redistribution with Growth*,

Michael Lipton and E. F. Schumacher, all of whom are discussed in the following chapter.

But if the moral or philosophical dimensions of pre-1945 neo-populism are less pronounced or less apparent among modern-day theorists, they are none the less still present. The difference may be simply in language and expression. Whilst the nineteenth-century Russian populists spoke the language of philosophy and literature, modern neo-populism is expressed largely in the language of economics. This means that ethical or moral issues may not be openly displayed – 'on the surface' – but instead semi-hidden in apparent economic technicalities, in discussion of production functions and of income distribution. Despite this difference and the greater theoretical sophistication of modern neo-populism, its central moral concern remains unchanged, for it addresses the problem of inequality, of minority wealth amid mass poverty. And in the tradition of Sismondi, Owen, the Ricardian socialists and Proudhon, as well as of the populists and neo-populists of Russia and eastern Europe, this concern takes the form of an attention to the issue of a more just distribution of society's wealth and income. In modern neo-populism, just as in its predecessors, this issue is seen to be central in itself and not, as for the conventional economists and the Marxists, merely in its impact upon production and growth.

4

Neo-populism in modern development theory

This chapter examines the ideas of three individual neo-populist thinkers who have made important contributions to present-day theories about development in the Third World: President Julius Nyerere of Tanzania, Michael Lipton and E. F. Schumacher. It deals also with the ideas put forward by intellectuals connected with two major organizations engaged in promoting neo-populist development strategies in the Third World, the ILO and the World Bank. I am concerned here purely with the ideas expressed and their intellectual justifications, but in the following chapter I shall examine two cases often seen as embodying neo-populist ideas in action – Tanzania and China – as a basis for evaluating neo-populism as a practical development strategy.

One preliminary comment is necessary. In moving from the demise of the east European peasant parties after 1945 directly to the ideas of theorists and policy-makers active in the 1960s and 1970s, I have left unexplored many important by-ways in the history of populism in the Third World. In addition to Latin American populism, which is not touched upon in this book (see, however, Hennessy in Ionescu and Gellner 1969, for a preliminary account), it is clear that much British colonial policy both in Africa and India had a distinct populist slant at times, notably in attempts to maintain or shore up supposedly 'communal' forms of land tenure against the 'individualism' produced by agricultural commercialization (see, for example, Sorrenson 1967, Stokes 1978). The ideological roots of these attempts would be interesting to explore. Curious though it may seem now, an important minority of colonial officials from the late nineteenth century onwards thought of themselves as 'socialists', and conceived at least part of their task in that light. It is certainly possible that Owenite ideas, for example, may have penetrated, by devious routes, to some surprising parts of the British Empire.

In addition, to take a rather better known example, Mahatma Gandhi's ideas on rural development and village industries are known to have owed something to his reading of the Russian anarchist aristocrat and novelist, Leo Tolstoy, who himself was powerfully influenced by Russian populism. So here we have a direct link between the populism of eastern Europe and an important part of the Third World (Bandyopadhyaya 1969). And finally, to take just one more example at random, the first great Chinese nationalist, Sun Yat-Sen, put forward in 1912 an outline programme for Chinese development which was markedly populist in form. Sun Yat-Sen in turn was one of the strongest influences on the intellectual and political development of the young Mao-Tse Tung (Lenin 1912, Leng and Palmer 1961, Schram 1966).

Of course one should not suppose that the resonance of populist ideas among policy-makers represents the meanderings of intellectual influence winding its devious and hidden way through history. The ideas recur so frequently simply because a similarity of problem and context gives rise to a similarity of intellectual response. For leaders and policy-makers with the need or desire to change societies made up overwhelmingly of peasants and other small-scale producers, there will always be a certain attraction in a tradition of thought which suggests both that change and development is possible and that all that is conceived as best in existing institutions and practices may be maintained, and that this double objective can be fulfilled without creating massive extremes of wealth and poverty. The real situation determines the selection of ideas, and this is what is important, the selection of ideas. Ideas themselves are almost always in abundant supply.

This said, we may turn to our four examples of modern neo-populist thought, three individual and one collective/organizational. In reading this chapter, you should remember that all four of the examples are responding explicitly or implicitly to the supposed failure of a growth orthodoxy which dominated development planning in the Third World through the 1950s and early 1960s (see Mehmet 1978 and Todaro 1977). Some of the salient features of that orthodoxy were set out in Chapter 1, and you may wish to refer back to that briefly before proceeding further.

JULIUS NYERERE

President Nyerere's importance as a populist thinker derives from the fact that he is Executive President of a developing country (Tanzania) and thus, unlike all the other thinkers discussed below, he has had some opportunity to implement his ideas, to try and form them into a practical development strategy. In the following chapter I assess the success of the attempt. Here, the concern is simply to lay out the major elements in his thought.

Evocation of a traditionally socialist Africa

President Nyerere, and indeed many other nationalist leaders in Africa (see Friedland and Rosberg 1964), echo the nineteenth-century Russian populists in identifying a traditional form of socialism in Africa, partly corrupted by colonialism but still largely intact in the modern world and capable of providing a basis for future socialist development. Just as in Russian populism, this idea is used to deny the need to develop capitalism in Africa as a prelude to socialism. Thus:

European socialism was born of the Agrarian Revolution and the Industrial Revolution which followed it. The former created the 'landed' and the 'landless' classes in society; the latter produced the modern capitalist and the industrial proletariat.

These two revolutions planted the seeds of conflict within society, and not only was European socialism born of that conflict, but its apostles sanctified the conflict into a philosophy. Civil war was no longer looked upon as something evil, or unfortunate, but as good and necessary. As prayer is to Christianity or to Islam, so civil war (which they call 'class war') is to the European version of socialism – a means inseparable from the end. . . . The European socialist cannot think of socialism without its father – capitalism!

Brought up in tribal socialism, I must say I find this contradiction quite intolerable. It gives capitalism a philosophical status which capitalism neither claims nor deserves. For it virtually says 'without capitalism, and the conflict which capitalism creates within society, there can be no socialism!' This glorification of capitalism by the doctrinaire European socialists, I repeat, I find intolerable. African socialism, on the other hand, did not have the 'benefit' of the Agrarian Revolution or the Industrial Revolution. It did not start from the existence of conflicting 'classes' in society. Indeed I doubt if the equivalent of the word 'class' exists in any indigenous African language; for language describes the ideas of those who speak it, and the idea of 'class' or 'caste' was non-existent in African society.

The foundation, and the objective, of African socialism is the extended family. . . . '*Ujamaa*', then, or 'familyhood' describes our socialism. It is opposed to capitalism, which seeks to build a happy society on the basis of the exploitation of man by man; and it is equally opposed to doctrinaire socialism which seeks to build its happy society on a philosophy of inevitable conflict between man and man. We, in Africa, have no more need of being 'converted' to socialism than we have of being 'taught' democracy. Both are rooted in our own past – in the traditional society which produced us. Modern African socialism can draw from its traditional heritage the recognition of 'society' as an extension of the basic family unit. (Nyerere 1962)

In a later work President Nyerere makes more explicit and detailed his view of pre-colonial Africa as basically socialist. He argues that 'the traditional African family lived according to the basic principles of *ujamaa*. Its members did this unconsciously, and without any conception of what they were doing in political terms'; but none the less, in abiding by three cardinal principles, the members of the traditional African extended family were implicitly socialist in their life styles. These three principles were:

1 Mutual respect: 'Each member of the family recognized the place and the rights of the other members, and although the rights varied . . . there was a minimum below which no one could exist without disgrace to the whole family.'

2 Sharing of property and income: 'All the basic goods were held in common, and shared among all members of the unit. There was an acceptance that whatever one person had in the way of basic necessities, they all had; no one could go hungry while others hoarded food and no one could be denied shelter if others had space to spare.'

3 The obligation to work: 'The work done by different people was different but no one was exempt. Every member of the family, and every guest who shared in the right to eat and have shelter, took it for granted that he had to join in whatever work had to be done. Only by universal acceptance of this principle was the continuation of the other two made possible' (Nyerere 1967d).

However, whilst Nyerere looks back to the traditional extended family as a basis for modern African socialism, he idealizes it less than some of the more romantic Russian writers did the *obshchina*. In the same work, for example, as he sets out the three basically socialist principles of the traditional extended family, President Nyerere notes that there were two 'basic factors' also operating in the extended family which prevented its 'full flowering' as a socialist institution. These were:

1 The position of women: 'Although we try to hide the fact, it is true that the women in traditional society were regarded as having a place in the community which was not only different but was also to some extent inferior. It is impossible to deny that the women did, and still do, more than their fair share of the work in the fields and in the homes.'

2 General material poverty: 'Certainly there was an attractive degree

of economic equality, but it was equality at a low level. The equality is good, but the level can be raised' (Nyerere 1967d).

Elsewhere too Nyerere stresses various 'corruptions' of the *ujamaa* spirit by colonialism, especially the growth of economic individualism, and thus of growing class cleavages among Africans in town and countryside. It must be the aim of government policy in Tanzania both to eliminate these inequalities and to modernize agriculture so as to raise material standards of living. However, both these things can be done

> without affecting the validity and applicability of the three principles of mutual respect, sharing of joint production, and work by all. These principles were, and are, the foundation of human security, of real practical equality, and of peace between members of a society. They can also be a basis of economic development if modern knowledge and modern techniques are used.   (Nyerere 1967d)

Stress on the primacy of agricultural development and opposition to large-scale industrialization

Nyerere's stress on the central importance of agriculture in Tanzania's development has two strands of argument behind it, and it is difficult to tell which he considers most important. One strand is simply instrumental. He emphasizes that Tanzania is a country made up overwhelmingly of peasant people (more than 85 per cent), and that agriculture provides the bulk of the Gross Domestic Product (51 per cent in 1978) and of exports (90 per cent in 1977). Moreover, as one of the world's poorest countries, Tanzania simply has not got the capital to industrialize rapidly, and cannot obtain it from abroad on a sufficient scale without crippling debt and unacceptable dependency (Nyerere 1967a and 1967c).

However (and less instrumentally), the traditional extended family earned its livelihood in agriculture, and Nyerere's vision of Tanzania's *ujamaa* future is essentially an agricultural one. Tanzania is to be made up of a mass of self-reliant rural villages (*ujamaa* villages) producing and consuming co-operatively, and dependent on agriculture at least for the foreseeable future. Moreover, his hostility to industrialization as a primary goal in the present phase of Tanzania's development, a hostility which seems to have strengthened over time, has social and moral grounds as well as purely instrumental economic ones.

> From a social and economic point of view it is better if our industrial development is scattered throughout the United Republic. . . . We in Tanzania would infinitely prefer to see many small factories started in

different towns of our country rather than one big factory started in any one of them. Such a dispersal means that we are saved very many social problems of too rapid growth in any one city, and from the consequent break-up of all our traditional social organization; it promotes agriculture in the different regions of our country by providing local markets of wage earners, and a communication centre; and it spreads an understanding and familiarity with the possibilities and requirements of modern living and modern working.

(Nyerere 1965)

Moreover, in so far as industrialization is contemplated, it is not only to be spread throughout the country, but must also be labour intensive (Nyerere 1967c). However, unlike the ILO and World Bank (see the following section), Nyerere is not primarily concerned with the employment generation effects, since he conceives the bulk of employment being provided in agriculture, but with the need to match industrial technology to the limited skills available in Tanzania. The most advanced technology may be beyond the present technical capacity of Tanzanians (Nyerere 1967c).

Anti-urbanism

In the true populist tradition Nyerere sees towns and cities as exploitative of the peasantry and agriculture.

Our emphasis on money and industries has made us concentrate on urban development. . . . We spend most of our money in the urban areas and our industries are established in the towns. Yet the greater part of this money . . . comes from loans. . . . The largest proportion of the loans will be spent in . . . the urban areas, but the largest proportion of the repayment will be made through the efforts of the farmers. This fact should always be borne in mind, for there are various forms of exploitation. We must not forget that people who live in towns can possibly become the exploiters of those who live in the rural areas. (Nyerere 1967a)

At times too he seems to see the city (or at least very large cities) as potentially or actually dehumanizing, 'a great soul-less mass, in which people live in isolation while crowded among their fellow citizens' (Nyerere 1965), in contrast to the close, integrated communities of traditional rural Africa which are to be maintained but modernized in the form of *ujamaa* villages.

Co-operation and the middleman 'exploiter'

In his view of the middlemen and merchants as exploiters buying the peasant's produce cheap and selling it dear to the cities, Nyerere is again a very orthodox populist (as indeed were many other leaders of newly independent Africa). He also has the usual concomitant, a faith in co-operation as a mechanism for eliminating this exploitation.

> There is . . . another institution in rural life which has brought a very great change to many of our peasants and which does stem from the socialist principles of avoiding the exploitation of man by man. A large part of our farm produce is now marketed by co-operative societies which are owned and governed by the farmers themselves, working together for their own benefit. Many criticisms have been made of our co-operative societies; much practical improvement is necessary if they are really to serve the farmers and not to replace the exploitation of man by man by the exploitation of inefficiency and bureaucratic dishonesty. Yet there is no doubt that marketing by farmers, without the intervention of middlemen who are endeavouring to pay as little as possible to the farmer and receive as much as possible from the consumer, can be to the benefit of both the farmers and the rest of the community. In criticising the workings of existing co-operative societies, we must not make the mistake of blaming the principles of co-operation. (Nyerere 1967d)

Money and education

There are also traces in Nyerere's thought of the old populist distrust of money, though in his case it does not take the form of demands for labour money or direct and equal exchange between producers. Rather, he insists (as did Owen and and the Ricardian socialists) that wealth and development lie not in the acquisition of money *per se*, but in the production of useful products through labour or, as he says, 'hard work' and 'intelligence' (Nyerere 1967a). He also distrusts the moneylender and financier; though for Nyerere this is transferred to the international sphere, the reason for wariness is shared with the Ricardian socialists – loss of independence through debt (Nyerere 1967a).

In his major work on education (Nyerere 1967b), Nyerere echoes almost exactly Lavrov's view that the only possible justification for endowing a minority with higher education in a poor country (in which many do not even have a primary education) is the public service which the educated can undertake.

'Justice' and 'fairness' in distribution

Finally, Nyerere is squarely in the populist tradition in his primary concern with distribution and with equality in distribution. In fact it is not too much to say that socialism, for Nyerere, *is* equality or at least 'fairness' in the distribution of society's wealth. The traditional African extended family was socialist or proto-socialist because it observed this principle, and the socialist Tanzania of the future must in turn observe it. All of Nyerere's writings are peppered with the concepts of 'fairness' and 'justice'. The farmer must receive a 'fair' price for his produce, the countryside must obtain a 'fair return' in services and administration for the taxes it pays, educated people in a poor and illiterate society must receive no more than is 'fair' or 'just' for them to receive. In all these cases neither 'fairness' nor 'justice' is defined, nor are any general criteria adduced by which a given distribution of goods or services may be judged 'fair' or 'unfair'. It seems to be supposed that the meaning of these concepts is self-evident to any sensible person and that, almost invariably, they imply greater rather than lesser equality. Here too is a moralistic language and mode of argument that an Owenite or Ricardian socialist would have found entirely congenial:

> what have we . . . done, so far, as regards the distribution of incomes in Tanzania? And what are our plans for the distribution of the wealth we create – how do we propose to divide it fairly?
>
> First, ever since independence we have been gradually making our taxation more progressive. . . .
>
> Second, we have put a stop to any future large-scale exploitation of our workers and peasants through the private ownership of the means of production and exchange.
>
> In February we . . . restricted opportunities for exploitation of this type by nationalizing the banks, the insurance business, a number of large firms involved in the food industry, etc. . . .
>
> Thirdly, we have put a stop to wage and salary increases at the top level and have even . . . succeeded in cutting their incomes. . . . But the number of people involved at this level is very small indeed. . . . The real problem in Tanzania is not redistribution between the rich and the poor, but a fair distribution of wealth and of contribution to national expenses, between the very poor and the poor, between the man who can barely feed himself and the man who can barely clothe himself. (Nyerere 1967e)

He then mentions wage increases for urban workers and the setting up of peasant co-operatives 'to avoid the exploitation of peasants by middle-men' as examples of measures which have been taken to help the poor.

This does not mean that Nyerere is unconcerned with production. Indeed in the speech from which the above quotation is drawn, he explicitly makes the point that even if Tanzania's total wealth (in 1967) was absolutely equally divided, 'each person would receive goods to the total value of Shs. 525/–'. Hence 'our major preoccupation must be to increase our wealth, and the amount of time and energy we spend on squabbling over what we now have should be very limited indeed' (Nyerere 1967e).

But none the less, for Nyerere, no method of increasing wealth which would lead to increased inequality (even temporarily) is acceptable. The aim must be to maintain or even increase equality of distribution as economic development takes place, and it is significant that his discussion of nationalization and of peasant co-operatives occurs in the context of distribution, not of production. Reduction of inequality between individuals, between regions and between town and country, a hardworking but spartan public service, decentralized to be nearer the people, serving a mass of small-scale, co-operatively organized, rural villages – this is Nyerere's vision of a socialist Tanzania. It would certainly have found favour with the Ricardian socialists, with Proudhon and with many of the populist and neo-populist thinkers of eastern Europe. We shall see, in the next chapter, how it has worked out in practice.

THE ILO'S 'WORLD EMPLOYMENT PROGRAMME'

The World Employment Programme of the International Labour Office (ILO) was launched in 1969, in response to what was seen as the major failure of the first United Nations Development Decade (1960–70). It was a response to the continuing, and perhaps even worsening, presence of absolute and relative poverty in developing countries despite the reasonably good growth performance of many Third World countries over the decade. ILO figures for 1972, for example, estimated that there were 706 million people who were 'destitute' in Asia, Africa and Latin America in that year, and 1210 million who were 'seriously poor' (ILO 1976b, p. 22). These people were reckoned to represent 39 per cent and 67 per cent respectively of the total population of the Third World. Knowledge of and concern about this problem was not, of course, restricted to the ILO, but the original contribution of the latter was to interpret the problem of 'poverty' in an interesting and original way. Put simply, the ILO saw the problem of poverty as essentially an employment problem. One reason for this was in fact the large amount of open unemployment in the Third World (the ILO estimated there to be some 47 million people in this category in 1975). More importantly, poverty was essentially an employment problem because the bulk of poor people in the Third World could not find uses for their labour which were significant enough or remunerative enough to provide them with a minimum standard of living. This latter problem, the problem of the 'working poor' as the ILO termed it, could also be subdivided.

In the first place there were those people (the ILO estimated there to be some 281 million of them in 1975) who were 'underemployed', i.e. they wanted to work more hours in the day or week, but could not find the means to do so. Since their remuneration for the time that they did work was low, underemployment kept them in poverty. But the largest category of the poor (some 700 million people in the world, using the ILO's estimates) were people who worked long hours of hard and back-breaking toil (the ILO frequently uses the Chayanovian term 'drudgery'), but who received such a small return for each hour of labour that despite their hard work they remained in poverty. The bulk of these people were peasant farmers on small or infertile holdings and landless agricultural labourers. The problem here was to raise the return for work for these people, to make their employment more productive and remunerative. For the ILO this was still essentially an employment problem but the need was to provide not just more but better work (ILO 1976a, pp. 15–23).

The net result of this analysis was that the ILO came to see the task of the second UN Development Decade as being to devise 'employment-oriented' development strategies for the Third World, and to this end it has made a number of 'country case studies' (of particular developing countries) with the aim of designing such strategies. As of 1981 the programme has encompassed major studies in Colombia and the Dominican Republic in Latin America, Kenya and the Sudan in Africa, Iran in the Middle East, and Sri Lanka (Ceylon) and the Philippines in Asia. The aim of this next section is to summarize the main findings of these studies and the broad strategy which emerges from them (ILO 1970, 1971, 1972, 1973, 1974, 1975, 1976). There are of course significant differences of emphasis between the various reports from which a general account must abstract, differences mainly produced by the varying situations in the countries involved, and the reader is referred to the individual reports for a fuller account.

The ILO strategy

First, the ILO takes its main aim – the generation of an 'employment-oriented' development strategy – very seriously. Even its first report, on Colombia, makes it clear that the full logic of the strategy must be followed through: the generation of more and more productive employment must be the primary objective in development policy, to which all others, including growth, must be subordinated. It recognizes that it would be self-defeating in the long run to concentrate purely on employment generation at the expense of growth since the resources used to raise incomes would dry up. So it does give great attention to policies which it believes will aid both growth *and* employment generation. None the less in the short term, where there is a choice between growth maximization and employment maximization, the ILO is unambiguous in opting for the latter, and in this respect at least its approach marks a significant break with growth orthodoxy.

Primacy of agriculture

Beginning from the undisputed evidence that the bulk of the world's poorest people are peasant farmers or landless rural labourers, all the ILO reports recommend that future development policy must give priority to agriculture and rural development. More concretely, it analyses the problems of peasant agriculture in essentially Chayanovian terms. The poorest peasants in the world, it suggests, are mainly using family labour and very simple technologies to produce for their own subsistence, plus a small surplus which they sell for cash. Either due to lack of land (parts of Colombia and Kenya, the Philippines, Sri Lanka) or due to lack of sufficient labour (the traditional sector in Sudan and in Iran), all this 'drudgery' still only produces sub-subsistence incomes. The first aim therefore must be to provide all, or as many as possible, of the peasants with sufficient land. The ILO recommends quite radical land reforms in Colombia, Sri Lanka and the Philippines, and extensions of existing reforms in Kenya and Iran. However, although land reform may increase employment by allowing peasants and the labourers they employ to invest more of their labour time in the extra land, it is unlikely to raise incomes significantly; peasants typically do not have either the technology or the capital to work the land intensively enough to raise output and incomes significantly. Generally, therefore, the ILO reports recommend improving the access of peasant farmers to credit (but not artificially cheap credit – see p. 76) and to new types of agricultural technology. However, consistent with the overall objective (increasing remunerative employment), the ILO favours technologies which are labour enhancing rather than labour displacing, i.e. forms of modernization of peasant agriculture which allow the same number of people to work the land but to increase the productivity both of their land and labour. Hence, extensions or improvement of simple irrigation systems, new seeds and plant varieties, more and better fertilizer applications, improved hoes, wheelbarrows and simple spraying equipment are the kinds of innovations which find favour with the ILO, unlike large tractors, mechanized harvesting or threshing equipment and highly mechanized irrigation or storage systems.

All this does not mean, however, that the ILO reports are uniformly hostile to large-scale agricultural production or to labour-displacing mechanization. In their report on the Sudan, for example, the ILO notes that the large-scale mechanized farming of sorghum and sesame in Kassala Province, southern Kordofan and the Upper Nile has 'undeniable advantages':

> It uses sparsely settled or empty productive land which is difficult, or even impossible, to work without mechanization. It makes a valuable contribution to expanded food supplies for domestic consumption and export. It does not demand so much in the way of public services as irrigated or traditional farming. It mobilizes private investment, and compared with other modes of agriculture it progresses rapidly.
>
> (ILO 1976b, p. 47)

And even in Sri Lanka, where the pressure of population on land is far greater than in the Sudan, and where the ILO mission suggested a quite radical land reform, it remained neutral over whether the large rubber and tea plantations should be broken up. In Sri Lanka, as against other parts of the world, 'it is the bigger, not the smaller units that are higher yielding, more labour intensive and better managed'. It drew particular attention to the management problems which were likely to arise from breaking up large plantations into a multiplicity of smallholdings (ILO 1971, pp. 96–8).

In short, in its recommendations on agriculture, as on everything else, the ILO combines firmness about the general objective (maximizing productive employment) with a marked pragmatism about the means to be used. Whilst in general its overall objective leads to support for the expansion of peasant agriculture (through land reform) and its subsequent modernization, it is prepared to depart from this strategy where particular conditions seem to warrant it.

The same pragmatism is to be found in the ILO's attitude to peasant co-operation. Whilst in general it supports schemes for co-operative processing of agricultural produce and for marketing, it is generally opposed to collective or co-operative production. And even in the case of processing and marketing (and especially the latter) it stresses the need for efficient management and for competition between co-operatives and private traders for the peasant crop as a way of maintaining efficiency in marketing and the maximum possible price to the producer.

Labour-intensive industrialization

In its reports on Colombia, Kenya, Iran and the Philippines, the ILO draws attention to what is essentially the same problem. Rapidly growing population and land shortage in the rural areas has led to an ever more rapid process of urbanization. At the same time, industrial employment in the cities has risen only very slowly or not at all. As a result the bulk of rural–urban migrants, and the young people constantly being added to the urban labour force (by population growth in the cities as well as migration), have had to find employment elsewhere. This has usually been in public bureaucracies for those with high formal educational qualifications, or in a rapidly expanding sector of small-scale production and service activities (the urban 'informal sector') for those without such qualifications. Because, typically, output and demand in the informal sector have not expanded with the numbers of people entering it, earnings there are usually very low, certainly far lower than either in the public sector bureaucracies or in larger scale 'formal sector' industry. Hence, a large proportion of the poorest people in the urban areas of Colombia, Iran, Kenya and the Philippines are found in the informal sector.

Predictably the ILO tends to favour policies which can raise productivity in the informal sector and thus, perhaps, allow rising levels of remuneration to be combined with employment generation in that sector. Policies typically recommended are the removal of restrictive legislation or discrimination against informal sector enterprises in city centres, the increased provision of credit to employers in the sector, and various forms of assistance (including co-operative organization where appropriate) with both marketing and management. Where small-scale artisan activities are involved, the ILO tends to favour research and development to find non-labour-replacing technologies which can reduce 'drudgery' and raise output per worker.

But again all this does not mean that the ILO is hostile to large-scale, capital-intensive industry *per se*. Its attitude is rather that such industry is perfectly acceptable where it can be shown that it is highly efficient and is increasing output rapidly. For in this case, even if the direct employment benefits are few, the indirect benefits may be considerable. Capital-intensive industry can be taxed and the money used to fund employment elsewhere, or money may be saved on imports and/or obtained from increased industrial exports, which may also be used to provide employment in other sectors.

The ILO's argument against capital-intensive industrialization in most of the countries it has studied is simply that in the vast majority of cases none of the above conditions hold. The industries in question are in fact neither efficient nor increasing output rapidly. On the contrary, they are often producing products which cost more than they would if they were directly imported. Even though they have often raised productivity by becoming more and more capital intensive, i.e. providing each worker with more or better machinery with which to work, this has usually not gone along with output increases. All that has happened is that the same output, or only a slightly increased output, is produced with fewer workers (thus providing more profits to the owners of such enterprises but few benefits to the countries involved).

The reasons for this state of affairs are similar in at least four of the countries studied (Colombia, Kenya, Iran and the Philippines). In all these cases industries were begun as a way of substituting domestic production for imports of manufactured goods from advanced industrial economies. Import substitution was usually justified by arguments about increased economic independence, and by the conviction that industrialization was the only way to increased growth and better standards of living. However, in order to get either local capitalists or (more frequently) multinational firms to set up such factories, measures usually had to be taken to make such investments 'attractive'. Such policies made it 'artificially' cheap both to import capital equipment and to set up factories. One favourite method was to 'overvalue' the local currency for certain capital imports, i.e. for certain transactions the government subsidized its own currency so that it would 'buy' more in dollar or pound or deutschmark terms. Tax measures were also used to subsidize new industries in various ways.

In addition, especially where local markets were small, firms setting up factories in these countries usually asked for, and obtained, various amounts of 'protection' of their products. Imports of competing commodities were either banned altogether or strict quotas laid upon them, or a tariff or duty was applied to ensure that imports were more expensive than the locally produced product. Where the government itself was the agency setting up the new industries, such protection was of course applied automatically.

The net result of this effective monopoly, argues the ILO, is that such industries have no incentive to operate efficiently. In addition the 'artificially' cheap access to capital actually provides an extra incentive to adopt capital-intensive production methods. Moreover, where the factories involved are producing consumer durables rather than raw materials or 'producer goods' they often have to import raw materials, machinery or spare parts in order to maintain production. They may not make much, if any, contribution to reducing imports – rather they just substitute imports of machinery, fuel, spare parts, etc. for imports of consumer goods. Because they are so inefficient they cannot compete on export markets either. Thus there is the worst of all possible worlds: high costs (and prices), little or no employment, no reduction of imports and no contribution to exports.

The ILO's recommendations with respect to capital-intensive industry are therefore generally twofold. In the first place the missions usually recommend the abolition of all the exchange, tax and other mechanisms which make capital artificially cheap. They also recommend that interest rates for lending to any producer (whether a large industrialist, a small urban artisan or a peasant farmer) must reflect the shortage of capital which actually exists in most developing countries. 'Cheap' capital provides no incentive to efficiency, encourages the substitution of capital (in the form of machinery) for people, and tends to lead, especially in the case of peasants, to frequent defaulting on loans.

Second, the ILO missions tend to recommend the dismantling, more or less gradually depending on circumstances, of the protection afforded to local industries. The aim here is to enforce efficiency on local industry through admitting foreign competition, and at the same time (through that efficiency and through the lowering of input costs for all imported industrial inputs) to increase export earnings by industry. The report on the Philippines is particularly interesting in this regard (ILO 1974). In that report the ILO mission presented data on capital intensity and labour productivity in a large number of manufacturing industries in the Philippines employing from five to more than 200 workers. They found that the most efficient firms (defined in this case as those having the highest amount of value added per unit of capital invested) were of varying sizes from the smallest to the largest, but that even where they were large (200+ employees), they tended to be fairly labour intensive, i.e. they employed more workers per unit of capital than most large firms. Moreover, all the firms, large and small, which ranked highest in terms of efficiency tended to be among the most successful exporters. They were producing such commodities as embroidery, clothing, glass containers, rattan furniture, pharmaceutical products, cigars, shoes, wood furniture, veneer and plywood, cordage, rope and net. All these products were made in comparatively labour-intensive ways, and therefore exploited the Philippines' abundant supply of comparatively cheap labour. Low wages and high output made them efficient (in terms of value added per worker) and enabled them to compete in export markets.

Hence, concluded the report, if protection were ended, these and similarly organized industries would be likely to do well. Other less efficient, capital-intensive industries, most of which were large enterprises, would either alter their production techniques to take advantage of the same cheap labour (and thus would increase employment) or go out of business.

Thus, it is made clear in the Philippines report especially that the issue is not one of large versus small scale, but of efficiency. The most efficient scale of industrial production may vary from product to product and from time to time (ILO 1974, pp. 140–54). The important thing is to ensure that both large and small enterprises are efficient; and in most developing countries where labour is abundant and capital scarce, if the cost of capital is allowed to reflect its scarcity, the most efficient production methods will often be the more labour-intensive ones, and thus also the ones which generate most employment. A large scale of enterprise (in the sense of employing a large number of workers in one establishment) is not incompatible with relative labour intensity.

Industry and urbanization

In several of the countries studied by the ILO, modern industry was not merely large scale and capital intensive, it was also spatially concentrated in a few large cities, and especially in the capital city. This was markedly true in Iran and the Philippines, but was also a feature of development in Kenya and Colombia. In all these cases, the mission reports advocate some decentralization of industry in order to spread employment opportunities and to arrest or slow down the tendency for mass migration to a few already crowded urban centres, with all the social and economic problems (especially of housing and employment) which go with this. However, once again the arguments in favour of deconcentration are very modulated and pragmatic. In the case of industrial deconcentration in particular, the mission reports stress that the matter cannot be resolved by general formulae, and must be approached industry by industry and case by case. Thus in Colombia

It seems that the provision of infrastructure in the largest towns is more expensive than in smaller ones. Costs appear to rise rapidly as towns grow larger for such projects as sewerage and fresh water systems, and also for roads. . . . This is . . . partly due to the high cost of land . . . and partly to the general structure of costs, wages, etc. in the major towns.

However,

> On the other hand the further growth of significant sectors of modern manufacturing will probably have to be planned for a strictly limited number of major centres, as economies of scale, supporting services, transport problems, vertical integration and so on all point to the need to avoid too great a dispersion of efforts.

But,

> There is clearly a need in general to pay much more attention than in the past to the smaller urban centres. These will have to play an essential role in the provision both of alternative employment opportunities to agriculture, such as handicrafts, food-processing industries, and small-scale manufacturing, and of welfare services to the population in the surrounding rural areas.   (ILO 1970, pp. 99–100)

In the Philippines, which had the most spatially concentrated industrial structure of any of the countries examined, 'about 80 per cent of all employment in manufacturing is centred on Manila and its adjacent provinces' (ILO 1974, p. 154). Here the mission's recommendations are even more qualified and moderate. It first notes that the very form of import substitution industrialization tended to favour location in and around Manila:

> Import substitution was heavily dependent on imported materials and intermediate goods, as well as capital equipment. This helped to determine location near the principal port – Manila. Those manufacturing industries which relied on materials from Philippine natural resources, and which were therefore more dispersed regionally, were not favoured by the protection system hence their growth was relatively retarded. In addition financial and governmental institutions also show a heavy concentration in Manila to obtain the various tax and credit favours offered.

However, the mission hoped that if its policies for rural and agricultural development were successful, this

> would mean a more rapid development of new markets in the rural areas for relatively inexpensive wage goods that could be produced by local, small-scale labour intensive industries. Examples might include processed foods, clothing, sandals and shoes, building materials, school supplies, simple toys and even guitars. At the same time, inputs into agriculture (such as farm implements, pumps, tube wells and so on) could be produced efficiently.

Moreover,

> Footloose industries that depend more on imported inputs can also
> export, especially if they are labour intensive. And they need not
> locate near Manila. Export Processing Zones could be set up near
> other major . . . ports throughout the country. These would increase
> the demand for labour drawn from the rural surplus and reduce the
> tendency to migrate to Manila. Moreover, they would help to develop
> an industrial labour force in the provinces, from which could also
> come small and medium scale entrepreneurs for new industries that
> could spring up as a result of the income and spread effects from the
> Export Processing Zones.   (ILO 1974, p. 155)

But while these are possibilities, the mission to the Philippines, just like
that to Colombia, noted that there were real economic and social factors
which tended to reinforce concentration once it had begun:

> The presence of other industries, the concentration of financial and
> commercial services, the concentration also of the institutions of
> government and cultural life and of educational institutions, together
> with a well developed infrastructure, all combine to reinforce the
> desire on the part of private investors to remain concentrated in
> Manila.

The concentration of infrastructure was a particularly important factor
and tended, the mission noted, to dissuade even the most determinedly
decentralizing government from carrying this policy too far. The basic
problem was the 'lumpy' nature of infrastructural investment:

> when port facilities or a railhead are created, it seems most economical
> to design them in such a way that they will be sufficient to handle the
> traffic expected some years hence. This means that at any one time an
> urban centre will inevitably find itself with excess of capacity of some
> kinds of infrastructure but with shortages of others. Hence it will
> appear that there is a bargain to be had in expanding the supply of the
> scarce categories rather than in constructing a whole new set in a new
> urban complex.   (ILO 1974, p. 156)

But while recognizing these centralizing forces and the economic
rationality behind them, the mission still recommends that new urban
infrastructure should be developed away from Manila, and that a conscious policy of decentralizing industry should be pursued. They even
suggest an especially high industrial property tax in Manila to dis-
courage further investment there. However, this decentralization is not
to occur in a vacuum. A general development of small-scale agriculture

and rural enterprise will be encouraged and in fact should follow rather than precede the trend of market forces. As rising rural real incomes create an effective demand away from Manila, industrialists, large and small, will want to meet it and will move to rural areas or smaller towns. This stress on the totality of the strategy, of the likely inefficacy of some parts of an employment-oriented development strategy if other complementary parts are not carried through, is a hallmark not only of the report on the Philippines but of all the reports.

Employment, income distribution and production

We have already noted that for the ILO the poverty problem in developing countries is essentially an employment problem. But of course the reverse is also true: the 'employment problem' is also a poverty problem. The need therefore is not simply to create more work − the ILO missions make clear in report after report that they are not interested in 'make work' schemes − but to create or expand employment which can produce a sustained and considerable rise in real incomes for workers. Hence they are looking not merely for labour-intensive activities but for labour-intensive activities which can be made more productive and remunerative by 'appropriate' technological modernization and other policies. This is the common thread in ILO recommendations. It is to be the central aim in modernizing peasant agriculture, in support for urban artisan and service activities, in schemes for labour-intensive housing and construction projects and in labour-intensive 'rural works' schemes.

And it is in this context that the issue of the distribution of income and wealth is considered. Concentration of industries in particular urban centres, a fragmented labour market with a highly paid minority of skilled manual and white-collar jobs and a mass of poorly paid unskilled work in the formal and informal sectors, concentration of ownership (of industry, housing, urban real estate and, above all, land) − all these of course imply a very unequal distribution of income and wealth. They make for minority affluence, even opulence, amidst mass poverty. The ILO reports always attempt to produce data on the distribution of income and wealth when these are available, and a separate chapter or chapters (usually at the beginning of the reports) is devoted to the issues of poverty and inequality. Where the government of the country in question is actually or rhetorically committed to policies of socialism or social justice (as for example in Kenya or Sri Lanka), this governmental rhetoric is usually quoted to justify recommendations aimed at, for example, land reform or more effective taxation of income and property.

Thus in the best populist tradition, the ILO reports are highly preoccupied with inequality of income and wealth. However, their originality resides in the fact that their analysis does not stop there but, unlike most populist writing, attempts to make a complex and multi-faceted connection between the structure of consumption (i.e. of demand or distribution) and the structure of production. However, the logical structure of this argument is still identical to that presented by Sismondi in 1815 and quoted on pages 24–5 above. The only changes are those deriving from the rather different structure of production in the present-day Third World as compared with early nineteenth-century Britain.

We can best follow the argument by going back to earlier points about capital-intensive industry. We noted earlier that in developing countries capital (machinery) is used to replace people in industrial production. However, this often does not go along with a net increase in output. As a result the productivity of labour is increased, and also the profits of the employer, but there is little or no increase in employment. More than this, several of the ILO studies found that many modern capital-intensive industries did not use all their capacity. They had machines standing idle for a large amount of the time, since there was no need or incentive to run them to their capacity (for example by multi-shift working). Lots of spare capacity in turn increases costs, since the price of the machinery has to be spread across fewer products than would be the case if output was greater.

And this is the central point. For the ILO found that in Colombia, in Kenya, in Iran and in the Philippines, owners and managers of industrial plant explained lack of output increases and idle capacity by stating that local demand for their product was inadequate. High cost production for a small market in turn led to demands for protection, because that is the only way such industries could survive.

But why is demand inadequate? In part because some of the countries involved (e.g. the Dominican Republic or Kenya) are small, but mainly because a very unequal income distribution combined with mass poverty means that only a very small proportion of the population in these countries can actually afford to buy the sophisticated consumer goods produced in many of the more capital-intensive industries. A general rise in incomes, plus a more equal distribution of incomes, would spread purchasing power through the economy and increase demand – and presumably encourage more output and lower unit costs.

In addition, however, the ILO argues that as incomes rise from a very low base, the kinds of goods which tend to be demanded (better quality and processed food, new housing, simple clothing and footwear, furniture and hardware, etc.) are, in the late twentieth century, precisely those products which tend to be relatively labour intensive, even in industrial production. Conversely, the most capital-intensive consumer goods (e.g. electrical and electronic goods, highly processed food and drink, sophisticated leisure equipment, etc.) tend to be those goods which only those people with absolutely high levels of income are able to buy. This argument can be extended from consumer goods to producer goods. Primitive peasant agriculture and artisan activities can be improved enormously in productivity by the addition of relatively simple tools (e.g. better hoes and cutters, simple sprays, better hand tools and lathes), which not only do not displace labour in operation but are relatively labour intensive to produce. Conversely, sophisticated agricultural and industrial producer goods (tractors and automatic attachments, computer operated lathes, etc.), which tend to be labour displacing, are also capital intensive in production.

Thus, using a central neoclassical concept of the 'income elasticity of demand', the ILO analysis 'moves back' as it were from a call for a more equal distribution of income to the argument that such a distribution, in a society in which incomes are growing from a low base, will be congruent with a more labour-intensive structure of production. The former will tend to lead to the latter (if capital and labour markets are not 'distorted'), and the latter will in turn reinforce the former. Hence growth and a more equal distribution of income and wealth can proceed hand in hand. Hence, just like Sismondi, the ILO theorists believe that if none are rich but none deprived of an 'honest competence', this can lead not only to a more equal structure of distribution but to a more equal and employment-generating structure of production.

Conclusions

In the reports and analyses of the ILO, the neo-populist vision of development reaches what is in some ways its most advanced expression. In this work, a sophisticated understanding of peasant agriculture derived from Chayanov, and incorporating some of his arguments for the greater efficiency of small-scale over large-scale agriculture, is supplemented by a sophisticated critique of large-scale, capital-intensive industrialization as this has occurred (mainly as import substitution) in developing countries. This critique appears to take full cognizance of the more conventional arguments for such industrialization (based on labour productivity, economies of scale and unit costs) and shows that, in the particular circumstances of the countries it has examined, most of these arguments are vitiated by very distorted 'factor markets', especially for capital, and by the acute limitations on demand and output.

In addition, a modulated but sophisticated argument for industrial deconcentration is made, largely on the grounds that such factors as 'external economies' arising from agglomeration are very time and product specific, and may be outweighed by other factors. The argument for support and modernization of small-scale peasant agriculture, and for similar policies towards small-scale urban artisan and construction activities and services, is based not on the old populist grounds of the 'beauty' or 'completeness' of the peasant or artisan way of life, but on what appear as hard-edged economic analyses of the capacity of such enterprises for employment generation and increased output and income. The insistence that credit to small-scale enterprises should be made easier of access but on fully commercial terms reflects a tendency to support successful small enterprises, not merely to 'featherbed' employment for the poor.

Indeed, by the time we reach the ILO reports, virtually all the social and moral language of the old populists and neo-populists has gone. Official reports written for national governments of various ideological hues and for an international organization trying to balance many competing national demands and ideologies necessarily shun emotive or rhetorical language. Instead, the discourse of economics and what has been called 'unospeak' holds sway. There is no romanticization either of the peasant or the artisan; rather the life of the poor is firmly Chayanovian − a life of 'drudgery' to be relieved and improved, not mused upon. Cities and towns are not, as in classical populism, dens of iniquity, nor the fount of all exploitation and double-dealing; at worst 'agglomeration' is 'economically dysfunctional' and has 'social costs'.

But despite all these differences we should note that the essential vision of development remains unchanged. A world of small enterprise, with some (labour-intensive) large enterprises, a world of small towns and cities arranged in ordered hierarchy (rather than of metropolis and 'megalopolis'), a decentralized world, a more equal but competitive world and, at least for the foreseeable future, a predominantly agricultural world. For most of the ILO theorists this is less a utopian vision than a pragmatic recognition of realities − the need to adjust to a situation in which population growth, vastly increased capital intensity (compared with the nineteenth or even early twentieth century) and fearsomely rapid rural–urban migration have made repetition of the old crash industrialization strategies impossible as well as undesirable. We have already noted how the neo-populists of inter-war eastern Europe, sitting amidst 100 million peasants, relied increasingly on not dissimilar arguments from practicability. We shall consider the viability of these arguments in the following chapter. For the moment, however, we should simply note two more points before ending this discussion of the

ILO. First, the same strategy, somewhat generalized and built into a formal econometric model, can be found in the World Bank's *Redistribution with Growth* (Chenery et al. 1974). As well as indicating the increased popularity and acceptability of the ILO strategy among international agencies, this book is also a good source for an overview of the strategy, which has otherwise to be disentangled from the empirically richer but infinitely longer and more diverse ILO country reports.

Second, because of the major concerns of this book, I have not by any means discussed here all the dimensions of the reports. All of them have some extremely interesting sections on the reform of education systems in developing countries in line with their general strategy. This dimension is of central importance in the report on Ceylon (Sri Lanka). The reader is strongly recommended to read these sections as an invaluable source on education and educational reform in developing countries.

MICHAEL LIPTON AND E. F. SCHUMACHER

The absence or muting of the traditional moral and social dimensions in populist thought in the more recent work of the ILO and World Bank does not mean that it has disappeared altogether in modern development theory. Michael Lipton and E. F. Schumacher between them reproduce almost all the arguments (political, moral and economic) which have been the hallmark of populism since its beginnings. Michael Lipton's major work, *Why Poor People Stay Poor: Urban Bias in World Development* (Lipton 1977), has in fact been described as 'populism in the high tradition' (Byres 1979), whilst Schumacher's *Small is Beautiful* (1973) reintroduces as a central theme (and not merely as an ancillary argument) many of the traditional moral objections to industrialization associated with nineteenth-century populism.

Michael Lipton

Much of Lipton's critique of 'urban bias' in Third World development uses economic arguments which overlap markedly with those advanced by the ILO theorists. He too points to the inefficiency and inequity of concentrating on capital-intensive industrialization in a situation of capital shortage and labour abundance, and he too notes the distortions and waste produced by protection and subsidy of import-substitution industries. However, he makes two distinctive arguments. First, he adds to the economic arguments we have already examined an argument that, even with all these 'artificial' advantages, industry in the Third World is markedly less efficient than peasant agriculture in that its capital/output ratios are far lower. He argues that in a capital shortage situation peasant agriculture uses capital far more efficiently than industry (i.e. gets more output from each unit of capital). This argument is used, along with a number of others, to support a call for a massive increase in the amount of capital allocated to agriculture. Moreover, says Lipton, peasant agriculture comes out as more efficient in the use of capital, despite the fact that the price measures one must use to measure capital efficiency are usually distorted in most Third World countries. Policies designed to make industrial input costs low and output prices high, and (conversely) policies which keep agricultural input prices high and output prices low, are responsible for these distortions. Were these 'price twists', as Lipton calls them, to be removed, then agriculture would show up as even more efficient than industry.

Some of the arguments he uses to demonstrate price twisting in favour of industry are identical to those of the ILO analysis, i.e. exchange rate and other measures designed to make imported capital goods and raw materials for industry artificially cheap, and protectionist policies which allow high output prices to be charged. But in addition he argues that, almost universally, government policies of providing 'cheap food' to urban consumers (to keep wages down, in the interest both of urban workers and employers) mean that the official prices of most agricultural output in Third World countries are below what they would be in a free market situation, and thus overstate the capital/output ratio for agriculture. His argument for over-pricing of agricultural inputs is more partial and hesitant, but it rests on the charge that most subsidies on agricultural inputs (cheap or free fertilizer, cheap credit, subsidized sale or hire of agricultural machinery) benefit a minority of commercial farmers rather than the mass of poor peasants and that, in any case, input subsidies to industry are usually far greater than to agriculture as a whole, and thus the relative imbalance is maintained.

But as well as these additional economic arguments in favour of peasant agriculture and against industry (capital efficiency, price twists), Lipton's originality in current development theory derives from his analysis of the cause of anti-agriculture, pro-industry development policies in the Third World. One can say '*the* cause' because Lipton's theory is, at the most general level, mono-causal: all these policies derive from one source – *urban bias*.

For Lipton, urban bias is 'a state of mind' (Lipton 1977, pp. 63–6). It is a 'disposition' to take decisions about allocating resources in a way which cannot be justified either on the grounds of efficiency (since agriculture is more efficient than industry, at least in its use of capital) or on the grounds of equity (since income and welfare differences between rural and urban areas are far greater than could be justified by any argument from efficiency or productivity) (Lipton 1977, pp. 49–56). This 'dispositional bias' is itself explained in a variety of ways, by belief in economic theories of growth which, through favouring industry, also favour urban areas; by the greater political pressure which urban interest groups (both workers and employers) can exert on policy-makers; but above all, perhaps, by the simple fact that policy-makers (politicians of all ideological persuasions and bureaucrats) are themselves urban dwellers, and thus benefit directly from urban-biased policies. This does not mean that they are, in the majority of cases, consciously corrupt or dishonest in their decision-making (Lipton 1977, p. 63). It does mean, however, that they are likely to give great credence and weight to those theories which favour and justify (in terms of 'growth' or 'development') giving preference to the urban interest.

Lipton specifies his concept of urban bias very carefully, and he makes it clear that for him it represents an alternative explanatory principle to those more commonly adduced for pro-industry policies in the Third World. Thus, for example, such policies get adopted because they are pro-urban, not because they are pro-industrial.

> The daily contacts of, and pressures on, central decision-takers in poor countries come overwhelmingly from small groups of articulate, organized and powerful people in regular contact with senior officials and politicians; but it is wrong to describe such groups as 'industrial'. Though they are often influenced by the interests of industrial workers, firms or ideologists, such interests represent too few people in most poor countries to succeed frequently alone. Leaders of labour, and of public and private capital and management, in construction, railways and government service; prominent academics and other intellectuals; influential editors and radio producers – these, and not just leaders of industry, are the threateners, promisers, lobbyists, dinner companions, flatterers, financiers and friends to senior administrators and politicians in all countries, rich and poor. They are almost always 'urban' but seldom just 'industrial', in their interests, preferences, friends, places of residence, and above all perceptions. (pp. 61–2)

He also argues that 'urban-biased' policies discriminate against all rural people and not just agriculturalists, that they favour all towns and cities and not just capital cities, and above all that they polarize Third World countries into two distinct and opposed interest groups (he even uses the term classes). These are rural and urban classes, not the conventional classes of Marxist analysis. He returns to this point again and again. His book in fact begins: 'The most important class conflict in the poor countries of the world today is not between labour and capital. Nor is it between foreign and national interests. It is between the rural classes and the urban classes' (p. 13). Or again:

> The state is acting as an executive committee, but for managing the common affairs not of capitalists but of townspeople: not a bourgeois state but a burghers state. Communist development, like capitalist development draws the farm sector into the cash nexus in ways making it dependent on the city; communist states, like capitalist states, in the interests of primitive accumulation in early development, manipulate prices to increase the resource drain out of the villages.   (p. 117)

We have seen that anti-urbanism has been a major theme of populist thought since the early nineteenth century, and that the city as a centre of exploitation of all rural people (themselves conceived as a broadly uniform mass) was a central plank in the ideologies of most of the peasant parties of inter-war eastern Europe. But in Lipton this strand reaches a high point of development. For round the concept of urban bias he constructs not only his own version of the class struggle, but also a sophisticated defence of peasant agriculture and a critique of industrialization drawing on all the neo-populist economic theory which we have examined in earlier sections, and adding original economic arguments of his own.

Whilst here, as elsewhere, I am not primarily concerned with evaluating populist ideas, but simply with presenting them as a historical tradition, it is necessary to look at one or two of the problems in Lipton's analysis, as a prelude to what is said in the next chapter. In the first place, he does have considerable difficulty in maintaining his notion of a uniform urban and rural class in the face of empirical evidence. In the case of the 'urban class' he tends to rely heavily on the argument that a solidarity on the need for 'cheap food' keeps the urban alliance cemented in the face of other divisions. In the case of the 'rural class', however, he faces severe difficulties, principally because in other parts of his analysis he himself draws attention to what might seem to be fundamental divisions; for example, between larger scale commercial farmers and the bulk of poor peasants, in getting subsidized inputs, or between landlords and moneylenders and their poor tenants and debtors. In these cases he tends to adopt one of two stratagems. He either argues that, though there are rural privileged, they are not as privileged *vis-à-vis* other rural dwellers as are the urban privileged *vis-à-vis* other urban dwellers (or more importantly as are all urban dwellers *vis-à-vis* all rural dwellers) or he simply defines the rural privileged as 'rural urbanists' and the urban disprivileged as 'urban fringe villagers'. He argues that in the former case the rural rich benefit either because they have powerful urban connections or are themselves urban dwellers (e.g. absentee rural landlords), and that in the latter case one is dealing with:

> Village born students with poor prospects or unemployed migrants living on rural savings or remittances and likely to return to the village after a few years; and 'engulfed villagers' who, without great changes in their agriculture based environment and life-style, have been gradually surrounded by the sprawling city.   (p. 150)

These arguments do seem rather thin, and appear to involve large stretching of the categories 'rural' and 'urban' so as to maintain his urban and rural classes intact definitionally.

In addition, however, some of Lipton's economic arguments for urban bias seem to have rather questionable theoretical roots and very questionable empirical support. In the former case, his data on comparative capital/output ratios for agriculture and 'non-agriculture' depend on imputing monetary values to fixed capital in peasant agriculture (Lipton 1977, pp. 189–215). Many peasants construct irrigation ditches, fences, stores and cattle byres, with their own family labour, using raw material locally available. They do not pay for these facilities in the market, nor do they even hire labourers for the work. If the raw materials (such as wood) are also 'freely' available, there may actually be few or no cash costs in such 'capital formation'. Economists have therefore to find some way of imputing or giving a monetary value to these capital goods. The usual method is to try to work out what the peasant would have had to pay for the whole facility, or for the labour and raw materials if he had paid cash for them. Since in labour-abundant economies rural labour may be relatively cheap, and labour is the main input into capital formation in peasant agriculture, this tends to lead to a low evaluation of fixed capital in peasant agriculture and hence to low capital/output ratios. This may be justified insofar as it reflects the relative abundance of labour in some − though not all − rural areas of the Third World. But some economists at least would argue that, for precisely this reason, the 'capital/output' ratios obtained can scarcely be compared with those for industry where the types of capital involved (plant and machinery or expensive infrastructure most or all of which must be purchased with − comparatively scarce − money) are very different. This argument does not deny that, in a static comparison based upon such evaluations, peasant agriculture may well come out as a more efficient capital user. But it questions whether such very different processes and objects can actually be counted as a single thing – 'capital' – with a single 'output' for the purpose of this comparison. Lipton considers a number of objections to his method of measuring comparative capital efficiency in agriculture and non-agriculture, but oddly he does not consider this obvious one.

There are also objections to Lipton's mode of procedure which rests on its static or short-run nature, i.e. its failure to take into account possible long-run benefits to growth and employment that may accrue from investments which at one moment look to be 'inefficient' and 'inequitable'. This argument refers specifically to investment in highly capital-intensive producer goods industries, and is generally known in development economics as the 'Dobb–Sen' thesis on choice of techniques. It will be explained in the next chapter. We should simply note that Lipton himself refers vaguely to a similar position which he identified with Hirschmann (Lipton 1977, pp. 213–14), but offers no theoretical critique of it, contenting himself with a description of what he believes to have been the baleful effects of such ideas in practice.

> Such defences . . . sheltered much wasteful equipment – made profitable to rich men by high levels of protection – in the name of 'import-substituting industrialization'. The inefficiency of installing machines to assemble motor vehicles in Latin America – machines that produce cars available on world markets for less than the landed cost of the imported inputs – is an extreme case, heavily supported by subsidized public services.   (p. 213)

But this is simply a restatement of the static comparison (in this case between domestically manufactured and imported cars) and begs the question about long-term, dynamic benefits. Of course much depends on how long the long term is, and how likely the future dynamic benefits are to materialize. It is clearly Lipton's view that the present palpable costs, in inefficiency and inequity, are not worth the 'vague' hopes of 'potential potentials' (p. 213).

At the empirical level, Lipton's thesis has been subjected to severe attack by Byres (1979) who claims that:

1   The evidence adduced by Lipton on income distribution in rural and urban areas of the Third World does not support his basic contention that intra-rural income distribution is less unequal than intra-urban income distribution.

2   The evidence on India (on which a lot of Lipton's argument and analysis is concentrated) does not support his view either that agriculture is more heavily taxed than industry, or even the

argument that it is heavily taxed at all. Moreover, Lipton's arguments on 'price twists' against agriculture are not supported by the Indian evidence on the inter-sectoral terms of trade between agriculture and industry. Work by Tharmarajakshi and Mitra (see Byres 1979) shows a consistent movement of both the net barter and the income terms of trade in favour of agriculture between the mid-1950s and 1973, with that movement actually accelerating through time.

3   Contrary to Lipton's view that remittances of money from urban to rural areas 'are not very large', there is a lot of evidence to suggest that in many Third World countries such remittances are considerable. Since Lipton himself admits that if 'large sums of money are remitted by urban migrants to their families in the villages [this] could counteract much of the damage done to the village by urbanization, and perhaps revive one's faith in its alleged power to reduce rural–urban inequalities', the evidence (cited by Byres 1979, pp. 218–20 and 223–32) showing large remittances in many parts of the Third World obviously constitutes a serious undermining of the urban bias thesis.

Lipton and industrialization   I have presented Lipton as an anti-industrialist, but in fact in the introduction to his book he goes out of his way to deny this:

> I do not believe that poor countries should 'stay agricultural' in order to develop, let alone instead of developing. The argument that neither the carrying capacity of the land, nor the market for farm products, is such as to permit the masses in poor countries to reach high levels of living without a major shift to non-farm activities seems conclusive.
>
> (p. 21)

In other words, Lipton recognizes the power of the central theoretical argument for industrialization (from the shifting structure of demand with rising income) which we examined in Chapter 1. What Lipton terms 'populism' is an absolute opposition to industrialization on the grounds that it is destructive of the total human reality found in simple rural life; and he equates this with the nineteenth-century English Romantic poets, and with Gandhi and Maine. In 'A note on pastoralism and populism' Lipton makes clear his rejection of such views as backward-looking and sacrificial of what he regards as the real 'rural interest', a 'prosperous, scientific, labour-intensive and egalitarian agriculture'. What then is his position? He states it at the close of his introduction: 'This book does not . . . say to those who work in and on poor countries: "Don't industrialize". Rather it says "A developed mass agriculture is normally needed before you can have widespread successful development in other sectors",' The 'most fundamental' reason for this is that

> In early development, with labour plentiful and the ability to save scarce, small farming is especially promising, because it is the part of the economy in which a given amount of scarce investible resources will be supported by the most human effort. Thus it is emphasis upon small farming that can most rapidly boost income per head to the levels at which the major sacrifices of consumption, required for heavy industrialization, can be undertaken without intolerable hardship and repression. (p. 23)

Byres simply disbelieves the sincerity of Lipton's protestations in favour of some long-run industrialization. He uses some of Lipton's worries about whether industrialization of the Third World will be possible, even in the long term, given finite world resources and growing ecological problems, as evidence that in fact Lipton supports an essentially agricultural future for the Third World (albeit at gradually improving productivity levels) more or less *ad infinitum* (Byres 1979, p. 239). However, we do not have to take sides on this matter. Neo-populist schemes have always had somewhat vague time horizons, since their main aim is to demonstrate the costs and shortcomings of industrialization in the 'present' (whether that be Russia in 1880, Romania in 1925 or India in 1975) and for the foreseeable future. What may or may not be possible in some distant future is, understandably enough, not the first focus of concern. In fact, it is doubtful whether any neo-populist thinker since Vorontsov and Danielson has openly opposed industrialization absolutely. All of them have called for different forms of industrialization (more decentralized, small scale and labour intensive) and/or have supported industrialization in the long term. In fact a limited coming to terms with industrialization in some form or another is one of the characteristics which distinguishes neo-populism from its populist predecessor.

This is precisely what makes Lipton's situation of himself within development theory so odd. For he has a whole chapter devoted to this task (under the title 'Ideologies of rural and urban development') in which, as we have seen, he explicitly distances himself from populism. But this distancing seems to rest, as Byres notes, on an almost complete ignorance of the neo-populist tradition, from Vorontsov and Danielson through Chayanov to the theorists of the east European peasant parties (Byres 1979, p. 237). Byres himself suggests why it is proper to call

Lipton a 'liberal populist', and since I do not feel that his justification of the application of this label to Lipton can be bettered, I shall end this section of the chapter by quoting it:

> Lipton is a populist inasmuch as urban bias embraces . . . recurring characteristics of classical populist ideology. These include a repeated implication that inequality is the greatest of all social evils . . . a theory of why inequality persists, and an agenda for eradication; an almost mystical faith in the mass of the people . . . not some of the people, but all of them, who are capable, under proper circumstances, of uniting against their urban oppressors and establishing an egalitarian utopia; a belief . . . that all evil lies in the city; a certainty that all farmers – the single rural class – are being mulcted, squeezed, exploited; an underlying assumption that there is an urban conspiracy against the countryside; an insistence that the small farmer is more efficient – more worthy, more wholesome – than the large, along with proposals to populate the countryside with as many small peasants as possible; a distaste for industry and a conviction that industrialization – and especially large-scale industry and heavy industry – is undesirable; an anti-capitalist stance; a determination to confront and reject Marxism, allied to a curious fascination with Marxist ideas. . . . He is a neo-populist, however, in some important respects; in his defence, however mild of rich peasants; . . . in his claim that he actually accepts the need for industrialization – but in the distant future . . . and in his aversion to revolution and his proclamation that it is not necessary. This last characteristic, with its accompanying professed faith in reformist solutions and in the power of reason and argument to secure social justice . . . justify the description liberal populist.
>
> (Byres 1979, p. 238)

E. F. Schumacher

E. F. Schumacher's book *Small is Beautiful* (1973) covers a wide range of subjects in a comparatively short space and with considerable eloquence. It is not therefore surprising that it is one of the most widely read and influential books of the 1970s. In less than 300 pages Schumacher deals with such diverse topics as the energy and ecology crises which are facing the industrialized western world at the end of the twentieth century; the uniqueness of agriculture and energy sources, and a demand that both should be treated as unique specifically in economics, and not simply lumped together with industry as forms of 'production'; the substitution of a labour-intensive, small-scale technology for high-energy, capital-intensive industrialization in both the developed and the developing countries (he terms it 'intermediate technology' to indicate that it is both small scale and labour intensive, but not simply traditional); urbanization and political centralization in both the developed and developing world; nationalization in Britain, and even a call for a new type of economics ('Buddhist economics').

It will be seen that many of these themes overlap with much of what we have already discussed, while some (his ideas on energy and ecology) fall outside the range of our concerns in this book. I do not intend to present or criticize this full range of material, but simply to highlight one or two themes in Schumacher which echo the moral and social criticisms of industrialization first found in early nineteenth-century thinkers.

Industry and labour There is universal agreement that a fundamental source of wealth is human labour. Now the modern economist has been brought up to consider 'labour' or work as little more than a necessary evil. . . . It is . . . simply an item of cost, to be reduced to a minimum if it cannot be eliminated altogether, say, by automation. . . . The Buddhist point of view takes the function of work to be at least threefold: it gives a man a chance to utilize and develop his faculties; to enable him to overcome his ego-centredness by joining with other people in a common task; and to bring forth the goods and services needed for a becoming existence. . . . The carpet loom is a tool, a contrivance for holding warp threads at a stretch for the pile to be woven round them; but the power loom is a machine, and its significance as a destroyer of culture lies in the fact that it does the essentially human part of the work. It is clear, therefore, that Buddhist economics must be very different from the economics of modern materialism, since the Buddhist sees the essence of civilization not in a multiplication of wants but in the purification of human character. Character, at the same time, is formed primarily by a man's work. And work, properly conducted in conditions of human dignity and freedom, blesses those who do it and equally their products.

(pp. 54–5)

How could we explain the almost universal refusal on the part of the rulers of the rich societies – whether organized along private enterprise or collectivist enterprise lines – to work toward the humanization of work? It is only necessary to assert that something would reduce the 'standard of living' and every debate is instantly closed. That soul-destroying, meaningless, mechanical, monotonous, moronic work is an insult to human nature which must necessarily and inevitably produce either escapism or aggression, and that no amount of 'bread and circuses' can compensate for the damage done – these are facts which are neither denied nor acknowledged but are met with an unbreakable conspiracy of silence. (pp. 37–8)

It is not surprising that Schumacher actually advocates lowering the productivity of labour in the advanced industrial societies so that the physically productive part of total labour expenditure could be expanded (he estimates that it constitutes some 3.5 per cent of total labour time in modern Britain, and occupies less than a sixth of the total employed population).

We may say, therefore, that modern technology has deprived man of the kind of work that he enjoys most, creative, useful work with hands and brains, and given him plenty of a fragmented kind, most of which he does not enjoy at all. It has multiplied the number of people who are exceedingly busy doing kinds of work which, if it is productive at all, is so only in an indirect or 'roundabout' way, much of which would not be necessary at all if technology were rather less modern. (p. 151)

Size and humanity Today, we suffer from an almost universal idolatry of giantism. It is therefore necessary to insist on the virtues of smallness. . . . The idolatry of giantism . . . is possibly one of the causes and certainly one of the effects of modern technology, particularly in matters of transport and communications. A highly developed transport and communications system has one immensely powerful effect; it makes people footloose. . . . The factor of footlooseness is, therefore, the more serious, the bigger the country. Its destructive effects can be traced both in the rich and the poor countries. In the rich countries . . . it produces . . . 'megalopolis'. It produces a rapidly increasing and ever more intractable problem of 'drop outs', of people, who, having become footloose, cannot find a place anywhere in society. Directly connected with this, it produces an appalling problem of crime, alienation, stress, social breakdown, right down to the level of the family. In the poor countries, again most severely in the large ones, it produces mass migration into cities, mass unemployment, and, as vitality is drained out of the rural areas, the threat of famine. The result is a dual society, without an inner cohesion, subject to a maximum of political instability. (pp. 66, 67–8 and 70)

As Gandhi said, the poor of the world cannot be helped by mass production, only by production by the masses. The system of mass production, based on sophisticated, highly capital-intensive, high-energy-input dependent, and human-labour-saving technology, presupposes that you are already rich, for a great deal of capital is needed to establish one single workplace. The system of production by the masses mobilizes resources which are possessed by all human beings, their clever brains and skilful hands, and supports them with first-class tools. The technology of mass production is inherently violent, ecologically damaging, self-defeating in terms of non-renewable resources, and stultifying for the human person. The technology of production by the masses, making use of the best of modern knowledge and experience, is conducive to decentralization, compatible with the laws of ecology, gentle in its use of scarce resources, and designed to serve the human person instead of making him the servant of machines. I have named it intermediate technology.... I have no doubt that it is possible to give a new direction to technological development, a direction that shall lead it back to the real needs of man, and that also means: to the actual size of man. Man is small, and, therefore, small is beautiful. To go for giantism is to go for self-destruction. (pp. 153–4 and 159)

Why is it so difficult for the rich to help the poor? The all-pervading disease of the modern world is the total imbalance between the city and the countryside, an imbalance in terms of wealth, power, culture, attraction, and hope. The former has become over-extended, and the latter has atrophied. The city has become the universal magnet, while rural life has lost its savour. Yet it remains an unalterable truth that, just as a sound mind depends on a sound body, so the health of the cities depends on the health of the rural areas. The cities, with all their wealth, are merely secondary producers, while primary production, the precondition of all economic life, takes place in the countryside. The prevailing lack of balance, based on the age-old exploitation of countryman and raw material producer, today threatens all countries throughout the world, the rich even more than the poor. To restore a proper balance between city and rural life is perhaps the greatest task in front of modern man. It is not simply a matter of raising agricultural yields so as to avoid world hunger. There is no answer to the evils of mass unemployment and mass migration into cities, unless the whole level of rural life can be raised, and this requires the development of an agro-industrial culture, so that each district, each community, can offer a colourful variety of occupations to its members.

The crucial task of this decade, therefore, is to make the development effort appropriate and thereby more effective, so that it will reach down to the heartland of world poverty, to two million villages. If the disintegration of rural life continues, there is no way out – no matter how much money is spent. (pp. 203–4)

Education The whole matter can be summed up in the question:

What is education for? I think it was the Chinese . . . who calculated that it took the work of thirty peasants to keep one man or woman at a university. If that person . . . took a five-year course, by the time he had finished he would have consumed 150 peasant-work-years. How can this be justified? . . . These questions lead us to the parting of the ways, is education to be a passport to privilege or is it something which people take upon themselves almost like a monastic vow, a sacred obligation to serve the people? The first road takes the educated young person into a fashionable district of Bombay. . . . The other way . . . would lead to a different destination. It would take him back to the people who . . . had paid for his education by 150 peasant-work-years; having consumed the fruits of their work, he would feel in honour bound to return something to them. (p. 207)

Property As regards private property, the first and most basic distinction is between (a) property that is an aid to creative work and (b) property that is an alternative to it. There is something natural and healthy about the former – the private property of the working proprietor; and there is something unnatural and unhealthy about the latter – the private property of the passive owner who lives parasitically on the work of others. . . . Private enterprise carried on with property of the first category is automatically small scale, personal and local. It carries no wider social responsibilities. Its responsibilities to the consumer can be safeguarded by the consumer himself. Social legislation and trade union vigilance can protect the employee. No great private fortunes can be gained from small-scale enterprises, yet its social utility is enormous.

It is . . . apparent that in this matter of private ownership the question of scale is decisive. When we move from small scale to medium scale, the connection between ownership and work already becomes attenuated; private enterprise tends to become impersonal and also a significant social factor in the locality; it may even assume more than local significance. The very idea of private property becomes increasingly misleading. (p. 264)

I have quoted Schumacher at great length, because it is only through quotation that one can get a sense of his thought and its expression. The prose is powerful and direct, the ideas are simply expressed, technical elaboration, even of economic ideas, is kept to an absolute minimum. Above all, the whole book is suffused with a passionate ethical or moral concern, and with a visionary image of a total alternative future for both the rich and poor countries to that held out in conventional economic theory. Whereas the ILO theorists, and even Michael Lipton, keep overtly ethical and political vocabulary (the vocabulary of value judgement) to a minimum, in Schumacher that vocabulary permeates all the discussion, even of economic or technological issues. Moreover, Schumacher is not in the least apologetic about this. On the contrary he acknowledges it and defends it pugnaciously:

> It will be said that this is a romantic, a utopian vision. True enough. What we have today, in modern industrial society, is not romantic and certainly not utopian, as we have it right here. But it is in very deep trouble and holds no promise of survival. We jolly well have to have the courage to dream if we want to survive and give our children a chance of survival.   (p. 152)

Nor, after all that has been said, should the intellectual antecedents of his thought be in any doubt. The passages on the fragmentation of the human personality and the loss of purpose in work and labour in modern industrial society would have drawn applause from Robert Owen, the Ricardian socialists, Sismondi and Proudhon. The passages on the city and the countryside are classically populist, the ideas on education are pure Lavrov, and the formulations on acceptable and unacceptable property echo Proudhon's views on *aubaine* almost exactly.

Unlike Lipton, Schumacher is to some degree aware of the antiquity of the tradition of thought to which he belongs. His most conscious and oft-expressed intellectual debt is to Gandhi, but in the book one can also find references to Aldous Huxley, Leo Tolstoy and Richard Tawney, whilst Theodore Roszak, in his introduction to the American edition, suggests that

> Schumacher's work belongs to that subterranean tradition of organic decentralist economics whose major spokesmen include Prince Kropotkin, Gustav Landauer, Tolstoy, William Morris, Gandhi, Lewis Mumford, and, most recently, Alex Comfort, Paul Goodman and Murray Bookchin. It is the tradition we might call anarchism, if we mean by that much abused word a libertarian political economy that distinguished itself from orthodox socialism and capitalism by insisting that the scale of organization must be treated as an independent and primary problem.   (p. 4)

In nineteenth-century Russia the overlap between populist and anarchist thought was very considerable; in any event Schumacher seems, at first sight, to belong to that tradition of populist thought which Lipton regards as 'romantic' and 'backward-looking'. But this I think is misleading. Schumacher is adamant, for example, that a world of 'intermediate technology' is a world which will make full use of modern science and technology. However, this will be a science put to the task of raising or maintaining high levels of output while preserving a rich and creative role for the worker. The rule will no longer be 'maximize output and lower costs whatever the social consequences', as demanded by conventional economics. Moreover, in his discussion of the role of intermediate technology in developing or poor countries, Schumacher makes it clear that the scale of operation is less important than lowering the cost of equipment per worker where capital is scarce − 'a small-scale enterprise with an average cost per workplace of £2000 is just as inappropriate as a large-scale enterprise with equally costly workplaces' (p. 179).

In short, Schumacher is in no simple sense either a romantic or a backward-looking thinker. It is rather that, as I have said, he thinks that neither economic judgements about the scale and type of investment nor technological decisions about the type of technology to be used can be made without some broader vision of the type of society and of human values and behaviour which are desirable − without, in short, the use of overtly ethical value judgements (what he in one place calls 'meta-economic' judgements). It is in the use of an explicitly ethical mode of discourse that Schumacher looks back to the classical roots of populism, whilst his supplementation of ethical and political concerns with scientific and economic arguments puts him firmly alongside the modern neo-populists. In this section I have stressed the former dimension of his thought, principally in order to demonstrate the recent renaissance of classical populist ideas and values, but the student who wants a complete view of Schumacher's remarkable book must also read his arguments on the exhaustion of renewable energy resources, the dangers of nuclear power, the decentralization of nationalized industries, the possibility and reliability of computer prediction and many other 'technical' topics.

CONCLUSIONS

It has been the aim of this and the two previous chapters to trace a continuing tradition of thought over some 180 years of world history. I have aimed to show that whenever predominantly peasant societies have been confronted with the possibility or actuality of industrialization, ideas which I have termed 'populist' have come to the fore. These ideas have sought to confront industrialization and urbanization with an alternative 'vision' of development, concentrating on small-scale enterprise, on the retention of a peasant agriculture and of non-agricultural petty commodity production, and on a world of villages and small towns rather than large industrial cities.

I have also sought to show how these ideas have metamorphosed over time, and I have made the broad distinction between classical populist thought and 'neo-populism'. The latter is distinguished by its far greater command over economic theory and interest in economic issues, its partial acceptance of industrialization and its attempts (partly, but not only, through co-operative schemes) to modernize peasant agriculture and raise both the productivity and incomes of peasant farmers. In modern neo-populism, which has emerged in and about the Third World since the late 1960s, a far greater stress than ever before has been placed on the incapacity of large-scale, capital-intensive industrialization to provide sufficient or sufficiently remunerative employment, and this has become the main focus of many modern neo-populist schemes (particularly in the work of the ILO, but also in Lipton and Schumacher). However, both populism and neo-populism share an over-riding concern with problems of inequality in distribution, and a desire for a future in which the eradication of poverty is combined with forms of social and economic organization able to guarantee a considerable equality of income and wealth in a world of small-scale property. Both populists and neo-populists want a world in which ownership is always justified, so far as is possible, by work and direct use of productive assets (whether this be land or other non-agricultural means of production).

However, if an historical analysis of modern theories of development shows them to have unsuspectedly deep roots, in a whole tradition of opposition to industrialization and urbanization – if we see in fact an extraordinary continuity hidden behind apparent novelty – it is also important to recognize that there have been changes within that continuity.

One very important change, occurring gradually as industry has spread across the world but very noticeable if modern (post-1945) neo-populism is compared directly with the populism of the early nineteenth century, is that modern neo-populism is much less a doctrine of conservation or recreation than its populist predecessor. That is to say, for Robert Owen or the Ricardian socialists, for Proudhon, even for some of the earlier Russian populists, a major aim, perhaps the prime aim, of their schemes was to place a barrier in the way of industrialization and of the rapid growth of industrial cities swollen with a new propertyless proletariat. They wanted to preserve a pre-industrial world of peasants and small-scale artisans from the destruction and depersonalization which was thought to be inherent in proletarianization and an enforced existence in urban factory and slum.

However, as industrialization spread from its first home in Britain, across western Europe, to Russia and eastern Europe and then to the non-European world, so it gradually became impossible to conceive a populist world purely in terms of protection or recreation of a pre-industrial economy and society. Gradually the critique came to focus on the form of industrialization and urbanization, and on the role which small-scale agriculture was meant to play in the industrialization process.

In the context of the Third World in the late 1960s, that meta-morphosis was taken one step further, in that most modern neo-populists profess an agnosticism about whether, in the abstract, large-scale, capital-intensive industrialization is 'desirable' or not. They concentrate much more on its alleged failure in practice, i.e. its inability to deliver employment and the alleviation of mass poverty, especially in rural areas. Modern neo-populist schemes seek not to arrest industrialization but to direct it into new forms and channels, to maximize employment, increase equality and stem the drift to the swollen cities.

Thus one should not be misled, for example, by the reappearance of the urban artisan at the centre of modern populist thought, or by schemes for the support of the urban 'informal sector'. For most of the artisans involved in the Third World are *not* pre-industrial producers struggling to preserve an existence in the face of industrial competition (as in the early nineteenth century). They are, on the contrary, often pursuing activities which depend for their very existence on modern mass production industry. They may be involved in motor car or bicycle repair and maintenance, they may 'recycle' industrial raw materials, for example the manufacture of rubber sandals and other goods from car tyres, or they may provide essential wage goods for, among others, urban industrial workers, such as tailoring and food preparation and provision (Gerry 1979). In short, the urban informal sector in many Third World countries has expanded together with the spread of industrialization, partly because the latter has been unable to provide sufficient employment directly, but also because it has indirectly provided a range of other income opportunities.

Similarly, there is no doubt that the degree of capital intensity of modern industrial plant in the Third World (and thus the enormously high cost of industrial job creation and the very small amount of employment created by industrial investment) has produced a qualitatively different situation in the Third World today from that which existed in Europe in the nineteenth or early twentieth centuries. Broadly, it can be said that with each industrialization experience, across Europe and into Japan, the technology in use became ever more capital intensive and labour saving. But for countries commencing upon industrialization in the late 1950s or early 1960s, and also experiencing very rapid rates of population growth, the degree of capital intensity and thus the scale of the 'employment problem' faced are qualitatively different from anything ever known previously. Modern neo-populism, with its primary emphasis on employment generation, reflects in its theory that qualitative change in reality.

Finally, a change is also noticeable in modern neo-populist attitudes to the peasantry. Although in Schumacher we have a restatement of the old populist view that industrial work is dehumanizing and stultifying to human creativity, making workers slaves to machines rather than masters of them (on this, see also Braverman 1976), none the less, even in Schumacher, we do not find this contrasted to an idyllic image of the fulfilled, creative and wise peasant, so beloved of the old Russian *narodniks*. On the contrary, for Schumacher, rural life in the present-day Third World has 'lost its savour', has 'atrophied'. It is only something to escape from to the ever-swelling cities. We saw earlier how the ILO reports echo the Chayanovian image of peasant life as one of unremitting 'drudgery', while Lipton too is more impressed by the poverty and exploitation of the present-day peasantry than by the beatitudes of rural living. To be sure, frankly romantic images of peasant people are not totally absent in modern-day development studies literature (see, for example, Hyden 1980, p. 2), but generally they are much less common than they were 100 or 150 years ago in Russia and eastern Europe. The explanation of this does not lie in any major material differences in the condition of the peasants involved (the nineteenth-century Russian peasantry probably had as mean and hard a life as the present-day Indian peasantry), but very largely reflects the different type of intellectual involved in modern neo-populism on the one hand and in classical populism on the other. There are far fewer poets, theologians and philosophers and far more economists, social anthropologists and others for whom a certain degree of field exposure to actual peasant life is usually incumbent. This, together with the much greater availability of empirical data on the living conditions of the peasantries of the present Third World, make the more extravagant images of idyllic 'pastoral' rather difficult to sustain. Hence modern neo-populists are unanimous in their desire not simply to preserve the peasantry, but to improve and modernize their way of life. This is even true of Nyerere, who perhaps comes nearest to the old populists in his image of the traditional extended family in Africa.

None the less, even when all these discontinuities have been recognized, one is still struck by the extraordinary vitality and durability of the essential populist 'vision' − a world of equality, of small property, a minimally urbanized world, an agricultural world, a decentralized world − and by its capacity to manifest itself again and again in various situations, even though invested in somewhat different vocabulary and arguments. It is clearly a vision with many attractive qualities and, above all, a vision which speaks strongly and repeatedly to nations and peoples faced with the economic and social problems of industrialization and urbanization. But does it in reality provide a coherent, practicable, long-term development strategy which can be set against conventional models of growth and industrialization? The next chapter tries to answer that question by examining two case studies of 'non-industrial' development in action, Tanzania from 1967 to the present and the People's Republic of China from 1949 to the present.

5

Populist development in action?
Tanzania and China

This chapter departs from the previous concentration on populist texts and ideas and examines two developing countries whose experience throws considerable light on the practical implication of those ideas. Given the analysis of President Nyerere's thought in the previous chapter, the choice of Tanzania as one case study is perhaps predictable. The choice of the People's Republic of China does, however, require some explanation, for many students of China would vigorously deny that China is pursuing policies which could in any way be categorized as 'populist'. And in fact I shall argue precisely this, that China's development model is not populist. However, there is no doubt that China's 'success' in development has been hailed by many who are sympathetic to populist ideas as a demonstration of what populist strategies may achieve. Thus, China is held in high esteem by the World Bank (1980, p. 78), by Michael Lipton (1977, pp. 27 and 74) and above all by many of the advocates of Schumacherian 'intermediate technology'. And the reasons for this are not far to seek. With an estimated population of over 900 million people, over 80 per cent of whom live in rural areas and of whom some 320 million (adults) are employed in agriculture, China has none the less been able to claim full employment in agriculture (and in fact now complains of acute labour shortages in agriculture) and this despite densities of population on her scarce cultivable land which often exceed 700 per square km. In addition until very recently China had cut rural–urban migration virtually to zero, and indeed had sent tens of millions of people out of the urban areas and into the countryside. In addition her small-scale rural industries employ some 14–17 million people and are frequently noted as the best single example in the Third World of 'intermediate' or 'appropriate' technology in action (see, for example, Open University 1978). Above all, China is held in high esteem by many students of development because, starting from a situation in 1949 of widespread malnutrition and disease, endemic urban overcrowding and poverty (which shocked visitors to Shanghai,

Peking and other cities as they today shock visitors to Calcutta or Bombay), and enormous economic and social dislocation (after nearly thirty years of war, civil war and breakdown of civil order), by 1975 she appeared to have eliminated absolute poverty. Adequate food, clothing and shelter has been provided for all, whilst her near universal education and rural health services excite widespread admiration, and help to provide a minimum standard of social as well as material well being for all her 900 million people.

The Chinese experience also seems to have exciting implications because the bulk of the world's worst poverty overall is concentrated in South Asia, and China is the only 'successful' case of development in a situation which is demographically and (to a degree) economically similar to that prevailing in the Indian sub-continent. For all these reasons, it is not surprising that advocates of very different development strategies have wished to hold up China as 'supporting' in practice the policies which they advocate in theory, and the populists have been no exception to this generalization. In particular if China has achieved her transformation in a situation in which 60 to 70 per cent of her population is still dependent on agriculture, and indeed in which agriculture alone absorbed nearly 100 million extra workers in the period 1957–75 (Rawski 1979, p. 71), then surely this is proof that in an area like India or China one must, as Lipton suggests, have a 'developed mass agriculture . . . before you can have widespread successful development in other sectors', and especially before you can have 'successful' industrialization. In the second part of this chapter, I shall argue that appearances are deceptive and that in fact, if the Chinese case 'proves' anything, it is that a high degree of industrialization (and especially a considerable development of 'producer goods' industries) is a necessary precondition of successful labour absorption in agriculture. However, the Chinese case does call into question some part of the conventional thinking about industrialization, especially the general equation of 'producer goods' industries with large-scale production, and the conventional distinctions between 'labour' and 'capital' which are built into most models of industrial growth. However, this is to anticipate. For the moment we must turn to the Tanzanian case.

TANZANIA

The year 1967 (seven years after independence) is conventionally regarded as the turning point in Tanzania's development. In that year the Arusha Declaration resulted in the nationalization of most of the small industrial and commercial sector in the country, and also placed rural development on *ujamaa* principles at the forefront of development strategy. In theory at least rural development was to follow the lines laid down in *Socialism and Rural Development* (see Chapter 4), which was also published in 1967. Over 85 per cent of Tanzania's 13 million people (in 1967) lived in rural areas, and were directly or indirectly dependent on agriculture. Hence a policy of priority to rural development was defended both on grounds of equity (and especially of giving priority to the needs of the poorest people) and on the grounds that Tanzania's previous policy of giving priority to urban areas and to industrialization had failed. For, it was argued, the previous strategy could not be sustained without large amounts of foreign investment which were not forthcoming in the required quantities (Tanzania 1969, vol. I, pp. x–xi).

It took some time to reorientate plan priorities in Tanzania to the *ujamaa* philosophy, and in fact the second Five Year Plan (1969–74) had to be altered at a rather late date to reflect the change of political direction. In the estimates of planned development expenditure, items clearly earmarked for agriculture or rural development accounted for just over 17 per cent of the total, while the Kilimanjaro airport (designed mainly to attract tourist traffic) and road expenditure were by far the largest single item (nearly 30 per cent of the planned budget). In the current Five Year Plan (1976–81) agriculture and livestock are allocated nearly 15 per cent of the planned capital investment and 13.5 per cent of government development expenditure. In both cases this is markedly less than the allocation to industry, which received nearly 27 per cent of the capital budget and 24 per cent of the total development budget (Tanzania 1969, vol. II, p. 13; Tanzania 1976, part I, pp. 10 and 11). However, this is somewhat misleading in that reorientation of education and health expenditure to favour rural areas (a process which began during the second plan) means that the bulk of capital and recurrent expenditure under these heads, which totalled Shs. 2894.6 million or 19.4 per cent of total government expenditure in the second plan period, has to be accredited to the rural areas. The net result of these efforts in education and health was that the number of health centres in rural areas more than tripled between 1969 and 1974, while by 1978 an estimated 97 per cent of all children of primary school age were at school.

Moreover, the bulk of the expenditure on water supply (Shs. 1081 million) went to rural areas during the second plan (1969, vol. II, p. 35), and in addition an analysis of Tanzania's industrial structure in 1974 showed that most of it was devoted either to the processing of food or other agricultural products, such as coffee, tea, tobacco, cotton and wood, or to the production of fertilizer and other agricultural inputs. A large part of the 'industrial' budget for the 1969–74 plan could therefore be regarded as ancillary to rural development, and indeed the allocations for industrial investment for 1976–81 continue this trend (Tanzania 1976, part I, pp. 41, 42 and 45).

In short, after something of a lag whilst plan priorities and government expenditure caught up with political undertakings, there *has* undoubtedly been a major shift of Tanzania's development effort to the rural areas and to agriculture. In fact this seems, in keeping with Nyerere's anti-urban philosophy and the desire to slow the rate of rural–urban migration (running at 6 per cent annum in 1969), to have led to a relative neglect of urban areas, especially after their loss of administrative autonomy under the decentralization measures of 1972. We now have to look at this rural development effort more closely, outlining its structure and attempting to evaluate it.

Ujamaa and rural development

The centre of Tanzania's rural development strategy, as conceived in 1967, was to be the '*ujamaa* village', a nucleated settlement of peasants dependent mainly, if not totally, on agriculture and engaging in a variable degree of communal or collective production, although individual households were also to retain private plots on which they were to grow crops for their own consumption. As initially conceived at least, most of the village's cash crops were to be produced on the communal farm, and the proceeds divided on the basis of the labour performed on the farm by each village member. By 1974 over 2½ million Tanzanians were said to be living in over 5000 *ujamaa* villages, though the bulk of these were not in the agriculturally rich areas of Tanzania, but in the semi-arid areas of Dodoma, Iringa, Mtwara and Singida, where the population had previously been very thinly spread, and engaged in a mixture of pastoralism and shifting subsistence agriculture. After 1974 official accounts speak not of '*ujamaa*' villages but simply of 'villages'. For the acceleration of the programme in that year went along with an effective dropping of the demand that villages should have some form of communal production, in favour of a simple crash programme bringing peasants together into nucleated settlements. Official statistics suggest that all rural Tanzanians were living in 'villages or *ujamaa* villages' (the great majority in the former) by 1976, by which time there were 13 million village members. However, in some of the more densely populated parts of Tanzania, which were also the areas responsible for a great deal of the cash crop output (especially coffee) and for a large share of exports, many villages were simply created administratively by labelling a pre-existent administrative unit of dense settlement a 'village'. In such areas (Arusha, Kilimanjaro, Rungwe and West Lake), which tended to be the last to enter the villagization programme, there was in fact no change at all in residential or production arrangements 'on the ground'. There was not even the creation of planned nucleated settlements as in the less densely populated regions. The change was purely formal. There is no way of knowing from the currently available statistics, but given the weight of these areas in Tanzania's total population, it may well be that at least 40 per cent of the country's 'villagers' are in fact living in these purely nominal entities, with their substantive situation unchanged since the colonial period. Under the Villages and Ujamaa Villages Act of 1975, a registered village must have at least 250 households resident within it, but in reality villages have been very varied in size, from 350 people or less up to 2500 or more (see Mascenharas 1979, p. 154).

Supporting policies

As well as the creation of several thousand villages and *ujamaa* villages, Tanzania has also implemented a number of policies designed to support agricultural production and rural transformation in the villages. These policies included (1) the setting up of a Regional Development Fund (initially of Shs. 500,000 for each region) to fund village industries and other small-scale rural enterprises and (2) the decentralization in 1972 of ministerial and technical personnel to the regional and district level, and the allocation to each region of a regional budget to be allocated in a manner determined by the region for its own development projects. In theory, these allocations were to be made on the basis of regional development plans, which were in turn to be compiled by selection from plans coming up from district and village level. This decentralization of administrative responsibility for nearly all rural development programmes went along with an attempt to bring the administration far closer to the village level by the appointment of full-time 'ward secretaries' (in place of previously elected 'Ward Executive Officers') and by the allocation of full-time agricultural extension and rural development staff to each village. This process of 'closer administration' was completed in 1978 by the introduction of a 'village managers' scheme, by which a full-time trained executive manager was to be appointed to each village to co-ordinate the whole rural development effort there. This process of close administration has of course been facilitated by the villagization programme itself, since with the aggregation of scattered households into nucleated units there are now fewer units to which services have to be provided. In addition, in 1976 the agricultural marketing system of Tanzania was reformed. Marketing co-operatives were abolished and villages were allowed to sell their produce direct to local branches of state marketing boards.

Evaluation

With that outline of the institutional development and formal structure of rural development policy in Tanzania, we can now turn to an evaluation of its actual performance. To summarize a complex matter, there is no doubt that overall results have been very disappointing. We will examine the very poor performance of Tanzanian agriculture in the 1970s shortly, but before looking at the figures, it is important first of all to appreciate how *ujamaa* in practice differed from the vision which had been conceived in *Socialism and Rural Development*. In the first place the *ujamaa* village of Nyerere's vision was supposed to rest on the initiative of the peasants themselves. They were to come together voluntarily to try to extend the communal principles which had operated in the traditional extended family into a wider arena and new activities. The role of the government was to facilitate and encourage initiatives which had been taken at the grass roots, rather than to initiate or coerce. There was some warrant for such ideas in the very first *ujamaa* villages in Tanzania, those set up by ex-estate and mission workers in Ruvuma in the early 1960s and amalgamated subsequently into the Ruvuma Development Association. However, apparently as a result of the hostility of local state officials to this uncontrolled exercise in 'utopian socialism' (see von Freyhold 1979 and Coulson 1977), the autonomy of the RDA was effectively ended in 1969. From then on the formation of *ujamaa* villages owed more and more to state encouragement and (after 1974) coercion, and less and less to local initiative. Although the details varied, the process up to 1974 seems to have been broadly the same everywhere.

Regional and district officials tended to compete against each other to register the fastest possible increases in *ujamaa* villages in 'their' areas. Since coercion was not, at this stage, acceptable to the President or central government, it was used only occasionally, the much more common tactic being to make extravagant promises of state aid to peasants 'volunteering' to move to villages. In some cases the President himself played a direct part (as in 'Operation Dodoma' in 1971); and though he himself eschewed such promises, his very presence, and the fact that such promises were probably made on his behalf by officials both before and after his tour, rendered the effect much the same. In such cases spectacular results were obtained, with thousands of peasants (as in Dodoma) moving to supposed village sites in a matter of days or weeks. But the very speed of the operation tended to overstretch the capacity of the government to deliver the rewards expected, or indeed effectively to plan and administer the mushrooming villages at all. With the decision in late 1973 to speed up the process and to have all rural Tanzanians living in villages by the end of 1976, these problems of 'administrative overload' were compounded. In addition coercion began to play a much greater role in the process (see, for example, Coulson 1977, p. 93, and Hyden 1980, pp. 130 and 144).

Clearly a process on this scale (perhaps as many as 5 million Tanzanians were moved into villages between the beginning of 1974 and the end of 1976), and undertaken at this speed, is a far cry from the slow organic growth of local socialism from traditional roots which had been posited in *Socialism and Rural Development*. As a result it is scarcely surprising if many of those who found themselves in *ujamaa* villages (or indeed in villages) had little conception of what they were required to do, beyond hoping for the receipt of massive government assistance, and were neither equipped nor motivated to cope with all the organizational and technical problems which arose. But in any case it is doubtful whether, in many parts of Tanzania, there was any real basis of traditional *ujamaa* to build upon even in the genuinely 'voluntary' years from 1967 to 1972 or 1973. Von Freyhold's analysis of Tanga region (1979), van Velsen's work in Rungwe (van Hekken and van Velsen 1972), my own work in Arusha (Kitching 1972), Boesen's work in West Lake (Boesen, Moody and Madsen 1977), Raikes's work in Mbulu (1972) and Awiti's work in Iringa (1972) are some of many studies showing that by the end of the colonial period the emergence of cash crop farming and of wage labour in town and country had long produced *de facto* individual systems of land tenure, and had weakened or totally undermined inter-household traditions of communal work (which in any case had always been strictly ancillary to the individual household's own efforts). In short, as far as the most densely populated and agriculturally advanced regions of Tanzania are concerned, *Socialism and Rural Development* must be regarded not as a description of contemporary reality but as at best a somewhat idealized picture of a long dead past. It is significant in this context that the very first and spontaneous *ujamaa* villages (the RDA villages) were not founded by peasants but by ex-estate workers and others who had had experience of trade union organization, and had often lived and worked (for wages) outside their areas of origin for many years (Coulson 1977, p. 88). It is also significant that when the final push into the more commercially developed areas of Tanzania was made (in the period after 1973), the demand that villages have some form of collective farm was dropped altogether. Either President Nyerere himself or his advisers had clearly become aware (as a result of violent resistance in Iringa and West Lake) that the *'ujamaa* spirit' was somewhat thin on the ground in these areas.

A closer look

Given this general context – a programme going ever faster and eventually at breakneck speed, a vastly overstretched administration unable to provide the material or organizational support which had been promised, and a peasantry sometimes eager (where pre-village conditions had been harshest or the promises grander), sometimes suspicious or unwilling (especially in the more commercialized areas), but always with little or no understanding of the *ujamaa* ideology and policy – one might expect that results would not match either peasant expectations or President Nyerere's original vision. But the precise extent of the gap can only be grasped by detailed accounts such as the following (paraphrased) account of the process in Tanga region as outlined by a recent writer on *ujamaa*:

> There was a lack of applicable research recommendations on almost all crops except sisal, cotton and tea. . . . Contrary to official directives, localized research posts and field trials in different villages hardly existed.
>
> Villagers in the Tanga lowlands would have needed research into drought-resistant varieties of different food crops, on citrus trees with early and late harvesting times, on ways of handling the weed problems, on the most appropriate means of planting rice, on pests and plant diseases in different areas, on suitable pasture crops and forage trees, and on farm management problems such as the optimum crop combinations for different areas. There did not appear to be much research on these problems going on or, if there was, the farmers and the agricultural experts in Tanga had never heard of it. . . .
>
> Research into problems of livestock management was also not very abundant. There was one station supposed to test, select and eventually breed cattle according to their resistance to east coast fever, but records of illness were not kept, there was no veterinary officer at the station and most of the cattle there were beyond the age of reproduction. . . .
>
> In 1971, after more than a year of drought, farmers had run out of seeds for most of their traditional crops, and there was almost none on the market. For the communal plots all the registered villages received

free seeds financed through the regional development fund, but communal production was as yet only a small part of the total cultivation. Not all the free seeds were satisfactory. Some were too old, some had been treated for food preservation, some were not suitable for the particular environment. . . . More serious was the lack of seeds for less conventional crops, in both private and communal farming. . . .

There was a lack of all implements except hoes and *pangas* [machete-like knives] in the villages. Digging of holes was done by digging sticks which had pieces of metal tied to their ends. Distribution of green manure and weeding of seedbeds was done by hand, watering of vegetables was done with milk tins, huge trees were felled with *pangas*. . . . Application of fertilisers was not practised by any private farmer in the villages of our study. In 1971 the villagers were given free fertilisers for the communal plot, but the bags arrived too late and without any instructions on how and where the fertiliser was to be used. . . .

The biggest problem almost everywhere was vermin control. There seemed to be a vermin control unit in the region which had been sent to some villages, but the peasants asserted that this unit was not effective and rarely shot anything. Villagers attributed this to the fact that the members of the unit did not have any real hunting experience, and that they got paid even when they did not shoot anything at all. . . .

Communal livestock production was neglected. There was one station in Tanga engaged in breeding dairy cattle, but experts in the station did not consider any of the cattle fit for the doubtful management practices in the villages. In 1971 most of the villages . . . had been waiting to receive cattle which they had been promised one or two years previously. But the cattle had not yet been purchased by the Agricultural Department. By 1977 one village had received a few oxen which had died, and all the other villages were still waiting or had given up hope. . . .

Communal crop production was not mechanized. Between 1962 and 1976 about seventy farmers had been trained in the region to plough with oxen or donkeys. Only two farmers in the region who had gone through the local courses were reported to be doing some ox-ploughing. One of the reasons was the inadequacy of the training. . . . Farmers were not sufficiently informed about technical practices and farm management details without which the successful use of oxen was impossible.

Existing training facilities in the region were inadequate. In mid-1971 there were only two ox-training centres which between them had two fully qualified ox-trainers, four assistants and eight trained oxen. The ox-training centre at Segera gave the oxen better accommodation than the neighbouring peasants and there was an obvious reluctance to move the precious animals to a village. . . . By 1975 the ox-training centres in the region had been reduced to one. The other one had been closed down because the precious oxen had died, reportedly due to negligent dipping. . . .

In 1971 the Ministry of Education, the Co-operative Union and the Ministry of Agriculture had all allocated some funds for the purchase of oxen, equipment and for the training of farmers, and until 1975/6 the Agricultural Department continued to allocate increasing amounts for the purpose of ox-mechanization. All the animals that arrived, however, died or were allocated to ranching schemes, or were sold before they reached the peasants.   (von Freyhold, pp. 94–9)

And so it goes on. And it is supplemented by further details of negligent or incompetent agricultural extension and rural development officials who, when they were present in the village (their 'permanent' residence there often being purely fictional), could offer little useful help or advice; by details of erratic activity or total inactivity by district and regional officials; by statistics on inadequate and vastly expensive state crop marketing; by details of wrongly sited villages, and so on. Von Freyhold's account is supplemented by many others from other areas of Tanzania which tell an almost identical story (see Hyden 1980, chapters 4 and 5, for a composite account and further references).

Of course most peasant farmers in Tanzania had grown used to this kind of ineffective 'rural development' which had been the norm long before *ujamaa* (Coulson 1977, pp. 74–87). But then they had been living in areas which they knew well, operating a form of household or family agricultural organization to which they were accustomed, and handling ecological and climatic problems which, no matter how severe, were at least familiar. But 'villagization', particularly when it was allied to communal production, changed all this. It altered the settlement pattern (so that fields were often some distance from the village, rather than surrounding the individual homestead as had been the case previously); it brought historically unprecedented numbers of people together, often from different clan or tribal backgrounds; it placed people on soils with which they were unfamiliar, in rainfall regimes about which they knew little or nothing. Above all, perhaps, it required them to enter a form of large-scale communal production, sometimes of unfamiliar crops and to use a type of work organization which was complex and likely to have many teething troubles, even if (as was not the case) experienced, committed and technically skilled help and advice had been available. As a result, in the *ujamaa* villages which attempted it, the experience of communal production was almost totally negative, and rapidly productive of either hostility or, more frequently, indifference, and a speedy return to concentration on private plots.

Most of the village members were not used to any conscious planning and had no idea of how their private experiences on their small farms could be of any use to a larger enterprise. Nor were they used to depersonalized discussions on farm management problems. If there was anybody with any talent for such issues they would elect him as a leader and expect him to make the suggestions and they would normally agree without asking for particular reasons.

Where the leadership was not too interested in communal production, the village council would in the end decide according to outside pressure that a minimum of outside work needed to be done, and most of the work would be done without too much concern about results. Where leaders were ambitious they would run the communal enterprise like an estate. Less than a handful of people would make all the decisions, and the ordinary members would abide by these decisions, either because they were forced to, like in Segera where the village militia went to the houses to summon people to the farm, or because ordinary villagers did want their village enterprise to succeed and trusted their leaders to make the correct decisions to achieve this success. . . .

In villages where most members were only interested in their private farms they would sabotage any system designed to tie them down to communal farming, even if they did not voice their objections against the communal venture in public. If it had been decided that all members should spend a certain number of hours or a certain number of days per week on the communal farm, those who were not keen would either not appear at all, or would hang around saving their strength for the private farming later in the day. If it had been decided that each villager would be given a certain piece to complete each day, those who were not keen on communal work first pressed for keeping that piece as small as possible, and then finished it sloppily and in a hurry. There was little leaders could do against this kind of sabotage. Even punishments . . . were difficult to apply when other villagers rallied around the deviants protesting against the treatment. The idea that all members should contribute the same amount of labour to the communal enterprise so that they would derive the same benefits from communal work had its origin in the pioneer villages where the majority of members were committed to communal progress. The application of this idea to politically much more heterogeneous villages turned out to be an obstacle to . . . progress. What emerged as a norm . . . regarding the time and energy to be spent by everybody on the communal farm could only be what . . . the more reluctant members were prepared to accept. So in effect the less committed members set the standards of communal labour to be followed by the rest of the village. . . .

The most serious problem in nearly all *ujamaa* villages was the absence of any reliable system of financial control. With the exception of Kabuku Ndani and Moa, no village in Tanga had any regular and comprehensive system of book-keeping and of public control over the use of communal cash. More often than not the chairman or treasurer kept some or all of the communal money in his own house and was allowed to spend at least part of it for the village without prior consultation with anybody. . . . For the leaders the temptation to embezzle some of the funds was very strong.

(von Freyhold, pp. 84–8)

Given these experiences it is hardly surprising that in many villages communal plots were neglected in favour of family land, or in most cases were never more than a fiction at all. Such studies as are available all agree that productivity per acre and per worker was always much lower on the communal plots than on the private holdings in *ujamaa* villages (Mapolu and Phillipson 1976), and indeed although data are limited they strongly suggest that earnings from communal work in most *ujamaa* villages were very low (Hyden 1980, pp. 115–16). In short, faced with complex organizational difficulties of communal farming, and lacking any real support or necessary services and inputs from government, most villagers simply retreated into familiar forms of traditional subsistence agriculture.

How did all this affect agricultural output in Tanzania? The following two tables show the estimated harvest of Tanzania's principal food crops and sales of her principal cash crops to state marketing agencies in the 1970s (Table 2) and the export volume of six major export crops from 1965 to 1975 (Table 3).

As will be seen from Table 2 there is something of a contradiction between the harvest figures for the principal grain crops and the much more reliable sales figures, the former showing an increase or steady trend through 1972–4, while the latter show sharp falls in all cases, particularly between 1973 and 1974. The harvest figures seem particularly difficult to credit, when we know that large quantities of all

Table 2 Output and sales of major food and cash crops in Tanzania, 1971

Crop	Output (000 tons)						
	1971	1972	1973	1974	1975	1976	1977
Maize	—(43)*	847 (106)	761 (74)	1367 (24)	1499 (91)	1673 (114)	1455 (144)
Paddy	—	189 (63)	223 (60)	265 (25)	346	314	337
Wheat	—	81 (51)	85 (31)	82 (12)	69	64	53
Sisal	181	157	155	143			
Coffee (clean)	46	51	55	45			
Cashew nuts	126	126	146	154			
Tea	11	13	13	13			
Tobacco	12	14	13	18			
Sugar	96	89	105	96			
Pyrethrum	4	4	4	3			
Cotton	65	78	65	72			

* Figures in brackets show food sales to marketing agencies.

Sources: Tanzania Food and Nutrition Centre (1980 Table 12.1), Hyden (1980 Table 4.3, p. 120) and Tanzania (1974).

Table 3 Indices of export volume of six major export crops in Tanzania, 1965–75

Crop	1965	1966*	1967	1968	1969	1970	1971	1972	1973	1974	1975
Cotton	65	100	71	73	66	70	64	75	70	57	44
Coffee	56	100	88	97	98	89	70	108	119	81	108
Sisal	107	100	103	95	86	109	81	77	57	47	51
Cashew nuts	89	100	98	110	114	107	133	156	152	158	135
Tea	68	100	97	106	121	110	132	146	151	152	165
Tobacco	97	100	144	153	147	226	194	209	209	356	253
Total	75	100	88	92	88	93	82	99	95	82	82

* 1966 = 100.

Source: Hyden (1980, p. 146).

three grains had to be imported in these years to meet domestic demand. Thus, imports of maize rose from 92,000 tons in 1972 to nearly 300,000 tons in 1974, rice imports shot up from 23,000 tons in 1973 to 73,000 tons in 1974, and wheat imports were 46,000 tons in 1972, 8000 tons in 1973 and 47,000 tons in 1974 (Hyden 1980, p. 141, and *Economic Survey* 1974, p. 53). Cash crops show a much more variable trend as far as sales are concerned, and, with the exception of cotton and sisal, export volume mainly held up through the early 1970s.

Two good harvests in 1976 and 1977 helped to stabilize the food situation and were aided by the beginnings of a World Bank funded food production programme. In 1978, however, there was a sharp fall in the world price of Tanzania's coffee, and floods in 1979 were followed by drought in 1980. These latter events produced a need for further massive imports of food and indeed for food aid (200,000 tons of maize, rice and wheat were imported in 1980). In 1980, in response to the food shortages and the low prices for export crops – made worse by very inefficient state marketing – there were reports of peasants refusing to harvest their cash crops, or uprooting them and planting food crops (*Guardian*, 2 December 1980).

But one would would be ill-advised to link these problems directly to villagization, for most observers agree that their major cause was the weather conditions which prevailed across Tanzania from 1971 onwards, and which were particularly severe in 1974, 1979 and 1980. In fact in the early 1970s output of both food and cash crops were to some degree insulated from the chaotic effects of the *ujamaa* and villagization campaigns for a number of reasons:

1   Peasant 'retreat' into private plot food production probably helped maintain subsistence food output in all but the worst weather conditions.
2   Some of the cash crops, especially coffee, tea and pyrethrum, were produced in areas which were experiencing only 'nominal' villagization in any case, and there is some evidence to suggest that, despite the apparent commitment to *ujamaa*, these areas continued to get a large share of the expenditure on rural development and agriculture (see von Freyhold 1979, pp. 108–9).
3   From 1973–4 onwards, the government responded to the food problem (and the massive balance of payments problem which it was helping to exacerbate) by dropping the demand for communal production, raising the price of maize massively, putting far more resources into production of food on state farms, and obtaining large quantities of aid from the World Bank, especially for the

National Maize Project (NMP) in which heavily subsidized inputs were provided to 100 selected 'progressive' villages in a very conventional production campaign. This abrupt change in policy, and above all the more abundant rain from 1976 onwards, all helped to stabilize the food situation, at least temporarily. In fact in 1978 Tanzania exported some maize.

But whilst there can be no warrant for seeing the failure of *ujamaa* as the primary cause of Tanzania's food problems, and indeed no warrant for seeing Tanzania's agricultural performance overall as disastrous, there can be no doubt that the chaos, disappointment and cynicism which the campaign from 1971–4 has left behind have been major contributors to a political malaise in Tanzania, a malaise which goes far deeper than the simple question of agricultural output or exports. There are several dimensions to it. In the first place there are general economic difficulties of which the agricultural problems are just a part. For throughout the 1970s drought and food imports coincided with the massive increase in oil prices and were followed shortly thereafter (1978–9) by the massive foreign exchange costs of the war with Uganda.

The net result was an enormous balance of payments problem. In the two years 1979 and 1980 Tanzania's total balance of payments deficit was £620 million, and Green has estimated that the total losses to the Tanzanian economy through the 1970s (from collapse of coffee prices, oil price rises, the Ugandan war and adverse harvest conditions) were about £750 million, equal to 32 per cent of Tanzania's (1979) GDP, 125 per cent of her annual government revenue, or 200 per cent of her annual export earnings (Green 1980, p. 7).

The balance of payments problem would have been far worse had it not been for the receipt of large amounts of aid from the World Bank, IMF and other sources after 1975, but even with this aid the foreign exchange constraint has led, along with a very inefficient system of state commodity distribution, to periodic shortages of even very basic consumer goods. It has also led to production difficulties for many of Tanzania's industries, which, like many 'import substitution' industries in the Third World, are heavily dependent on imported inputs. A chronic shortage of cement and other building materials has been a major problem in many sectors.

In the second place, however, there is some evidence of a growing disillusion and cynicism, and perhaps even of attempts at sabotage and passive resistance by many senior and middle level officials in Tanzania (Hyden 1980, p. 137; Green 1980, p. 8). This probably has its origins in the Leadership Code formulated by President Nyerere in 1967 in which strict upper limits were placed on official salaries, while investments by civil servants in land, houses or other private business ventures were outlawed. Official figures suggest that these and related policies had reduced the ratio between the top and bottom salaries in the Tanzanian Civil Service from 26:1 in 1966 to about 9:1 in 1977 (Pratt 1979, p. 216). But the cost has been an unknown amount of evasion of these regulations and probably increased official involvement in the black market through misappropriation of state-distributed goods. There must also be a suspicion that some of the chronic incompetence and administrative chaos from which *ujamaa* villagers suffered had roots in factors other than simple technical shortcomings or administrative overload (see von Freyhold 1979, p. 120). Thus a whole network of factors, of which the failure of *ujamaa* is just one, has produced serious economic problems and formidable political difficulties for Tanzania's development strategy. The most serious of these political problems is not perhaps the bureaucratic disaffection itself, but rather the fact that the chaos and disappointments in rural development, and now the frequent and widespread shortages of even essential goods (in which, of course, bureaucratic incompetence has been a contributing factor) have spread dissatisfaction deeply among workers and peasants themselves. The 1980 Tanzanian general election, in which 50 per cent of the incumbent MPs lost their seats, was an eloquent testimony to this mass dissatisfaction.

But if the formidable economic and political problems now facing Tanzania have their roots in a complex of problems, some of which (droughts and floods, oil price rises or the Ugandan war) could not have been foreseen or controlled by President Nyerere or anyone else, is it fair or justified to relate these failures to the shortcomings in the President's populist development philosophy at all? I think that at least some of Tanzania's present difficulties (and perhaps those with the most gloomy long-term implications) do have their roots in that philosophy. This is so for a number of reasons. First, because of the very curious social and political situation which Tanzania found itself in at independence, President Nyerere has had (and probably still has) considerable latitude to make state policy in line with his own political beliefs. His capacity to have that policy implemented as he would wish is perhaps more problematic. But there is no doubt that the broad thrust of government policy since independence has been entirely determined by him. Indeed major policy statements by the Executive Committee of the ruling party are nearly always written by him, even when they do not formally bear his name (for example, the Arusha Declaration). To a far greater extent then than is common in the modern world, Tanzania has been a sort of huge laboratory for testing out its President's ideas on development, and to that extent it is justified to judge those ideas by the results obtained in practice.

Second, it is clear that President Nyerere's frankly romantic vision of the socialist nature of pre-colonial Tanzania *did* lead him to under-estimate the extent to which attempts at communal production would be unpopular with and/or strange to the vast majority of Tanzania's peasants. Indeed, it can be argued that even before the emergence of commercial agriculture and cash crop production in East Africa, 'traditional' systems of land tenure were in fact highly individualistic, or at least allowed great autonomy in land use and crop disposal decisions to individual household heads. Such inter-household work groups as there were, and such sharing of food crops and other produce as there was, were always seen as strictly ancillary to an individual household's right and obligation to provide for its own subsistence and prosperity. In fact, it was this 'proto-individualist' form of pre-colonial social organization which allowed *de facto* individual land tenure and rural differentiation to emerge so rapidly once colonialism provided access to greater sources of accumulation (see Kitching 1980a, especially chapter 10). In so far as the romantic images of African peasant life contained in *Socialism and Rural Development* influenced the making of the *ujamaa* policy in Tanzania, they did predispose its President to underestimate the difficulties that were likely to be encountered. In creating nucleated villages which were to depend for the bulk of their income on communal production on a collective farm, Tanzania was *not* simply extending 'traditional' practices in new directions. It was creating completely novel forms of social and economic organization that were totally strange and alien to the vast majority of the people who found themselves 'villagers'. Further, these new forms required the solution of complex technical and organizational problems with which these 'villagers' were not remotely equipped to cope.

Third, and above all perhaps, Tanzania's development has suffered from the effects of that thoroughgoing egalitarianism which is at the centre of President Nyerere's thought and policy-making and which marks him most thoroughly as a populist. The decision to try to imple-ment *ujamaa* quickly and universally (rather than on a slow localized basis), the decentralization policies, the comparative neglect of the cities and urban areas, and especially of Dar es Salaam, as well as the attempts to enforce a rigid Leadership Code — all these policies reflect President Nyerere's determination (for which he is widely admired) that Tan-zania's development should not lead to widening inequalities between Tanzanians, but rather should be accompanied by narrowing differentials between town and country, between regions, between peasants and workers, between government officials and the rest of the population. Lack of reliable data makes it difficult to assess the results in all these dimensions, but we have already seen that in the official figures at least, public service differentials have been reduced, and indeed at the top levels official wage restraint policies have been so severe that top officials probably suffered a fall in real incomes of 20 to 25 per cent between 1971 and 1974, when inflation accelerated rapidly. On the wider front, one well-informed observer has suggested that:

> It is likely that average peasant incomes were at best static over 1961–66 and rose relatively more slowly than real wages over 1966–74. . . . It appears that about 30% of peasants in 1974 had consuming power equal to or greater than the minimum wage earner, another 30% had consuming power that was between two-thirds the minimum wage and the minimum wage itself, and the remaining 40% had less than two-thirds of the consuming power of the minimum wage earner. (Green 1979, p. 24)

If the results have not been startling, very largely, one suspects, because of the failure of rural development efforts and the poor agricultural performance, the costs have been enormous. We have already talked of bureaucratic discontent (for it is the bureaucrats, above all, whom egalitarianism has hit hard). But more importantly, a determination that none should lag behind, that all should receive a 'fair' share of the resources available, *has meant that all resources (personnel, money, agricultural inputs) have been spread so thinly over the country and the population that 'critical minimum' levels, necessary for any effective impact, have not been obtained anywhere.* In all the accounts of *ujamaa* one sees the same picture of inadequate resources stretched so thinly as to render them useless. Extension officers trying to cover several villages and a huge area. Not enough transport, not enough surveyors and natural resource analysts (so that villages were wrongly sited in remote, badly watered, tsetse-infested, soil-poor areas), not enough fertilizers and insecticides, not enough sprays, ploughs, oxen, not enough ox-trainers, not enough stores or marketing outlets, and so on. Even a highly competent and motivated public service would have struggled under such circumstances, and the evidence is that Tanzania had no such thing. Thus the basic problem was exacerbated by incompetence, neglect, demoralization and even perhaps malevolence. And of course the resource constraint was not only quantitative but qualitative as well. Tanzania did not have enough agricultural and rural development cadres, many of those it had were not very good, and attempts to produce more by 'crash' short courses only compounded the problem. We shall see in the next part of this chapter that this crippling lack of sufficiently motivated and technically competent cadres is not present in China, and this is one – but only one – of the crucial reasons why a genuinely effective egalitarian rural development has been possible there and not (as yet) in Tanzania. One cannot escape the conclusion that given its severe constraints in skilled and motivated manpower, Tanzania should have either sacrificed some equality by concentrating resources on 'the strong' areas and farmers or gone rather more slowly and concentrated *ujamaa* efforts initially on the most underprivileged areas and peasants. The latter alternative would presumably have been much more congenial to President Nyerere, though its impact on regional and social inequalities would certainly have been much less than the policies which have actually been followed.

It also seems likely that President Nyerere's essentially rural and agricultural vision of Tanzania's socialist future led him to underestimate the extent to which a particular sort of industrialization is in fact a prerequisite of effective agricultural development. In particular, it is essential, as the experience of China shows, to have an industrial structure capable of providing the capital goods and other inputs which are necessary to raise agricultural productivity. As we have already seen, although Tanzania has a number of industries which process agricultural output, either for export or domestic consumption, she does not have enough industries providing the chemicals, implements and machinery on which any agricultural development effort depends. In particular, fertilizer production in Tanzania is small and actually fell in the course of the 1970s (see Hyden 1980, p. 174); it is also high cost. As a result fertilizer has also to be imported, cannot be obtained in the required quantities (since oil price rises have massively increased its price) and is distributed through a very inefficient and high cost state distribution system. In addition, Tanzania's engineering industry for the production of agricultural and related machinery is small, very inefficient and totally incapable of providing either the technology or the technological knowledge that the peasants require to raise their output and productivity. Hence the situation of continued working with the most primitive tools which we saw outlined by von Freyhold.

It must be stressed that this is not the result simply of an inadequate investment in industry, but rather of investment in the wrong sort of industry and of the very inefficient manner in which all Tanzanian industries (including those which should provide agricultural inputs) are managed and operated. One observer has suggested that this latter problem too owes something to naive egalitarianism, especially a lack of industrial discipline consequent upon worker participation legislation (Hyden 1980, pp. 156–81). Nor does it seem that this situation is likely to change much, at least in the immediate future. For though Tanzania's long-term industrial plan (to 1995) does promise a growth in the capital goods and engineering sectors through a new 'Basic Industries Strategy' (BIS), it seems that for the immediate future Tanzania has 'placed a high priority on the satisfaction of domestic basic need. Thus the production of food, textiles, shoes and construction materials will have particular emphasis' (Tanzania 1976, p. 43).

Conclusions

Does all this mean then that Tanzania's socialist development strategy has 'failed'? It does not, because there are some positive features and some potential for the future, and also because development strategies are not to be judged as 'successes' or 'failures' in this sort of time span. After all, Tanzania has just been independent for twenty years, and her present development strategy is barely fourteen years old. Fundamental changes in the economic and social structure of human societies, total shifts in their forms of production and ways of life, do not, even in this century of government-directed development efforts, occur overnight. They do not even occur in a decade or two, even in the most dramatic cases (such as Japan or the Soviet Union). On the contrary thirty years is the minimum for even basic changes, and other shifts, in social practices and in values and attitudes, may take fifty years or even a century.

What are the positive features of Tanzania's performance to date? There seem to be three principal ones. In the first place, she has made considerable strides in the provision of basic social services to her rural people, notably near-universal primary schooling and an apparently quite successful adult literacy drive, a system of basic preventive and curative health care (partly modelled on the more famous Chinese system), and much increased provision of clean water supply in rural areas (see Green 1979, pp. 25–6 and Tanzania 1976, pp. 65, 79, 83 and 89). In the second place, the process of villagization is now complete. The villages exist, and over time both the quantity and quality of the services made available to them can be improved. If these services include the provision of the inputs needed to increase output and productivity, and a marketing system which leaves a reasonable proportion of the consumer price in the hands of peasant producers, then agricultural output may begin to grow more rapidly. The impact of this on peasant incomes will depend, though, on world prices for Tanzania's major export crops and on the pattern and growth of domestic demand for food and agricultural raw materials. The latter of course depends in turn on the progress of industrialization (as does indeed the provision of adequate agricultural inputs). However, all these other conditions being satisfied, it is undoubtedly true that the provision of all types of economic and social services is much easier and less costly when directed to a few thousand nucleated settlements rather than to hundreds of thousands of separate households, and this is particularly true in the more sparsely populated, semi-arid areas of Tanzania.

Third, it should be noted that despite drought, the dislocation caused by *ujamaa* and villagization, and problems with industrial discipline and maintenance of industrial output, Tanzania's growth performance has been far from disastrous. The World Bank suggests that Tanzania's GDP grew by an average of 5 per cent between 1970 and 1978, and Green provides the same figure for the period 1964–73. However, population growth in the 1970s is thought to have been about 2.5 per cent, so the growth in per capita income was about half the GDP growth rate. More important, it seems that much of the growth appearing in the national accounts may reflect the growth of services (especially government services) rather than increases in agricultural or industrial output.

However, as against all this it must be said that while 'Tanzania's development strategy' cannot as yet be said to have failed, *ujamaa* (which was our primary concern in our analysis of President Nyerere's thought) must certainly be said to have failed. It had until very recently been totally abandoned in the realization that the experience of communal agriculture for some Tanzanian peasants had been so disastrous. It may in fact be politically impossible to resuscitate it in practice, despite its recent reappearance in Tanzania's formal development objectives. More gloomily, the very poor performance in food production (it rose at 'barely 3 per cent a year' or at little more than the rate of population growth over 1964–72 according to Green) and the even worse performance in food and commodity *distribution* and crop marketing have all led to some suffering and mass political discontent. If these trends worsen or even do not improve, they may fuse with élite disaffection to produce a major political shift, perhaps by the most frequently employed tactic of political displacement in Africa – the military coup.

CHINA

An important insight into China's development strategy since 1949 can be obtained from Table 4. The crucial comparison here is in the lines

Table 4   The economic structure of Tanzania and China

	China %	Tanzania %
% of population in rural areas (1975)	81	85
% of labour force employed in agriculture (1975)	76	83
% of GDP (1974) from:		
1 Agriculture*	20	40
2 Industry*	54	18
3 Services*	26	42
Estimated GNP per capita (1978)	$230	$230

* Agriculture includes forestry and fishing; industry includes factory and small-scale industry, mining and quarrying, handicrafts, public utilities and construction; and services include transport, trade, government and other services.

Sources: Rawski (1979, p. 35), World Bank (1980, Tables 1 and 19), Eckstein (1977, p. 229) and Tanzania (1974, p. 7).

showing the structure of GDP in China and Tanzania in 1974. It will be seen that though China has a very similar proportion of her population living in rural areas, and an identical GNP per capita to Tanzania (in 1978), she is none the less much more industrialized, and derives a much smaller proportion of her national wealth from agriculture. Although China's agricultural labour force was proportionately rather smaller than Tanzania's, it still amounted to some 329 million people (or over 76 per cent of her total labour force) in 1975, and yet these people produced barely a fifth of her GDP (Rawski 1979, p. 39). Conversely, a 'mere' 47 million workers, or less than 11 per cent of her total labour force, produced 147 billion of the 273 billion *yuan* of China's GDP in 1974. In other words while the 'average' agricultural worker produced some 166 *yuan* of output in 1974, the 'average' industrial worker produced over 3000 *yuan*. Although figures like this must be treated only as rough orders of magnitude, and while these averages of course disguise enormous variations, other sources do confirm that this scale of differential exists (see Rawski 1979, pp. 120 and 162–3). As we will see shortly, it is the coexistence of these sorts of productivity differentials with much smaller income differentials between agricultural and industrial workers which provides a clue to the central mechanism of China's economic development.

However, China is not merely an extraordinarily industrialized country given her level of per capita GDP (Eckstein 1977, p. 229); the structure of her industry is very different too, as Table 5 shows. As already noted, Tanzania'a industrial structure is largely oriented to the

Table 5 The structure of industry in Tanzania and China

	Tanzania %	China %
% of value added in industry from:		
1 Producer goods (including construction)	32	62
2 Consumer goods (1974)	68	38

Sources: Eckstein (1977, p. 215) and Tanzania (1976, p. 41).

production of durable and non-durable consumer goods, mainly as a way of substituting for imports, whilst China's industrial structure is, by contrast, much more oriented to the production of industrial raw materials (iron, steel, cement, energy) and of industrial machinery.

Conventionally, an industrial structure oriented strongly to producer goods, and employing such a comparatively small number of workers in proportion to its output, would be found to be very capital intensive, and indeed this is the case in China. In 1974 urban industry accounted for 75 per cent of the gross value of industrial output, and large-scale urban plants in the metallurgy, machine building, automotive, aircraft, electronics and oil extraction industries accounted for the bulk of this (OECD 1977, p. 149). The core of this highly capital-intensive producer goods sector is still the 150 or so plants which were built and equipped by Soviet engineers and technicians under the massive programme of industrial aid to China during the first Five Year Plan (1953–7), many of which are located in Manchuria. One authority holds that the bulk of the growth in China's industrial output between 1957 and 1965 was attributable to these plants (Field 1975). However, the massive expansion of the highly capital-intensive oil industry occurred after the Sino–Soviet split of 1960 when China lost access to her main oil supplier, and the considerable growth of this industry (especially the Ta-Ching oil field) and of the chemical fertilizer and farm equipment industries have been the principal forces keeping the Chinese industrial sector as a whole on an upward slope of capital intensity since the mid-1960s (Eckstein 1977, pp. 215–18).

As against this, the rural small-scale industry for which China has become internationally famous makes a comparatively small economic contribution, no matter what criterion is used. Data presented by Rawski suggest that in 1975 rural small-scale plants in the '5 small industries' (energy – mainly coal mining or small hydro-electric power stations for rural electrification – fertilizer factories, small-scale cement production, iron and steel plants, and agricultural machinery manufacture and repair) accounted for just 7 per cent of the gross value of industrial output and 11 per cent of total industrial employment. Moreover, their level of output per worker was less than half that in the large state run plants. As Rawski states, 'it is . . . evident that despite the expansion of rural industry, large-scale urban industry has retained its position as the leading force in Chinese industrial expansion' (1979, p. 62). In addition, a great deal of China's 'rural small-scale industry' is neither rural nor small scale. For example, of the 52 plants visited by the American Rural Small-Scale Industry Delegation, 18 were located in county towns, produced an annual average gross output of 2.9 million *yuan* and employed on average 379 workers. Even the 'commune'-owned plants, of which there were 13 in the sample, employed an average of 145 workers. Only the 5 brigade-level plants in the sample were. genuinely small scale, employing an average of 15 workers (American Delegation 1977, p. 68). The county-level plants in particular account for the bulk of small-scale producer goods output (in the 5 small industries). Moreover, the general thrust of Chinese policy appears to be to make their rural industries more mechanized and capital intensive – at least in the actual production processes – as time goes on (see, for example, American Delegation 1977, pp. 93, 98, 102).

So, with a highly capital-intensive industrial sector and a comparatively small administrative and service sector, China continues to employ the vast majority of her labour force in agriculture, and indeed absorbs the huge annual increases in her labour force overwhelmingly into agriculture. Rawski shows that between 1958 and 1975 the Chinese labour force increased by 148.5 million people. Of these, 58 million were absorbed into all forms of non-agricultural employment (29.6 million of them into all forms of industry including construction), which left over 90 million people to be absorbed into agriculture. Rawski suggests that not only was this accomplished, but each agricultural worker was required to work more hours and days, and seasonal labour shortages were experienced in many areas. As a result the Chinese pushed ahead with a process of rapid mechanization in agriculture (particularly of harvesting and threshing processes), and indeed their plan was that by the beginning of the 1980s '70 per cent of the main work in agriculture, forestry, animal husbandry, side-occupations and fisheries will be done by machines' (Chou Chin 1977).

How was this possible? How could agriculture absorb such huge increases in manpower in a country which has population densities on crop land of over 700 per square kilometre, and how could mechanization of agriculture proceed without threatening massive unemployment or underemployment? The simplest answer is that China's agricultural system, particularly in the rice-growing river valleys of southern China (which bear the highest population densities), is more akin to intensive horticulture or market gardening than it is to peasant agriculture as conventionally understood. The Chinese peasantry, whether working on individual plots or (since the Revolution) on collectivized land, is engaged in a type of cultivation which is so intensive and painstaking that its capacity for labour absorption is, if not exactly infinite (we shall see later that there is some evidence of declining returns to labour in Chinese agriculture), then at least well capable of absorbing the increases in the agricultural labour force which have occurred to date.

The most labour-absorbing activity in Chinese agriculture today, as for many centuries past, is the collection, treatment and application of organic fertilizer from both animal and human sources. For despite the very rapid increase in the use of chemical fertilizer in the last two decades with the spread of rural fertilizer plants, over 80 per cent of the fertilizer applied to China's agricultural land still comes from organic sources. Rawski estimates that:

> At two hundred and seventy five working days a year, the increased direct human labour (exclusive of animal tending) required to compost and process the manure of the animal population annually is equivalent to 11.5 million man-years for hogs and 23.3 million man-years for large animals [horses, mules, donkeys, cows, buffalo and oxen]. The combined total of 34.8 million man-years amounts to more than one-third of the . . . 97.3 million workers added to China's agricultural labour force between 1957 and 1975.   (1979, p. 94)

And this of course is exclusive of the labour absorbed in the collection and treatment of human 'night soil' and of the highly labour-intensive process of manure application.

In addition to this, huge quantities of labour are absorbed in the planting and transplanting of crops (especially rice seedlings), in the hulling and threshing of grain by traditional methods, and in the expansion of a whole range of farm management tasks which follow from the extension or improvement of the irrigated area and from more multiple cropping and inter-cropping. These latter in particular demand more careful weeding and pruning, and they also of course increase the volume of harvesting, sometimes spreading all these tasks into what had previously been slack seasons, by adding new crops to the annual cycle. Moreover, there is some evidence that both the new crops adopted and the increasing stress on animal husbandry to provide draught power, meat, milk and manure have meant that more and more of China's agricultural output is labour intensive in nature (see Rawski 1979, pp. 106–7). When to all this one adds the labour absorbed in what was previously the slack season in Chinese agriculture (November to February) in mass mobilization campaigns against human, animal and plant pests, in irrigation construction and maintenance, and in a vast range of construction and reconstruction projects (from rural factories and hydro-electrical power stations to land levelling and terracing), it is small wonder that, on the most conservative estimates made by Rawski, the Chinese not only succeeded in absorbing over 90 million new farm workers between 1957 and 1975, but that the average number of days worked per worker per year rose from about 160 in 1957 to at least 215 in 1975 (Rawski 1979, pp. 113–18). In fact the problem now in many areas of China is to release labour from agriculture so that it can be more productively employed either in rural industry or, more importantly, in those capital construction projects that are the essential prerequisite of increasing labour productivity both in industry and agriculture. And it is here that the real originality of China's development strategy since 1949 lies. For the Chinese have squeezed to the limit the possibilities inherent in using labour to make capital. Particularly in the rural areas, their aim and their achievement have been to use labour in capital construction projects which both enhance the productivity of land and increase the amount of productive land (through irrigation and other water control schemes, by land levelling and terracing, and by fertilization of previously poor land), and which in turn make more productive the use of other capital equipment in agriculture. Thus, for example, in North China a predominant aim is to level hilly land for tractor use, as has occurred in the famous Tachai area. But even in industry, labour mobilization programmes have meant that rural hydro-electric stations, cement plants, fertilizer plants, steel furnaces and smaller consumer goods factories (for footwear and textiles, for example) have been built and, to a degree, equipped using local labour and materials and minimizing the use of imported materials whether from outside the country or from outside the particular commune.

Thus, as existing agricultural practices become ever more intensive (in part simply to cope with increased population pressure) and as the vast programmes of agricultural capital works in turn add to this, the Chinese aim is to alleviate the increasingly important labour constraint on development by shifting labour 'upwards' from less to more productive and remunerative tasks. For example, a great effort is being made to mechanize grain threshing and hulling operations (to release labour from this very onerous and unproductive task), and power tillers and mechanical transplanting machines are being introduced as quickly as possible to release labour from cultivation. In all cases the aim is to transfer that labour into agricultural capital works programmes (which will raise the long-run productivity of land and labour in agriculture) or to move it directly into industrial capital projects. One study even suggests that within the rural industrial sector itself there is now a conscious preference by Chinese planners for more and more capital-intensive technologies, so that, though employment may not be maximized in the present, 'future' labour will be released for more industrial capital works (American Delegation 1977, pp. 75–81).

However, there is a clear limit to the degree of capital construction, especially in industry, which can be attained from the massive mobilization of predominantly unskilled labour and the use of local materials alone. Plant design and the production of even 'simple' industrial equipment require specialist engineering skills. And many industrial processes require access to technology that may be beyond the capacity of a county or commune to produce alone. The Chinese achievement here has been to devise a system for the transfer of both equipment and expertise from China's industrial heartlands (in Manchuria and the coastal cities), so that local initiative and expertise can be supplemented from 'higher' levels when needed. In fact training programmes which allow brigade- or commune-level technicians to be attached to county-level factories for training, and county-level staff in turn to have access (through exchange and other programmes) to the industrial expertise of Manchuria, Shanghai or Canton, produce a constant upward shifting in the level of local technological skills. It seems particularly significant that the main role in technology development and diffusion in China has been played not by the Soviet-built Manchuria plants but by the smaller engineering works of Shanghai, Nanking and Canton, many of which, though merged into larger conglomerates, originated in the pre-1949 period as private enterprises. They employ an old and highly skilled working class and seem to have functioned continually since 1949 as the innovating and problem-solving core of China's industrialization effort (see OECD 1977, pp. 149–52).

Whilst China is a conventional communist developing country in her drive for industrialization, she is very different from the USSR in that this industrialization has not been funded by squeezing agriculture. On the contrary, since 1957 and especially since the food crisis which followed on the failure of the Great Leap Forward (1960–2), the real tax burden on agriculture has been progressively reduced. The terms of trade between agriculture and industry have constantly been improved for agriculture, both by raising procurement prices for crops and by actually lowering the prices of most industrial products sold in rural areas (see Lardy 1978, pp. 176–8). This has gone along with a large rise in health, education and welfare expenditures and their concentration in rural areas (Lardy 1978, p. 178). The net effect of all this, together with heavy constraints on urban real wages, has been to lower the urban/rural income gap continuously between 1957 and 1975.

But if industrialization has proceeded so rapidly and has not been funded by 'squeezing' agriculture in the 'traditional' communist fashion, how has industrial capital accumulation occurred? The answer seems to be threefold:

1 Labour mobilization for capital construction as already noted;
2 Massive Soviet aid during the first Five Year Plan which allowed the heavy industrial base in Manchuria and elsewhere to be re-furbished; and
3 Since 1957, in urban industry, prolonged wage restraint on urban workers. Lardy suggests that between 1957 and 1975 the product-ivity of Chinese industrial workers may have doubled, whilst their real wages remained virtually static. This policy seems partly to have been a response to the rapid rural–urban migration and urban unemployment which followed from the crash industrialization and rising urban real wages of the first Five Year Plan. But its net result has been to allow state and municipal enterprises to accumulate surpluses rapidly at the expense of the urban working class, and to use these surpluses not only for further capital formation but also to fund tax and other transfers to rural areas and backward regions (Lardy 1978, pp. 175–85). There is some evidence that a series of strikes and other labour problems in China's industrial cities in the period 1974–6 may have been partly due to the frustrations caused by nearly twenty years of wage restraint.

Yet despite all these efforts, China's recent economic policy changes indicate that the scale of capital accumulation and industrialization is still seen as inadequate by at least some of the current leadership. And the basis of the problem is almost certainly the continued massive absolute increases in China's population and labour force, even though the annual growth rate of population may not now be much more than 2 per cent. Given the age structure of China's population and the massive base on which increases occur, the best projections suggest an *annual* increase in the labour force of about 10 million workers, rising to nearly 17 million by 1990. Though the whole history of China suggests that if these workers have to be absorbed primarily into agriculture, this will be done, there is disturbing evidence that despite all the capital and input improvements in Chinese agriculture in the last twenty-five years, output per man day is declining, with the falls between 1957 and 1975 being in the range of '15 to 36 per cent depending upon which assumptions are chosen with regard to the labor intensity of cultivation and fertilizer preparation' (Rawski 1979, pp. 118–22).

Now we know that despite these productivity trends in agriculture, tax, subsidy and other policies meant that over the same period per capita rural incomes rose 15 to 19 per cent (Lardy 1978, p. 179). It seems unlikely that, if these diminishing returns are not arrested, 'squeezing' of industrial workers can continue on the scale required to maintain this kind of discrepancy between agricultural productivity and agricultural incomes (and indeed since 1977–8 urban real wages have risen). The only alternative therefore is to speed up even further the movement of labour out of agriculture into industry and services. Rawski has calculated that even with an annual increase of industrial employment of 5 per cent (the trend rate between 1957 and 1975), China's agricultural labour force will continue to rise until 1990, and that even with an annual increase of 7.5 per cent in industrial employment, probably the maximum which is feasible given the capital accumulation required, the peak would only be brought forward by five years (Rawski 1979, pp. 132–4).

But the problem is that with a tendency for China's industrial structure to become ever more capital intensive and the service sector of employment kept small until very recently by government policy, the capital requirements for such industrial employment expansion (on a scale of 15 to 20 million workers annually until at least the end of the century) are enormous, especially if there is to be capital 'deepening' (to lift productivity) as well as capital widening. The problem here is not simply or perhaps even primarily a monetary one. It is rather that there is a limit to which labour mobilization and use of indigenous expertise can substitute for access to the most advanced techniques of production. This is particularly true in the producer goods sector, which has been used, as we have seen, to provide both the 'hardware' and the 'know how' for China's rural industrialization drive, but which has itself become somewhat technologically backward (by world standards) after over twenty-five years of relative neglect. The current Chinese leadership has therefore opted for considerable imports of technology into this sector from the west. But of course this requires that China either have or obtain massive amounts of hard currency (i.e. it does introduce a monetary constraint) or engage in barter dealing of some form. The inability of most of China's industrial products to compete on the world market has meant that in opting mainly for barter dealing, China has had to offer her raw materials (oil, coal and other minerals) as her only internationally negotiable assets. That her present leadership has at times appeared prepared to do this, and on a massive scale, is a clear sign of the acuteness of the 'capital shortage' problem as they perceive it. China remains on a demographically induced treadmill. Though her astonishing achievements to date and the marvellous inventiveness and industry of her people give every cause for optimism that she can overcome her problems, there is no doubt that the effort to raise the mass of her people from the decent subsistence level which they now enjoy to a situation of even relative material prosperity (by western standards) will involve a further stupendous effort of resource mobilization and organization.

China and populism

Our close analysis of the Chinese development strategy shows very little which is populist, despite first appearances. It is true that the majority of China's vast population is still employed in agriculture, but the majority of the country's GNP does not come from this source. Moreover, there is a persistent pressure to mechanize agriculture (including tractorization, especially in the north) and to increase capital intensity in industry, including rural small-scale industry (much of which is neither rural nor small-scale and which, in any case, accounts for less than 5 per cent of total employment).

In addition, the continued thrust of China's development strategy is to accelerate the industrialization process, to remove labour from agriculture – through mechanization – even faster (so as to arrest diminishing returns). The prime constraint on this strategy is the phenomenal rate of capital accumulation required, especially if capital is to be deepened as well as widened. Recent changes in China's economic policy towards the west suggest just how serious this constraint may be.

The tremendous pressure of population on China's cultivated land and the small and unreliable 'surplus' over subsistence which this produces have meant that the Chinese communist regime has never (not even during the supremely 'orthodox' first Five Year Plan period) been able to pursue a policy of violently squeezing agricultural incomes in the interests of industrial capital accumulation. And indeed the mass starvation and misery which was induced by the one attempt to undertake anything like this (during the 'Great Leap Forward') convinced the regime that resources had to be devoted continually to raising agricultural output and incomes. This has been done largely by squeezing the urban working class and directing part of the resources so obtained to rural areas. It is the policies pursued in China's rural areas since the Great Leap Forward that have won her such popularity among those development theorists and agencies which I have termed 'populist'.

But, as I hope the above analysis has shown, the 'pro-agricultural', 'pro-rural' policies of the 1960s and 1970s all occurred within the context of a continued thrust toward industrialization. Indeed they were seen as part of that process, with the 'industrialization of the countryside' occurring through an ingenious broad-scale use of labour not to substitute for capital but to create capital. However, that process of 'labour mobilization for capital construction' was itself only possible because it could be supported with technology and expertise derived ultimately from the 'older' industrial centres of Manchuria and the coastal cities. It would be correct, I think, to say that agriculture has never been 'put first' in China, but one could also say that in so far as this did occur, it was only possible because a comparatively advanced industrial structure (with its concomitant, a skilled and adaptable industrial proletariat) already existed. The absence of such a structure and such a proletariat was one of the vital 'missing ingredients' in the Tanzanian situation. It meant that the Tanzanian peasants were, in every sense, 'left on their own' in the rural development effort.

Finally, we should note that many of the characteristics in China's development strategy which find approval from populists in fact depend upon institutional and political conditions they would presumably find unacceptable. Thus, for example, the massive labour mobilizations which have done so much to keep agricultural output ahead of population growth and to provide both employment and capital formation are only possible because of the 'dependent' situation in which the Chinese peasantry finds itself as the result of the collectivization of agricultural land. Since collectivization, peasant incomes in China depend upon the workpoints (calculated in a variety of ways – see Maxwell 1979, pp. 44–50) which they earn in agriculture and other work. The impossibility of earning an adequate subsistence income from the tiny 'private plots' and sideline crafts which remain to the peasants, together with the tremendous moral and social pressures which are placed on them to undertake any and all types of communal work, give the Chinese Communist Party a degree of control over the labour power of the masses in China which is without parallel in any other developing country.

Moreover, it is the total control over the industrial structure and commodity flows exercised by the central and local state in China which has allowed a policy of 'commune self-sufficiency' to be developed. Communes can be encouraged to be as self-sufficient as possible in a range of agricultural and industrial products because state planners know that only such commodities as they determine will be available to each commune from external sources. And conversely communes, brigades or work teams can construct factories for the production of iron and steel, cement, shirts or shoes, secure in the knowledge that no competing products will intrude into their designated markets. In part, of course, the sheer size of China and the still poor communications in some areas provide a measure of 'natural protection', particularly for heavy or bulky products like cement. But many of the smallest, most labour-intensive, rural industries are engaged in the production of light consumer durables. In this case, as in so many others in China, we have the paradox that it is only a massively centralized control of the macro-economic environment which makes this kind of 'local self-suffiency' viable. The small and beautiful, if it is not to be wiped out by competition, presupposes (ironically) the big and bureaucratic.

Examples of this sort could be multiplied but are, I think, unnecessary. The essential point is that China's overall development strategy is not in any way populist. On the contrary it is simply a conventional communist industrialization strategy modified in subtle and imaginative ways to cope with China's particular circumstances, and especially with a massive agricultural population crowded on to a small cultivated area. If this broad strategic context and thrust is abstracted away, particular characteristics may be found (employment generation in agriculture, labour-intensive rural industry, pro-agricultural terms of trade) which may appear to fit the populist mould. But when reinserted into that context they are seen to be adjustments to the crucial constraint on China's industrialization (the man/land ratio), and in fact are part of a long-term strategy to ease and finally remove that constraint. They also depend upon the maintenance of a highly centralized economic planning system in which the abolition of private control over investment, production and circulation makes the setting of relative prices and the patterning of product flows an essentially administrative business. They also exist within a context in which all agricultural production and management decisions have been removed from peasants as individuals or households, and are made in 'collective' ways which, to say the least, are highly susceptible to state and party influence. All this is a long way from the populist world of a small-scale peasantry competing 'fairly' under the indulgent eye of a minimalist state. It is even a long way from more modern neo-populist visions, which accept a more interventionist role for the state but only in support of the small independent peasant, artisan or trader. And these reflections lead us to examine some of the theoretical contradictions in the populist vision.

POPULISM AND NEO-POPULISM: SOME CENTRAL PROBLEMS

'They all want competition without the lethal effects of competition' – Marx.

The example of China is illuminating. This is a country in which agricultural incomes have been raised, both absolutely and relative to urban industrial incomes, while income differences between agricultural producers have been reduced and are now at some of the lowest levels in the developing world. At the same time independent peasant control over land and agricultural production was effectively ended over twenty-five years ago. There is in fact no meaningful competition among agricultural or industrial producers, and until very recently the role of international trade (except for grain imports) was of minimal importance in the economy. State control over agricultural and industrial producers is complete, at least in so far as the state sets all the most important parameters (of input costs and output prices) in which the peasantry must operate. To put the matter paradoxically, the Chinese peasantry appears to have been 'saved' by being abolished. A total loss of individual peasant autonomy (in the use of land and labour power) has been the price of a continual rise in living standards and of greater equality both among peasants and between peasants and others. However, a desire to separate these two phenomena is precisely the hallmark of populist and neo-populist visions of development. Populist visions imply that peasant living standards can be raised and equality increased while *at the same time* maintaining individual peasant households as landholding and labour-disposing units.

Unfortunately, there is no historical or contemporary example of this combination and, on reflection, this is hardly surprising. For whilst Chayanov may have been right to distinguish peasants from capitalist farmers, in that the former are not concerned to maximize output and minimize costs, and cannot treat labour as a variable cost, none the less peasants do compete. They compete for land above all, but they can also compete for hired labour and other inputs and in the sale of output. Moreover, some are always more able managers than others or enjoy a better land or market situation. Under these circumstances, it is hardly surprising if, in the absence of intervention, inequalities should emerge among peasants and possibly widen to the point where some become large-scale commercial farmers whilst others become landless labourers working in agriculture and elsewhere. Generally speaking, the greater the commercial opportunities available to the peasantry (i.e. the faster the market for agricultural produce is expanding), the more rapidly these tendencies will emerge. This market may of course be a domestic market within a given nation-state or the international or world market.

And this mention of the world market brings in another dimension of competition. For if peasants are producers of crops (either food crops or others) which are produced somewhere in the world by large-scale capitalist farmers or plantations, then in an economy which is 'open' to the world market, they may have to compete not merely with each other but with capitalist farmers in other parts of the world. The recent ex-perience of many of the oil-producing nations of the Third World which are or were also possessed of a considerable peasant sector (Nigeria, Algeria, Iran, Venezuela) is a powerful reminder of what this can mean in practice.

Broadly speaking, all these countries experienced the same pattern of events. The huge increase in revenue accruing from oil funded a large increase in urban employment, both in industry and in government and other services. Attracted by income opportunities not available in peasant agriculture, a huge drain of young people from the agricultural sector commenced and the urban food market expanded immensely. Although in theory this should have opened up considerable oppor-tunities for those remaining in peasant agriculture, the historical back-wardness of the sector and a total lack of supporting services meant that the peasants were unable to respond quickly enough to the opportunity. As a result it was easier to obtain the necessary food supplies by import-ing, which was in any event made easy both by the oil revenues and the abundant supply of cheap food – especially grain – from North America. As a result the migrant drain from a peasant sector, now in rapid decline and unable to compete with imports, continued, leading to an effective collapse or disappearance of the sector in two cases (Iran and Venezuela) and its marginalization in two others (Algeria and Nigeria). In three cases (Iran, Venezuela and Nigeria) attempts are or were being made to resuscitate domestic agricultural production, but through large-scale, capital-intensive 'agribusiness' ventures using multinational capital, not through the peasant sector (Bennamane 1980, Halliday 1979).

It is hard to resist the conclusion that if the desire is both to maintain a large proportion of the employed population in the agricultural sector and to equalize the distribution of income (both within that sector and between agriculture and other sectors), then necessary though not sufficient conditions of success in this dual populist objective are

1 to collectivize agriculture and
2 to 'close' the agricultural economy to the world market as far as this is possible.

Neither of these actions is likely to meet with much approval among populists or neo-populists, and in any case may simply not be possible in small open economies like Tanzania, or at least not without massive economic dislocation and suffering.

But it can be argued that for some at least of the modern neo-populists, particularly perhaps the ILO and even Michael Lipton, this cult of peasant agriculture and of equality is secondary. What is more important to them is opposing a blanket policy of large-scale, capital-intensive industrialization as the only route to development, and what they see as the consequent neglect of agriculture and small-scale enterprise in agriculture and industry. We have already argued that in this respect the neo-populists are on much firmer ground, especially when the discussion is of 'static efficiency', i.e. efficiency at one moment in time with respect to a given supply of capital and labour. Their critique is particularly convincing in situations where factor markets (i.e. the markets for capital and labour) are distorted in favour of capital and against labour. We have seen too that largeness of scale in employment terms need not imply capital intensity (see the discussion of the ILO report on the Philippines) nor need smallness of scale imply labour intensity. Many small-scale electronics enterprises in Japan are highly capital intensive. In agriculture Chayanov provided the beginnings of a theoretical account of why large-scale, capital intensive production need not be more efficient than peasant production, and the mix of large- and small-scale producers in different crops and even in the same crop (e.g. coffee or tea) across the world indicates that this is indeed so. In agriculture no general arguments from economies of scale or anything else can serve to establish the superiority of large-scale over small-scale production; both in theory and in reality the matter is decided by complex combinations of factors which may vary from situation to situation. They include the nature of the crop itself, the land and terrain, the skills of peasants and the structure and organization of markets.

When all this is said, however, the case of China acts as a powerful reminder that in development static efficiency is often less important than dynamic efficiency, i.e. the creation of the capacity to use future supplies of capital and labour more efficiently even at the cost of some inefficiency in the present. In its most developed form this idea is known as the 'Dobb-Sen' thesis on choice of techniques, and its essence is expressed by Dobb thus:

> the choice between more or less capital-intensive forms of investment has nothing to do with existing factor proportions, which are commonly asserted to govern such a choice. It depends not on the existing ratio of available labour to capital . . . but on precisely the same considerations as those which determine the choice between a high and a low rate of investment . . . namely the importance to be attached to raising consumption in the immediate future compared

with the potential increase of consumption in the more distant future.
. . . The same grounds which would justify a high rate of investment
. . . would justify also a high degree of capital intensity in the investment forms. [This approach] has the advantage of throwing into relief
the cumulative influence of investment in more productive methods in
making possible further investment, . . . of emphasising that one is
dealing with the slope of *a curve of growth* and not just a once-for-all
rise.   (Dobb 1955, pp. 149–50; see also Sen 1962, pp. 21–36)

In China it was the 'capital-intensive' producer goods industries of
Manchuria and the relatively capital-intensive engineering industries of
Shanghai and the other coastal cities which provided the machinery for
China's rural industrialization programme and which, even more importantly, provided both directly and indirectly the inputs (cement,
fertilizer, iron and steel, agricultural implements and machinery) which
made possible the continued expansion and intensification of China's
agriculture. In addition, it was in those industries that an industrial
proletariat and technical class were formed whose skills were then
diffused into the rural areas. We have already noted how the effective
absence of these 'motor' industries in Tanzania left the rural development effort there bereft of both inputs and expertise. In China in particular there is no doubt that the capital works programmes in
agriculture in the 1960s and 1970s (which were the prerequisite of
continued expansion of productive employment in that sector) were only
possible because investments had previously been made in capital-
intensive plants which were no doubt at their time of construction
statically inefficient with respect to given availabilities of capital and
labour. We should note too that in the 1950s China's factor markets were
severely distorted by the massive provision of Soviet industrial credits at
low or non-existent rates of interest. There is little doubt that an ILO
analysis at that time would have disapproved severely of this type of aid
because of its effect on employment.

But if a dynamically efficient capital goods industry was a necessary
prerequisite of employment generation in Chinese agriculture, and if its
absence was one factor undermining Tanzania's rural development
efforts after 1967, one should not be led to conclude that this is the magic
key to economic development. For if the comparison of China and
Tanzania reveals anything, it is the familiar truth that social, cultural
and historical factors may be as important in development as any
economic variable. Whether we are seeking to explain those organizational capacities of the state bureaucracy in China which are largely
absent in Tanzania, or the apparently wider diffusion of technical and

artisan skills among the Chinese peasantry than among their Tanzanian counterparts, or the incredible cultivating skills of the Chinese peasantry and the much lower levels of such skills among the Tanzanian peasantry, then in all cases we must have recourse to a detailed analysis of the history, culture and social structures of the two societies. For all these things point to a massive differential in the quality of the labour power available for the development effort in the two countries, to an 'X efficiency' factor, as economists call it, which may none the less be crucial in determining how organizations actually function and how land and machinery is actually used. In short, there are factors here unknown to the philosophies of either the populists *or* their conventional growth opponents, and their importance in the real process of development should not be overlooked merely because they fall largely outside the purview of the theories we are considering in this book.

All these qualifications notwithstanding, if we assert the central importance of capital goods industries in the process of development, the question arises as to how a particular developing economy should best obtain them. And in particular a central issue is whether it should attempt to create them by savings out of its own resources or should 'import' them from more developed economies, perhaps even under the control of foreign or multinational capital. This is just one of a series of questions which are considered in the second part of this book, when a particular strand of 'nationalist' development theory, often closely allied to populism, is considered.

The first part of this book has presented and examined a body of populist and neo-populist writing on development and has found it wanting. It has been argued that though the populist vision is in many ways very attractive and has frequently struck a chord amongst peasants and artisans faced with the traumatic experience of industrialization, it does not appear able to generate an alternative long-term development strategy which can be set against industrialization. Modern neo-populists have made telling economic criticisms of particular aspects of the industrialization thesis which require it to be modified in various ways (in particular as regards an uncritical cult of size and capital intensity), but they do not undermine its fundamental tenets. This marked theoretical weakness of populism as a total alternative is mirrored in the real world, where no successful examples of such an alternative are to be found. In short, populism makes good social and moral criticism, and has often produced very effective political sloganizing, but on the whole it makes rather flabby economic theory. I shall argue in the next chapter that precisely the same conclusions can be drawn about a tradition of nationalist economic theorizing about development, a tradition that partly overlaps with populism but has also taken other forms. One of those forms – 'dependency theory' – is analysed in the final part of the next chapter and points of similarity and difference between it and populism are noted.

6

Populism and nationalism

The 'classical' arguments for equating development with industrialization were laid out in the first chapter of this book in a very abstract form. They spoke of 'industry' and 'agriculture', of 'producers' and 'consumers', and of the changing structure of material needs as standards of living rise. But they told us nothing about *where* this industry or agriculture was situated, or *who* the 'producers' and 'consumers' were, and this of course is because these arguments are supposed to be universally valid. They are expressed in an abstract economic logic which is taken to hold irrespective of where or when production and consumption occur.

But in reality of course industrialization first occurred in the world at a precise place and time (Britain in the century after 1750), and this simple fact meant that, from the point of view of other (non-British) observers, the supposed universality of classical economic theory (whose founder was the Scotsman Adam Smith and many of whose principal advocates were British) could seem much more problematic. In particular, in a world in which Britain's massive industrial lead made her the 'workshop of the world', dominating both the production and export of virtually all industrial products, it was not difficult to suspect that many of the supposed universal postulates of classical economic theory were simply convenient rationalizations to justify and maintain British dominance. More sophisticatedly, one could argue that it would not have required any conscious rationalization of British industrial supremacy for Smith and his school to have ignored or downplayed the fact that 'economies' were, in the real world, largely coterminous with particular political entities − separate countries or nations − and thus to have failed to see some of the limitations on their own economic logic. In particular, it could be argued that the classical school's advocacy of free trade (on the grounds that unrestricted competition between all 'producers' and 'consumers' was the guarantee of increased economic welfare for all) would only hold if the world were one political and juridical entity. However, this was manifestly not the case and indeed the foremost

industrial 'economy' was in fact a specific nation, Britain. Hence acceptance of the free trade doctrine by the governments and producers of
other nations would condemn them to remain producers of food and
suppliers of raw materials (for British industry) in perpetuity. Moreover,
British industrial dominance also implied military dominance (and thus
its diplomatic dominance), as well as its dominance over production and
trade. And this too would be in perpetuity. Clearly the leaders of other
countries could not be expected to tolerate such a situation. Therefore it
was justified for the governments of such countries to take active steps to
support industrialization in their own countries, most notably by the
imposition of import duties and tariffs to protect their 'infant' industries
against British competition.

Such were the arguments of the German economist, Friedrich List,
who in his *National System of Political Economy* (1841) both made a
critique of Adam Smith and the classical school of political economy
from a nationalist perspective and provided the first full-scale theoretical
defence of industrial protectionism, a defence which has been reproduced, with slight variants, by every advocate of protection since that
time. List's critique of Smithian free trade doctrines depends upon its
nationalist perspective since it assumes that 'national' subordination is a
'bad thing' and indeed that 'national interest' is a meaningful notion.
Therefore we must note briefly the grounds on which List defended a
nationalist perspective. In his view, the central flaw in classical
economics was not its economic reasoning (a lot of which he agreed with)
but its 'anthropology', that is, its underlying conception of human
beings.

List argued that for Adam Smith and his school (he referred to it as
'the school'), human beings were conceived simply as isolated individuals endowed with a capacity for economic reasoning. This reasoning leads them to act in certain ways (as 'producers' and 'consumers')
and the sum total of these individual actions constitutes the workings of
'the economy' as a whole. Since the actions of the individuals are
rationally motivated, the overall pattern of actions is also rational and is
subject to certain laws. Though these laws are not known to most of the
individuals involved, they can be discovered through political economy.
Since for 'the school' all human beings, as human beings, are possessed
of this rational faculty, there is no meaningful way of aggregating them
as economic actors short of humanity as a whole. Thus in political
economy there are only two categories of human being, the isolated
individual and the universality of mankind. A particular, economic form
of rationalist individualism thus leads directly to universalism. But for
List both the individualism and the universalism of classical political

economy were spurious for, he argued, human beings are never isolated individuals but are always found as members of families, communities and cultures with their particular values, customs and forms of collective solidarity. These values, customs and sense of collective identity power-fully affect the way actual human beings think and feel. This in turn makes it misleading simply to abstract out individuals, and to conceive them simply as materialist calculating machines concerned purely with their personal advantage in production and exchange. The best way of putting this is to say that List thought that in analysing actual economies and societies one should not start from the individual but from collect-ivities of people. For in the real world individuals, born into or part of collective units of various sorts, will often sacrifice their individual material interests in the collective interest, and will do so largely because they obtain their values, beliefs and even their sense of identity in and through collectivities (from the family upwards). This applies especially to the nation, which stands predominantly between individual human beings and mankind as a whole.

> Between each individual and entire humanity . . . stands *the nation*, with its special language and literature, with its peculiar origin and history, with its special manners and customs, laws and institutions, with the claims of all these for existence, independence, perfection and continuance for the future, and with its separate territory; a society which, united by a thousand ties of mind and of interests, combines itself into one independent whole . . . and . . . is still opposed to other societies of a similar kind in their national liberty, and consequently can only under the existing conditions of the world maintain self-existence and independence by its own power and resources. As the individual chiefly obtains by means of the nation and in the nation, mental culture, power of production, security and prosperity, so is the civilization of the human race only conceivable and possible by means of the civilization and development of the individual nations.
>
> (List 1841, p. 174)

In this critique of Smith and the classical political economists for their 'individualism', 'materialism' and 'cosmopolitanism', List was by no means original. In fact in his arguments about the essentially 'social' nature of human beings and of the derivation of individual identity from collective (and especially national) identity, List was largely repeating the arguments of the German romantic school of theorists, including Fichte and Schelling. They had rejected the individualist rationalist doctrines of eighteenth-century France and Britain by attacking, in a very similar way but over a much broader range of issues, what they considered to be its false anthropology. In fact List did little more than apply to economic theory the philosophical arguments employed by German conservative thinkers in their rejection of the French Revolution (and of the Enlightenment doctrines which they believed had caused it). Even in the sphere of economics, List had his predecessors among fellow Germans like Jakob, Rau, Hermann and Adam Müller (Whittaker 1960, pp. 194–202). In America Alexander Hamilton's *Report on Manufacturers* (1791) had attacked Smith's free trade doctrine and defended a plan for protective duties and 'bounties' (subsidies) for American manufacturers on much the same grounds as List was to employ later. However, it is List's defence of protection, later endorsed (albeit briefly) by John Stuart Mill, which has passed into the mainstream of economic thought, and which provided the main intellectual defence of 'infant industry' protectionism, both in nineteenth-century Europe and, through transmission in countless economics textbooks, in today's developing countries (see Whittaker 1950, pp. 302–3, 307–8).

THE NATIONALIST ROOTS OF RUSSIAN POPULISM

We have already seen how the Russian populist movement sought to avoid the horrors of capitalist industrialization as it had occurred in western Europe. Instead it sought a direct transition to socialism based upon the traditional peasant *obshchina*, and we noted that this idea seems to have originated with Alexander Herzen. But Herzen himself became interested in the *obshchina* through two different influences: the researches of the German romantic conservative Haxthausen, and the writings of a group of Russian intellectuals who were particularly active in the 1840s and 1850s and who are usually known as the 'Slavophiles'. The three most outstanding theorists of the Slavophile movement were Ivan Kireevsky (1806–56), Alexei Khomyakov (1804–60) and Konstantin Aksakov (1817–60). The Slavophiles, like most of the Russian intellectuals of the nineteenth century, were primarily philosophers, theologians and literary critics. They were powerfully influenced by German literary romanticism and especially by Schelling, and like him their main aim was to defend what they regarded as the superior, more fully human values of a 'traditional' pre-Enlightenment world (especially the Christian religion) against the attacks of rationalism. The particular target of their wrath was the rationalist philosophical system of Hegel (which enjoyed great influence with other sections of the Russian intelligentsia, especially in the 1840s), and Hegel's central notion of an unfolding rationalist progress in human history. The

Slavophiles' total philosophy cannot concern us here (see, however, Walicki 1975, on which the following account is based). The main point of relevance for us is that a central role was played in the Slavophile world view by the peasant commune. Indeed the Slavophiles were the first group of Russian intellectuals to 'discover' the commune. However, its role in their thought was not as a 'proto-socialist' institution, but as the bearer of Slav culture and of Orthodox piety. In the Slavophile conception, traditional Slav culture (which was alive and well and living in the *obshchina*) had been distinguished by a total integration of the individual within the community, and thus with the total absence of that alienation and personal fragmentation which the Slavophiles, following the German romantics, saw as the necessary concomitant of rationalism and individualism. With this complete integration of the individual within the community (and the consequent sense of belonging, and of spiritual and psychological security which it brought) went a simple Christian piety expressed through the Orthodox church, and a rich and varied folk culture of artifacts, oral poetry and song (the Slavophiles, like the German romantics, were keen researchers of folk culture).

For the Slavophiles, then, the Russian serf, secure in his commune, was the bearer of the true Slav identity and way of life, and the principal bulwark against the 'westernization' or 'Europeanization' that had gripped an increasing part of the Russian intelligentsia and nobility following the reforms of Tsar Peter the Great (1682–1725) at the beginning of the eighteenth century. It was through this equation of rationalist individualism (and then of industrialization) with 'westernization', and of the peasant commune with 'Slav' identity and genuine cultural 'Russianness', that the Slavophiles added a central nationalist thrust to their conservative social philosophy.

Moreover, the Slavophile critique of Hegel also found echoes in Herzen, and thereafter in Russian populism. For the Slavophiles the single most objectionable feature of Hegel's philosophy was its evolutionism. In Hegel's philosophy the history of mankind was seen as the gradual development of a rationalist self-consciousness through which human beings came to understand themselves and their natural and social environment. Thus human societies past and present could be clearly ranked as more or less 'progressive' depending on the extent to which they manifested rationalist tendencies. In addition, however, Hegel identified stages in the development of reason in history, and explicitly drew the conclusion that all human societies must pass through those stages. Ultimately this 'necessity' derived from Hegel's fundamental premise, in which the growth of reason in history was the gradual unfolding of a creative design (identified with God). Thus

Hegel's philosophy was not merely evolutionary, it was what is termed 'teleological', that is, it predicated history as having an end or goal (the triumph of reason) which was already known (to God) at the beginning of that history. Thus human history was a literal 'unfolding' of a predetermined design or purpose and, as a result, no human society could avoid going through the predetermined stages of that unfolding.

The Slavophiles attacked this philosophy at its root, taking issue with its rationalist conception of God and thus with its teleology. They thereby denied that there was any basis on which societies in which rationalism played a greater role (they did not deny that such societies existed in 'the west' or in 'Europe') could be regarded as more 'advanced' or nearer to God's ultimate goal than those which were less rationalist and individualist. On the contrary, they argued, societies which were less rationalist and individualist, in which reason and individual self-consciousness played little or no role (more traditional collectivist societies like Russia, composed of its millions of traditional peasant communes), were not only happier but also more Christian and closer to God.

Now Herzen had little time for the Slavophiles' fundamentalist theology, anti-rationalism and anti-westernism, and in his early days was a convinced 'westerner' and disciple of Hegel. But his first-hand experience of industrialization and of bourgeois culture (in England and France where he lived in exile), and then the failure of the western European revolutions of 1848 to bring about the democratic and socialist changes for which he hoped, led him to revalue his original low opinion of 'traditional' Russian culture. He came to hope that the very 'backwardness' of Russia, her poverty, the comparatively slight impact of western rationalism and materialism, and the almost total absence of industry (and thus of a bourgeoisie) could prove an historical advantage. It might mean that there would be few or no obstacles to a direct transition to socialism, to a socialism based not on an industrial proletariat (which did not exist) but on the traditional peasant commune. If this were to occur, said Herzen, then Russia, far from being the most backward, least civilized country in Europe, with all the stages of historical progress still before her, could 'leap' into a position where she was the political and intellectual leader of Europe, able by her example to encourage the creation of socialism in the west. For this was something that the western proletariat, faced with a powerful and united bourgeoisie, seemed unable to do on its own. Indeed Herzen can be credited with formulating the concept, if not the term, 'proletarian nation'. In his view Russia had 'everything to gain and nothing to lose' from a leap into socialism. She was so backward, so poor, that there was both more to gain and fewer obstacles to overcome in a direct leap to socialism, but to a specifically 'Russian socialism' (Herzen 1956, pp. 199–200).

So the Slavophiles bequeathed to Russian populism – via Herzen – an obsession with the peasant *obshchina*, great hopes for Russia's role in history and a suspicion of, even total rejection of, evolutionist theories of history which would have condemned Russia to simple imitation of the stages of 'western' or 'European' history. They also bequeathed, though in a suitably modified form, an admiration for the 'simplicity' and firm sense of identity which the Russian peasant was supposed to possess (secure in his communal bonds). All this added up to a muted but persistent nationalism.

The Slavophile view of the Russian peasant – as the principal bearer of true Russian identity and culture, and as the hope of Russia – becomes more readily comprehensible if we understand that both the Slavophiles and the westerners in 1840s Russia were highly educated men, mainly of noble origin, who were *all* highly 'westernized'. For all of them had been exposed to western European thought and most of them could read one or more western languages. As a result virtually all of them suffered from a profound crisis of identity, an uncertainty about whether they were truly Russian or not, and a sense of being 'strangers', 'aliens' in their own society (Walicki 1975, pp. 336–455). Their conventional way of denoting this distinction was to refer to the nobility in general and the intelligentsia in particular as 'society', which was contrasted to 'the people'. 'Society' was highly individualist, alienated, constantly engaged in the analysis of the world and in self-analysis, whilst 'the people', secure in the Orthodox religion and in the communal bonds of their family, clan and village, knew no such problems of identity. Both Slavophiles and westerners shared this analysis of a fundamental cleavage in Russian society, and agreed that it had been created by the westernization of a section of the Russian upper class. But they disagreed violently about its implications. The Slavophiles saw it as a fundamental malaise which could be cured only by a thorough-going 're-Russification' of the nobility, who should learn from 'the people' (the peasants) what to believe and how to behave. The 'westerners' saw it as a personally painful but necessary stage in the growth of Russian society as a whole to rational self-consciousness. It is against this sociological background that we must see Slavophile/westerner disputes about the effects of rationalism and of tradition. For these were no mere scholastic debates, but sprang directly out of painful personal experiences of 'alienation', guilt and loss of identity, out of a 'crisis of the intelligentsia' in short.

Not only was this to be a continuing theme in Russian populist thought, culminating in the rather utopian movement 'to the people' in the 1870s (Venturi 1966, pp. 469–566), but it has been a repeated experience of westernized intellectuals in non-western societies, and particularly in European colonies and ex-colonies, from the late nineteenth century onwards. The intelligentsias of India, China (and South-East Asia generally) and Africa have all known this sense of alienation and of intense desire for identity and belonging which the Russian intelligentsia, of all political and ideological persuasions, experienced in the nineteenth century. The guilt theme, however, was perhaps uniquely strong in the Russian case. For there, unlike in many colonial and ex-colonial countries, the intelligentsia were predominantly of noble origin and, whatever their political views, often enjoyed extreme wealth and privilege. One must also say that the Russian intelligentsia did not experience direct imperial conquest and this made a difference to their social and political position as well as to their theoretical views. None the less this acute sense of personal and social disjunction, of being physically present in a society but culturally estranged from it, was enormously important in shaping the world view of the nineteenth-century Russian intelligentsia. It was a source of constant and violent fluctuations in their attitudes both to the west and to their own society (Herzen's own life and thought is a powerful example of this). It was also the main source of their nationalism. In fact it has been suggested that the Russian case is typical of modern nationalist movements in general which, so the argument goes, always have their origins in just such personal and social 'crises' in the intelligentsias of subordinated or dominated peoples (see Gellner 1964, pp. 147–78, and Smith 1971, pp. 109–50). However, it is beyond the scope of this book to comment on these theories of nationalism.

The major shift in Russian populist thought from the 1870s onward came, as we have seen, from the gradual emergence of capitalist industry in Russia (which seemed to throw into increasing doubt the possibility of a direct transition via the *obshchina* to a rural Russian socialism), but also from the replacement of Hegel by Marx as the primary 'western' thinker influencing the Russian intelligentsia. Yet in a curious way the populist response to Marx, and then to Russian Marxists (from the 1870s through to the 1917 revolution), was remarkably parallel to the Slavophile response to Hegel and 'the westerners' in the period 1830–60. Once again the primary point of criticism was Marx's evolutionism which, just like Hegel's idealist march of reason through history, appeared to condemn Russia to mere repetition of western experience. Once again, too, though Marx substituted the materialist development of the 'forces of production' for Hegel's idealist stages in the development of reason, the clear, indeed explicit, implication of his thought was that a considerable development of those productive forces and thus of material wealth was an absolutely necessary prerequisite of the construction of socialism. For capitalist development could only come about, he argued, in conjunction with the creation of a revolutionary proletariat possessed of both the desire for revolution and the technical skills required to run a socialist society.

Clearly acceptance of such a position entailed an abandonment of the idea of any unique Russian 'short cut' to socialism and thus of any idea of a unique Russian mission or 'leap' to prominence in history. It also logically implied that, in the early stages which capitalist development had reached in Russia, a consistent Russian Marxist should do all he or she could to encourage the development of capitalism whatever the social or human costs. For this was the only way to 'ripen' the conditions for ultimate revolution. We have already seen how the populist Mikhailovsky drew this implication in order to reject it scornfully (see pages 43–4); other Russian intellectuals like George Plekhanov and the 'legal Marxists' (such as Struve, Skvortsov, Chuprov and Tugan-Baranovsky) drew the same implication in order to endorse it wholeheartedly (Walicki 1969, pp. 132–94).

The response of Russian populists to Marx was twofold. Initially (through the 1870s) the major response was to reject Marx's evolutionism wholly or partly, and to assert that capitalist development had hardly touched Russia, so that a 'non-industrial' route to socialism still remained open via the *obshchina*. However, a second response, having its roots in some of Chernyshevsky's ideas, taken up by Flerovsky and most fully developed by the 'legal Populist' Vorontsov, was gradually to introduce the possibility of industrialization into the future of Russia but to make the Russian state (in Vorontsov's case a reforming Tsarist state) the agency of industrialization.

Significantly, this shift in populist thinking about industrialization became much more marked after the Russo–Japanese War (1904–5) when Russia suffered a humiliating defeat by a nation that had been regarded in Russia as a backward Asian island, but that, as Russian intellectuals now learned, had in fact embarked on a state directed programme of industrialization in the mid-nineteenth century. The connection between industrialization and military and naval capacity was made too clear to be ignored, and it was noted by the populists, especially Yuzhakov (Mendel 1961, pp. 57–8). At this point, too, Vorontsov moved decisively away from his earlier pessimistic theses on industrialization in Russia. Impressed both by the success of Witte's programme and by the humiliation of the Russo–Japanese War, he argued that, although it faced difficulties, industrialization under state control and direction was both possible and necessary. He even conceded that large-scale mechanized agriculture might be superior to modernized peasant agriculture, and therefore advocated a scheme whereby gentry farms were to be nationalized, with their former owners working as state managers. Peasants would be employed on these farms, where they would learn improved agricultural techniques, and would then 'naturally want to introduce this system into their own land' (Vorontsov quoted in Mendel 1961, p. 62). Thus they would unite their plots into larger farms and work under the direction of *zemstvos* agricultural technicians.

However, despite this nationalistically induced shift in his perspective, Vorontsov, like Danielson, still seemed to hope that industrialization could be made compatible with the improved welfare of peasants and artisans though, also like Danielson, he was rather vague about how this might be done. In the case of state industries, for example, Vorontsov wished them to provide employment for peasants in the winter months, whilst at the same time the peasant-workers would directly exchange the products which they produced in the factories on some direct barter basis (Mendel 1961, pp. 61–2). However, the very vagueness and contradictoriness of these schemes (what was to happen to these factories when the peasants returned to their farms in the summer?) prompted Engels at the time to dismiss them as 'bizarre', a product of the transitional stage in which Russia found herself. This stage allowed 'backward-looking', 'romantic' visions of a pre-capitalist utopia to coexist, with less and less conviction as industrialization advanced, with schemes for state-directed industrialization which were supposed, in some vague way, to avoid the social and human costs of capitalist industrialization (Engels 1895).

But, as Walicki points out, though the schemes of Vorontsov and Danielson may have struck Engels as bizarre and contradictory, with hindsight it can be seen that they were to be very typical of theories of development formulated in 'backward countries in conditions of a rapid and uneven growth of the world economy'.

The historical heterogeneity of the constitutive elements of Vorontsov's and Danielson's ideology was in fact a faithful reflection of the peculiar 'coexistence of asynchronisms' typifying all the backward countries in the process of modernization. Russian Populism, therefore, was not only an ideology of small producers, but also the first ideological reflection of the specific features of economic and social development of the 'latecomers', of the backward agrarian countries carrying out the process of modernization in conditions created by co-existence with highly industrialized nations. . . . [It was] the first attempt at theoretical explanation of these specific features and at deducing from it practical conclusions. And in this sense, it was a really representative ideology not in spite of the heterogeneity of its elements but because of it. . . . Flerovskii, Vorontsov and Danielson pointed out a double capitalist threat: the internal danger, threatening the Russian people [i.e. the peasantry], and the external threat, threatening the Russian nation as a whole. They were concerned not only with the problem of how to prevent the proletarianization of the Russian peasants, but also with the problem of how to avoid the proletarianization of Russia as a nation, how to prevent her from being exploited by more advanced countries and how to secure her an honourable place among the nations of the world.

(Walicki 1969, p. 129)

In fact with Vorontsov and Danielson we come as near as it is possible to get in the nineteenth century to those theories of 'underdevelopment' and 'dependency' which dominate the radical literature in 'development studies' today, and which I shall analyse in the next and final section of this work. Pessimism about the possibilities of indigenous capitalist development, hostility to free trade and a certainty that it leads to national exploitation, demands for state-led 'national' industrialization, sometimes socialist and sometimes capitalist in form, are all hallmarks of modern underdevelopment theory, through which runs a pervasive nationalism (just as in Vorontsov and Danielson). There is no doubt in my view that such thinkers as Paul Baran, Andre Gunder Frank, Samir Amin, Arghiri Emmanuel, and some at least of the Latin American, Caribbean and Indian dependency theorists, are much more the heirs of Flerovsky, Vorontsov, Danielson and other Russian populists and neo-populists, than they are of the Marxist tradition with which most of them consciously identify.

However, whilst this book has often been at pains to stress surprising and little-known historical continuities in unconventional or radical development theory, one must also, where necessary, give due weight to discontinuity. In this case there does exist a major historical chasm separating Russian populist theory from modern underdevelopment theory, a chasm which makes for substantial changes of emphasis (though not, I think, of fundamental premises) as one moves from one to the other. I refer to the experience of colonial conquest, and to the body of radical writing about imperialism, particularly by Marxists, to which it led. This experience, and the theories of imperialism to which it gave rise, are an essential background to a discussion of modern dependency theory, and are considered in the first part of the next section.

IMPERIALISM AND DEPENDENCY

Although the Russian populists were concerned to try to find a specifically 'Russian' route to development that would avoid the horrors of the western experience (horrors seen very much through the eyes of Marx and Dickens) and although both Slavophiles and populists were centrally concerned with what would today be called 'cultural dependency' (the loss of a specifically Russian or Slav culture and way of life through a 'westernization' spreading from the ruling class downwards), none the less the attitudes of the Russian populists to capitalist industrialization in Russia, and to Russia's place in the international economy, were somewhat different from those found in present-day radical dependency theories. The main difference is the even greater role of nationalism in the thinking of Third World intellectuals who, unlike the Russian intelligentsia, have been exposed to the humiliations of direct colonial conquest. As a result, even in the post-colonial period, they tend to be acutely suspicious of the role of foreign capital, and especially of multinational corporations (MNCs) in their economies.

In contrast even the most nationalistic Russian populists were not particularly concerned about foreign control over Russian industry – they had few worries about the 'Russianness' of Russian capitalism. Both Vorontsov and Danielson concluded, as we have seen, that Russian capitalism was doomed to be abortive, that it would not transform Russia as it had transformed western Europe, but they did not think that this was because it was under foreign dominance. They argued rather that Russian capitalism's inability to break into the international market (because western European economies were already dominant there) plus its necessary destruction of the internal market (by its destruction of peasant handicrafts) would mean that it would run into ever worsening crises of overproduction or underconsumption, and would finally grind to a halt.

This difference cannot simply be attributed to the different structure of foreign investment in nineteenth-century Russia and in the modern-day Third World. Much of the foreign investment in Russia was 'indirect', consisting of loans raised by the Russian government or public enterprises on foreign capital markets (mostly in France) and carrying a fixed rate of interest but implying no control by foreign investors over Russian enterprises. However, 'direct' foreign investment, with ownership of Russian firms by foreigners, was also important and grew in importance as the nineteenth century advanced:

> Between 1896 and 1900 a quarter of all new companies formed were foreign, and by 1900 foreign capital accounted for 28% of the total. By 1914 the proportion had risen to 33%. Foreign capital controlled 45% of Russia's oil output, 54% of her iron output. More than half the capital of the six leading banks of the country – themselves controlling nearly 60% of all banking capital and nearly half of all bank deposits – was foreign. (Warren 1980, p. 46)

Thus the much greater tendency among modern dependency theorists than among Russian populists to attribute the allegedly non-dynamic, non-progressive character of peripheral capitalism to its foreign control cannot be explained simply in terms of changed material circumstances (in this narrow sense). It is much more to do with the change in perspective wrought by the experience of colonial conquest.

Many parts of today's Third World are ex-colonial territories of the western industrial powers. They have known long periods of direct political conquest by a foreign power, with such direct control usually lasting at least a century (in Africa and South-East Asia), and over 250 years in the case of India. In Latin America direct colonial conquest (by pre-industrial Spain and Portugal) lasted for roughly three centuries and ended in the early or late nineteenth century (depending on the country) rather than in the middle of the twentieth. In addition to making a great difference to the social and political situation of the intelligentsias of the Third World (most of which were actually created by the colonial power), this experience of direct conquest also introduced theoretical questions about development and underdevelopment unknown to the Russians. Most especially, if (as in India) one was conquered and ruled for 250 years by a nation which, during that very period, itself became the greatest industrial power in the world and if, at the end of that time, one was not a highly industrialized country, but on the contrary was still dependent overwhelmingly on a peasant agriculture (which arguably was actually poorer at the end than at the beginning), then clearly it was logical to ask whether these two circumstances might be connected. That is, one may ask two distinct but closely related questions:

1 How far is the present-day poverty of an ex-colonial territory due to, or the fault of, the policies pursued by the colonial power?
2 How far did the industrialization of Britain, France and Germany depend upon creating and maintaining the poverty and de-industrialization of their colonies, that is, how far were development

in one part of the world and underdevelopment in another part interlinked processes, simply the opposite sides of the same coin?

The most comprehensive theory suggesting that development and underdevelopment *are* interlinked, indeed that underdevelopment in the Third World was caused by the development of the west, is usually identified with Andre Gunder Frank (1971). But, long before Frank, a whole series of writers concerned with nineteenth-century India had formulated arguments suggesting that British industrialization had rested on the 'draining' of wealth and capital from India and/or on the destruction of the Indian handicraft textile industry to provide a market for Lancashire cotton goods (see Kiernan 1981 and IESHR 1968). It may be noted in this context that the arguments used by the first 'drain' theorist, Digby (1901) paralleled very closely the arguments of Vorontsov, Danielson, Stepniak and others on the acquisition of peasant grain by taxes, on usurious credit and on the destruction of Russian handicrafts by Moscow's industries. For Digby, however, what was 'drained' was not grain but gold and silver; the drain went not merely out of the peasantry but out of India (to Britain), and the industries which destroyed Indian peasant handicrafts were not in Delhi but in Lancashire. In short, the 'drain theory' simply posits an 'international-ized' version of a mechanism that the Russian populists saw primarily in intra-national terms.

However, I do not wish to analyse these historical uses of theories of imperialism and dependency, partly because they would take us too far away from our primary concerns, partly because historical work on imperialism often contains arguments which are repeated in radical analyses of the post-colonial situation, and can therefore be dealt with in this context. One point, though, can be made. In all cases where one is attempting to assess the extent of the 'damage' to a colony's economic development caused by imperialism, or the extent to which the in-dustrialization of an imperialist power was due to the exploitation of its colonies, one faces a formidable problem of logic and method. In order to make such an assessment *one must know what would have happened if circumstances had been other than they were.* What would have been the form and speed of India's economic development if she had not been conquered by Britain? What would have been the extent of industrial development in Britain if she had not had colonies, or different colonies from the ones she actually had? One must make some assumptions, explicit or implicit, about these counter-factual situations. But the problem is that a large number of equally plausible situations can be imagined once one begins to move outside the real historical situation and consider alternatives. For example, if India is assumed not to have been conquered by Britain, is it more likely that she would have been conquered by another European power, or that she would have remained 'independent'? And if she remained independent, would she have had a modernizing internal government (such as that which appeared in mid-nineteenth-century Japan), or a weak traditionalist government, or no single government at all? Depending upon which of these, and other, assumptions one makes, one is likely to conceive of very different economic opportunities for India, and thus make very different comparisons with what actually happened under the British. And indeed it is precisely these kinds of issues that divide historians of India (see IEHSR 1968 for some very typical debates).

Rodney's work on Africa is also open to the objection that it relies heavily on very 'optimistic' assumptions about the possibilities for economic development in Africa if imperialism had not occurred (Rodney 1971). For while such assumptions have some plausibility, they are no more plausible, and arguably less so, than other, more pessimistic, assessments. Above all, in an historical situation, that is, a past situation which one cannot 're-run' to test different possibilities, such arguments are necessarily inconclusive and open-ended.

There is one logical escape from this indeterminacy. If in one's analyses of, say, nineteenth-century India, one can indicate constraints on development which were due directly to colonial control, e.g. the high tax burden induced by an extremely expensive army of occupation, or the refusal of a colonial government, under pressure from industrialists at home, to protect Indian industry, then one may argue not that these constraints would not have existed without the British (which leads, as we have seen, into necessarily indeterminate counter-factuality) but that these constraints could be got rid of by getting rid of the British. That is, if such analyses are directed not towards a dubious reconstruction of the *past*, but to the formulation of demands on the *present* and *future* (which of course is the way Indian nationalist scholars used them, as a basis of the demand for independence), then one can avoid the insoluble problems of hypothetical history. Of course when independence comes one may find that severe impediments to further economic development still remain, that political independence, while a necessary condition of 'real' economic development, is not in itself a sufficient condition. At that point the analyses will have to persevere in order to identify the new impediments and the means of removing them. And it is in precisely these conditions that theories of 'dependency' and 'neo-colonialism' have emerged. The bulk of writing on dependency in particular has originated in Latin America, and this is perhaps understandable given that the majority of countries in that area have been politically independent not for twenty or thirty years (as in Africa and Asia), but for 150 years or more. And yet most of them have levels of income and standards of living that are well below western levels, and all of them have large numbers of very poor people in their populations, most of whom are either peasants, landless agricultural labourers or 'marginal' urban workers of various types.

THE ROOTS AND CHARACTERISTICS OF 'DEPENDENCY THEORY'

Conventional accounts of the intellectual roots of Latin American writing on dependency stress two major streams of influence. First, they note a Marxist stream going back to Lenin and other classical theorists of imperialism (such as Hilferding, Bukharin and Hobson), with a major role in its transmission to Latin America being played by a small group of North American Marxists, notably Paul Baran (1957). Second, they identify a 'structuralist' stream originating in the work of Raul Prebisch and a number of other intellectuals active in the United Nations Economic Commission for Latin America (ECLA) just after the Second World War (see for example O'Brien 1975). However, more recently, a leading Brazilian writer on dependency, Fernando Henrique Cardoso, has taken issue with this conventional account, and has located dependency writing in a much richer indigenous tradition of economic and sociological analysis in Latin America, of which ECLA was just a part. He traces this tradition back to the 1930s, and sees the direct influence of Marx as just as important as that of Baran, while also stressing the contribution of a much more diverse set of 'external' influences including the 'bourgeois' thinkers Singer, Myrdal and Hirschman, as well as the explicitly Marxist theorizing of Sartre, Lukács and Gramsci (Cardoso 1977).

This issue of origins is less interesting for us than the central characteristic of dependency writing (certainly until very recently) which is – predictably enough we might now think – *a marked pessimism about the possibilities for capitalist development in Latin America*. Dependency writing in all its variants is concerned to locate the *blockages* or *impediments* to capitalist development (and especially to capitalist industrialization) in Latin America. These blockages are seen to lead to a 'distortion' of that development or to its 'stagnation'. For all the writers in this tradition the key to this 'blockage', 'stagnation' and 'distortion' in Latin American capitalism is its 'dependent' nature. Latin American capitalism is dependent upon western-dominated (and particularly American-dominated) international capital, and as a result plays a 'subordinated' or 'marginalized' role in world capitalism. This is reflected internally in a lack of structural dynamism, an inability of capitalism in Latin America to transform economies there in the dynamic or progressive way in which it transformed the west. At the level then of its broadest thrust – a blockage or stagnationist thesis – dependency writing is simply a re-run of Vorontsov and Danielson. However, the detailed arguments which are used to support this thesis are rather different from those employed by the Russian populists. In particular much less emphasis is placed on the destruction of the internal market as a built-in contradiction leading to stagnation. In the place of this rather simple argument, a much larger battery of arguments are employed by the dependency writers, with different weight being given to different arguments by different writers. Moreover, since most of the best dependency writing has been concerned with empirical analyses of specific Latin American countries and regions, changes of argument or of the weight given to various factors have reflected varying empirical conditions in Latin America, as well as differing theoretical perspectives. All this said, however, the following major arguments are almost universally employed.

1   An argument about *class structure and the role of the state* in Latin America. Here the main contention is that in a variety of ways the ruling classes in Latin America, both in the past and at present, are tied by their economic interests (and by their ideologies and cultural preferences) to international capital. Thus, unlike the 'bourgeoisies' of western Europe analysed by Marx, the ruling classes of Latin America have no interest in industrializing their economies in any 'autonomous' or 'independent' fashion. On the contrary, they are able to enjoy both wealth and high status by playing certain 'intermediary' or 'managerial' roles for international capital, and are quite content with this role. Thus they play no dynamic economic role themselves, and use their control of state power to protect the interests of multi-national capital in Latin America.

2   Arguments concerning the non-dynamic role of the *agricultural sector* in Latin America. This is generally characterized as technically backward and unable to provide 'surpluses' on a sufficient scale to allow for capital accumulation in industry. Sometimes this is because it is regarded as a 'feudal' sector implanted by the Spanish and Portuguese at conquest. Sometimes the problem is seen to lie in the particular form which capitalist penetration of agriculture took in Latin America, a form which involved the

'reconstitution' of certain forms of feudalist production alongside large plantations and commercialized, but technically untransformed, peasant production (Fernandez and Ocampo 1974).

3   Arguments concerning the *capital-intensive, luxury consumer goods nature of much industry* in Latin America. This creates problems of employment generation and also marked income inequalities between certain privileged urban industrial workers on the one hand, and the 'mass' of marginalized 'informal sector' workers in urban areas and rural dwellers on the other (arguments such as those considered in detail in Chapter 4 are repeated here).

4   A number of closely related arguments concerning mechanisms of *surplus transfer* out of Latin America in the interests of international capital. Mechanisms of this transfer which are frequently analysed include (a) persistently negative terms of trade for Latin American products in international markets, (b) profit repatriation and other forms of transfer payments (transfer pricing, royalty payments, management fees) by subsidiaries of multi-national corporations based in Latin America and (c) amortization payments and interest payments on loans contracted in international capital markets by Latin American governments. These debts are often contracted in the first place in order to meet balance of payments problems originating in the terms of trade, etc. All these mechanisms of 'surplus transfer' are seen to reduce the levels of investible surplus below what they might be, and thus slow down the pace of industrialization and structural change within Latin America. The central concept here (of surplus transfer reducing the 'actual' surplus below the 'potential' surplus) owes a great deal to Baran, whilst the specific propositions on the terms of trade originate with Prebisch and the 'structuralist' writers of ECLA with subsequent development by neo-Marxist writers like Emmanuel. The latter locates terms of trade imbalances in a much deeper process of 'unequal exchange' between developed and underdeveloped economies. We shall return to this shortly.

5   Arguments concerning *spatial inequalities* (between rural and urban areas and between regions) which often owe a great deal to non-Marxist writers on the causes of spatial inequality in economic development (writers such as Myrdal and Hirschman among many others). These can, as in Frank for example, be linked to arguments about 'surplus transfer' (from backward to advanced regions, from rural areas to cities) and to Marxist concepts of 'combined and uneven development' under capitalism deriving originally from Parvus and Trotsky.

In the rest of this chapter I shall be primarily concerned with the fourth of these five sets of arguments, that is, those concerned with surplus transfer. For they have been applied in almost identical terms to virtually all other parts of the Third World (Keller 1977, Amin 1976, Brett 1973, Leys 1975, Oxaal 1975, Palmer and Parsons 1977), and this set of arguments is central to the theme of this chapter: the role of nationalism in theories of economic development. However, before undertaking more detailed analysis, some general points about dependency writing in Latin America can be made.

First, it should be noted that although some (perhaps most) of the writers on this theme think of themselves as Marxist, and make frequent reference to the works of Marx, Lenin and others on imperialism, their writing in fact marks a sharp break with the classical Marxist writing on imperialism which dates from the late nineteenth and early twentieth centuries. For all the writers involved in that classical tradition (Bukharin, Luxemburg and Lenin) retained Marx's conviction (expressed in his writing on India for example) that imperialist conquest by the advanced capitalist powers, although it involved the crude exploitation of colonial peoples, would eventually lead to the creation of autonomous industrial capitalist economies in the colonies. They believed that although its short-run consequences were highly destructive, the long-run effects of imperialism (in destroying pre-capitalist economies and traditional ways of life) would be 'progressive'. And even though later Marxist writers like Lenin came to see imperialism as fulfilling a rather different role for capitalism than that identified by Marx – Lenin (1917) and Bukharin (1917), following Hobson (1902) and Hilferding (1910), stressed much more strongly the outlet for surplus capital provided by imperial conquest – *they never broke with Marx's conviction of the long-term 'progressiveness' of imperialism.* This is even true of Luxemburg, whose writing stresses much more insistently than any of the other early European theorists of imperialism the destructive nature of capitalism's initial impact on pre-capitalist economies (Luxemburg 1913).

However, whilst Lenin's *Imperialism* retains Marx's basic conviction about the long-term progressiveness of capitalism even in 'colonial and semi-colonial' countries, it has recently been argued that this work itself, and even more importantly Lenin's change of emphasis on this question in the early years of the Comintern, laid the foundations for a fundamental shift of Marxist thinking on this issue. After Lenin's death this shift was made final at the 1928 Congress of the Comintern when his 'formal obeisance' to the classical Marxist position was jettisoned completely and it was asserted instead that: 'Imperialism retarded both industrialization in particular and capitalism and the development of the productive forces in general. The resolutions of this congress formalized the surrender of the Marxist analysis of imperialism to the requirements of bourgeois anti-imperialist propaganda' (Warren 1980, p. 107). This movement away from the classical Marxist position had mainly political roots. It was the product of a situation in which the high hopes of support from a working-class revolution in western Europe, which had been entertained by the Russian Communists in 1917, were fading fast as the 1920s advanced. At the same time anti-imperialist nationalist struggles in the 'east' (India, China and elsewhere) were growing rapidly in strength and influence in the international Communist movement, and seemed to provide the best hopes of support to the still fragile and isolated Soviet regime (Warren 1980, pp. 84–109).

Baran's contribution to this shift (and certainly his main contribution to dependency theory) was to reinforce the post-1928 political position by a theoretical apparatus focused on the concepts of 'potential' and 'actual' 'economic surplus' and of 'surplus transfer'. Those specific theoretical ideas are analysed in the next section of this chapter. Here it should just be noted that in order to present his picture of a predatory, 'unprogressive' capitalism in the Third World, Baran had to contrast it, explicitly or implicitly, with the 'normal' 'progressive' capitalist development that had occurred in the west. Thus we have in Baran a tendency that is very noticeable in all dependency theory: isolating the 'blockages' or 'distortions' that afflict capitalist development in the Third World through contrast with a highly formalized and schematic historical account of capitalist development in the west, in which those blockages or distortions were not present. Thus he poses the question, 'why is it that in the backward capitalist countries there has been no advance along the lines of capitalist development that are familiar from the history of other capitalist countries?' (Baran 1957, p. 136). In attempting to answer that question he begins with a schematic description of capitalist development in the west:

First there was a slow but . . . appreciable increase in agricultural output accompanied by intensified feudal pressure upon the underlying agricultural population as well as ever more massive displacement and rebellion of peasants and consequent emergence of a potential industrial labour force. Secondly, there was a more or less far-reaching and . . . general propagation of the division of labor and with it the evolution of the class of merchants and artisans accompanied by the growth of towns. And thirdly there was a more or less spectacular accumulation of capital in the hands of the more or less steadily expanding and rising class of merchants and wealthy peasants. . . . In Western Europe, mercantile accumulations were particularly large and . . . highly concentrated. This was partly due to the geographical location of the Western European countries which gave them the possibility for an early development of navigation and with it of a rapid expansion of maritime and riparian commerce. . . . The resulting far-flung trade, combined with piracy, outright plunder, slave traffic, and discovery of gold, led to a rapid formation of vast fortunes in the hands of Western European merchants.

This wealth had a tendency to snowball. The requirements of navigation gave a strong stimulus to scientific discovery and technological progress. Shipbuilding, outfitting of overseas expeditions, the manufacturing of arms and other supplies required by them for protection as well as for the conduct of 'negotiations' with their overseas trading partners – all provided a mighty impulse to the development of capitalist enterprise. The principle that 'one thing gives another' came in full operation, external economies of various kinds became increasingly available, and further development could proceed at an accelerated rate. . . . Wealthy merchants entered manufacturing to assure themselves of steady and cheap supplies. Artisans grew rich or in partnership with moneyed tradesmen expanded the scale of their operations. Not infrequently even rich landowners became involved in industry (particularly mining) and thus laid the foundations for large capitalist enterprises. But most important of all, the state, ever more under the control of capitalist interests, became increasingly active in aiding and advancing the budding entrepreneurs. (Baran 1957, pp. 137–9)

The net effect of such lightning thumb nail sketches pointing to the dynamism of capitalist development in the west (which are then contrasted with the 'twisted', 'stagnant', 'backward' capitalism of the Third World) is to leave an impression, through brevity as much as anything, of western capitalist development as a relatively non-contradictory or unproblematic process. There is no doubt that Baran himself, steeped in *Capital* and other Marxist classics, was under no such illusion, and even in what is said above there are obvious clues to this, for example the 'displacement' and 'rebellion' of peasants, and mentions of 'plunder' and 'piracy'. None the less the brevity of treatment and the stress on dynamism (to provide a sharply contrasting backdrop to discussions of 'backwardness') can leave that impression. Moreover, such an emphasis is entirely in accord with the theoretical approach of Baran (and Sweezy) to advanced capitalism. They saw it as encountering its major structural problems only in its modern 'monopoly' phase, when severe 'stagnationist' problems are seen to set in (Baran and Sweezy 1966). Indeed in Baran's analysis part of the problem of capitalist development in 'backward' nations derives from the fact that they are penetrated by capitalism in its monopoly phase. It then becomes quite easy to postulate stagnation in the capitalist periphery as simply an offshoot of stagnation at the centre.

At any rate, in less historically informed hands than those of Baran, this tendency – to see capitalist development in the west as relatively or entirely uncontradictory or unproblematic in contrast with 'dependent' capitalist development at the periphery – has become much more marked. This in turn encourages isolation of such factors as regional or urban/rural inequality, or markedly dualistic labour markets, or 'marginalized' populations and regions, or rapidly expanding 'informal sector' activities, as unique hallmarks of dependency. And yet it can easily be shown that all these tendencies were also present at earlier stages of the development of the presently advanced capitalist countries. In addition, a strong concentration on British industrialization as the archetype of 'western' capitalist industrialization – which owes a great deal to Marx's *Capital* and later works based on it – leads to contrasts with the pattern or sequence of development on the periphery which are very problematic when the economic history of other advanced capitalist countries is examined (Kitching 1980b).

So we see an ironic contrast here. For Vorontsov and Danielson, and for other Russian populists, capitalist development in western Europe was viewed as a socially destructive, even horrific, process which had to be kept out of Russia at all costs (indeed one sometimes suspects that their stagnationist theses on capitalist development in Russia owed something to wishful thinking!). For the bulk of dependency theorists, however, capitalist development in the west appears as relatively unproblematic, or at least as relatively 'smooth' and 'straightforward' when compared with the 'distorted' and 'dependent' capitalist development in Latin America and other parts of the present-day Third World. This of course is because most radical dependency theorists are more or less enthusiastic industrializers (and thus must be contrasted with the Russian populists and neo-populists who were, at best, reluctant industrializers). Dependency theorists disagree on the form of industrialization which they want. Some believe in an independent 'national' capitalism; others think that only a socialist industrialization drive can succeed (O'Brien 1975). But all agree in condemning capitalism for failing to deliver a national industrial transformation of their economies similar to that accomplished in the west. The latter itself is not generally seen as undesirable. We must now consider one of their major means of explaining this 'failure': 'surplus transfer' from dependent economies.

'SURPLUS TRANSFER' AND 'UNEQUAL EXCHANGE'

The basic point of the concept of 'surplus transfer' is to suggest that a peripheral or economically dominated poor country has been and is developing slower that it might due to the fact that part of its resources are being transferred abroad. The underlying theory of the concept is most clearly set out in Baran. But it is one of the central concepts in Frank (for all Frank's 'metropoles' and 'satellites' are linked together through surplus transfer) and this concept, even if the name is not used, is a hallmark of virtually all writing on dependency, both theoretical and empirical. The central concept here is that of the surplus. In Baran this concept is divided in two.

1   The *actual economic surplus* defined as 'the difference between society's actual current output and its actual current consumption', that is, actual saving or capital formation.
2   The *potential economic surplus* defined as 'the difference between the output that could be produced in a given natural and technological environment with the help of employable productive resources and what might be regarded as essential consumption'.

(Baran 1957, pp. 22–4)

In Baran's subsequent analysis of both advanced and 'backward' capitalist societies it is the latter concept which is central. For his argument in both cases is that the potential economic surplus is far greater than the actual economic surplus, but specific mechanisms (different in the two cases but always traceable to the fundamental nature of capitalism, whether backward or advanced) ensure that large amounts of the potential surplus are wasted. In the case of the backward capitalist economies he says:

The principal obstacle to rapid economic growth in the backward countries is the way in which their potential economic surplus is utilized. It is absorbed by various forms of excess consumption by the upper class, by increments to hoards at home and abroad, by the maintenance of vast unproductive bureaucracies and of even more expensive and no less redundant military establishments. *A very large share of it – on the magnitude of which more is known than on that of others – is withdrawn by foreign capital.*

(Baran 1957, p. 228, emphasis added)

The mechanism of 'surplus withdrawal' to which Baran devotes most attention is profit repatriation. Indeed the quotation above is followed immediately by three pages of statistics on profits earned by foreign corporations in the Dutch East Indies, the Belgian Congo, India, Egypt, Mexico, Brazil, Chile, Bolivia, Northern Rhodesia and Iran, and remitted to their countries of origin. Subsequent writing on this theme has identified other mechanisms of surplus transfer including interest payments on foreign loans; payment for shipping, insurance and other 'invisible' services to advanced economies; patents charges and licence and management fees charged by multi-national corporations setting up subsidiaries in dependent capitalist countries; and also 'transfer pricing' by such corporations (which is in fact just another method of profit repatriation). Dependency literature has also drawn attention to the terms of trade between advanced and dependent economies, following Prebisch and the structuralist school of ECLA. Some dependency writers have even seen this as the primary mechanism of surplus transfer, even more important than profit repatriation. We shall look at this issue shortly, when we come to examine the theory of 'unequal exchange'. But here it is interesting to note that Baran himself explicitly rejects such a view, primarily on the grounds that, where changes in the terms of trade are mainly due to changes in the export prices of raw materials produced in the backward countries by multi-national corporations, then rises or falls in these prices affect mainly the corporations and their foreign stock holders, not 'the welfare of the peoples inhabiting the undeveloped countries'.

> A decline of profits may merely involve lower remittances abroad, possibly painful to the foreign stockholders of the companies involved or even disturbing to the countries the balance of payments of which are thus adversely affected; but this may be of no major consequence to the economy of the area the raw materials of which are being exported. Conversely, a rise of the profits earned by the raw materials enterprises may imply larger remittances on account of dividends or some investment in expansion of raw materials production – also . . . of no particular importance to the underdeveloped areas. In fact, since an increase of prices of raw materials and a corresponding swelling of profits of the raw materials enterprises does usually lead to larger payments to foreign capital, the higher prices of their exports do not result in an increased capacity of the underdeveloped countries to import foreign goods but rather in an expansion of their 'unrequited' exports. (Baran 1957, p. 233)

The central point here is that Baran, in many respects a very orthodox Marxist, examines surplus transfer from a class rather than a national perspective. He is continually aware that in a capitalist world economy resources are transferred from one class to another, or within one class –

the international bourgeoisie owning multi-national corporations – even when the transfers are simultaneously trans-national, that is, involve movement of resources from one country to another. Hence for Baran it cannot be assumed that, because resources move from country A to country B, either all of the classes in country A lose or all of the classes in country B gain. This *may* happen, but it is a matter for close theoretical and empirical investigation, not an assumption to be made. As we shall see, one of the crucial issues in the debate about 'unequal exchange' is how far it is possible to speak of countries 'exploiting' other countries. For that theory is a most sophisticated attempt to demonstrate in an economically rigorous way that *all* the classes in the countries benefiting from unequal exchange share, albeit to different degrees, in that gain, while *all* the classes in countries losing through such exchange lose, again to varying degrees. It thus attempts to give a rigorous theoretical foundation to the concept of 'national exploitation' (exploitation of one nation by another) by concentrating primarily on the terms of trade.

However, before dealing with that issue, we must complete this more general review of the concept of surplus transfer. Briefly, the central problem is the one already discussed in relationship to the historical uses of dependency theory: the problem of counter-factuality. This may be seen clearly if we look again at Baran's definition of the potential economic surplus. It is the difference between the output which 'could be produced in a given natural and technological environment . . . and essential consumption'. He then goes on to argue that in backward countries a lot of consumption is not essential (that is, it is luxury consumption by elites and therefore 'waste'). Together with other factors, including transfers to foreign capital, this inessential consumption ensures that what is produced is markedly less than what 'could' be produced if political and economic arrangements were other than they are. Hence the actual economic surplus is much less than the potential economic surplus. In the particular context of foreign capital investment he is forced to argue, explicitly or implicitly, that the additional output and other benefits (such as wage payments to local workers) produced by foreign capital are much less than those which 'could' have been available if such investment had occurred in some other, more 'independent' fashion. Dealing with this problem explicitly Baran says:

> It is undoubtedly correct that if the natural resources of the under-developed countries were not exploited, there would be no output to provide for the transfer of profits abroad. This is, however, where the firm ground under . . . the above propositions ends. *For it is by no*

means to be taken for granted that the now underdeveloped countries, given an independent development, would not at some point have initiated the utilization of their natural resources on their own and on terms more advantageous than those received from foreign investors.

(Baran 1957, p. 186, emphasis added)

Certainly, 'it is by no means to be taken for granted' that this would not have happened, but neither is it to be taken for granted that it would. So we are back once again in a necessarily indeterminate argument about hypothetical or likely possibilities. However, at least Baran does attempt to confront this problem explicitly. In later radical writing on dependency and underdevelopment it is simply assumed away (see, for example, Frank 1971 and Rodney 1971).

In addition to this intractable problem of counter-factuality, 'surplus transfer' formulations are often open to objection on technical grounds concerning the way in which the magnitudes of such transfers are measured. In the case of foreign investment for example, one frequently encounters a procedure by which the initial sum invested is compared with the total of profits and other monies, e.g. licence or management fees, which have been remitted abroad over some period of time since the original investment was made. If the flow of monies abroad is larger than the original investment, which it may often be, then the difference is said to represent a 'surplus transfer' of X amount. A similar procedure is adopted with foreign loans, the initial sum loaned being compared with the sum of the amortization and interest payments (see Leys 1975, pp. 137–8, and Shivji 1976, pp. 158–67). But of course such procedures fail to take into account the 'internal' benefits which may have flowed from the initial investment, e.g. a continuing flow of wage payments to local workers and of dividends to local investors, or external economies flowing from the initial investment and affecting other sectors. For example if the initial investment was in a railway, one has to attempt to assess the extent to which other monetary benefits – increased internal production and trade along the railway, or increased exports of other commodities – have been 'indirectly' a result of the railway. It is clear that similar considerations may apply to foreign loans, depending upon what the loans have been used for. Certainly a simple comparison of money capital inflows into developing countries with money capital outflows is an inadequate basis on which to assess even the monetary cost and benefits of foreign investment, and certainly a totally inadequate basis upon which to build a theory of exploitation.

In fact in ignoring both the physical impact of foreign investment – its contribution to increased physical production and/or exports – and its structural effects (such as changes in the internal division of labour, growth of the internal market, local acquisition of skills), such purely 'monetary' and 'international exchange' theories of surplus transfer can degenerate into a rather weak-minded economic nationalism. They leave the impression that by a simple monetary subtraction sum one can always demonstrate the 'undesirability' of foreign investment. In fact, at the very least what is involved is a sophisticated analysis of both the internal – 'structural' and 'dynamic' – impact of foreign investment and its foreign exchange costs. In some cases a sophisticated internal analysis may show that even the foreign exchange costs are less than supposed (because, for example, other exports have been 'indirectly' encouraged).

In short we are back at an old issue, the attempt to locate exploitation and the causes of inequality purely in the sphere of exchange relations and indeed purely in the sphere of monetary relations. We have noticed that this was a marked feature of populist thought, and brought down the wrath of Marx upon Proudhon's head. In the case of 'surplus transfer' theories, however, this tendency has been generalized out of the national sphere (where it dealt with relations between peasants and workers and merchant capitalists or financiers, or with relationships between the country and the town) into the international sphere, so that it now embraces relationships between countries. And in the case of Andre Gunder Frank, the 'national' and 'international' spheres are linked together, in that 'internal' metropoles within dependent countries, e.g. merchants or financiers in capital cities or provincial towns, pump out the (monetary) surplus. Part of it they keep, and part of it flows through them either to higher level local metropoles or abroad (Frank 1971).

But in either case the procedures adopted are all open to the same theoretical objections: the measures of 'transfer' used are naive and mis-leading, even as monetary measures, and underlying structural relation-ships and changes within the 'dependent' economy are ignored. The theory of 'unequal exchange' represents therefore an attempt to meet these sorts of objections by locating national exploitation between countries not in monetary relationships but in the underlying exchange of labour times. We have now to see how far this attempt was successful, and how far it is still open to the same fundamental objections.

UNEQUAL EXCHANGE

Before analysing the modern theory of 'unequal exchange' as set out in Emmanuel (1972), I will note what I hope the reader has already noted – that we are here in the presence of an old friend. We last encountered unequal exchange in Chapter 2, when we were examining the ideas of the early nineteenth-century Ricardian socialists. In that context it dealt with the exchange relationships between workers (primarily independent artisans) who, due to the monetary manipulations of merchants and financiers, were not able to exchange the products of equal amounts of labour time at equal prices. The Ricardian socialists looked to 'labour money' and direct 'labour exchanges' as a means of solving this problem. This does not mean that the concept was entirely lost between the 1830s and 1970s. We can find it, parenthetically, in the Russian populist work of Danielson, for example, who noted that in times of poor harvests Russian peasants were forced to exchange a larger amount of their labour time, embodied in their grain, for industrial commodities, necessary for their subsistence, which embodied a smaller amount of labour time (Danielson 1902, pp. 481–2). None the less, throughout the nineteenth century the notion of 'unequal exchange' of labour times received no theoretical development beyond that provided by the Ricardian socialists and, with the severity of Marx's attack on the idea of 'labour money' (Marx 1847) and then the waning popularity of the labour theory of value in general, it gradually faded away.

On its reappearance as a theory of international trade in Emmanuel, we find it backed up by a much more rigorous and mathematical economic theory (and there are thus direct parallels with the transition from nineteenth-century populism to modern neo-populism). But once again the essential idea is unchanged. To grasp that essential idea it is perhaps best to proceed by a simple example.

Imagine two equal-sized groups of workers in different countries. One group is producing an industrial product (say cloth) and the other group is producing an agricultural product (say sugar cane). In one hour the cloth workers produce one hundred yards of cloth, and the sugar workers produce one hundred pounds of cane sugar. If there is to be an 'equal' exchange of labour times, one hundred yards of cloth should exchange for one hundred pounds of cane (or one yard of cloth for one pound of sugar cane), and if the exchange is occurring through means of money then the prices of the cloth and the sugar cane should be set so that this ratio is maintained.

In Emmanuel's model of present-day international exchange, however, certain things have happened which guarantee that this equality of exchange is not maintained. For the cloth workers, who can be treated as exemplifying the workers of advanced capitalist countries, are now working with very advanced machinery so that in one hour they can produce not one hundred yards of cloth but, shall we say, one hundred thousand yards (a thousand times more). Meanwhile the productivity of the labour time of the sugar workers, who exemplify the workers of the dependent capitalist countries, has also increased, though possibly not as much as the productivity of the cloth workers (for technological research and progress has been heavily concentrated in the advanced capitalist countries). More importantly, however, even if the productivity increases have been exactly equal in the two cases, the effect of these increases on the groups of workers and on the prices of their commodities has been very different.

In the advanced capitalist countries the enormous increase in capital accumulation (which is what the new machinery and the massive increases in labour productivity represent) has meant that workers are in short supply relative to capital. This has happened because in the real world, though *capital* can move fairly freely between countries, immigration and other political restrictions mean that movement of *labour* internationally has been much more restricted. Hence workers from poor countries have not been able to move to rich countries in sufficient numbers to offset the relatively short supply of labour in those countries. This has given labour a much better bargaining position in advanced capitalist countries than in poor ones. In particular, it has allowed powerful trade unions to be formed by workers in advanced capitalist countries, and these trade unions have been able to ensure that as the productivity of workers' labour time rises (through increased capital investment), a larger and larger share of this extra productivity has gone to wages. In poor capitalist countries, however, labour is still very abundant relative to capital, and it cannot leave the poor countries in sufficient numbers to alter this situation. As a result, when there are productivity increases in poor capitalist countries through capital investment and improved technology, the major effect is not to increase wages (since trade unions either do not exist or are too weak to bargain effectively) but to lower prices.

In short, technological improvements in the advanced capitalist countries increase the productivity of each hour of labour, but they do not lower prices of production to the same degree as in poor countries since a much larger share of the increased productivity goes to wages, that is, real wages rise more or less continuously. In poor countries where the bargaining position of labour is much weaker (because of the relative excess of labour to the supply of capital), productivity increases lead to falls in prices of production. These two different trends in prices explain in turn the persistent tendency (to which Emmanuel draws attention at the beginning of his book) for the 'barter terms of trade' – the ratio of the prices of Third World commodities to the prices of 'First World' commodities – to be persistently in favour of the commodities produced in the First World. In addition, because the prices of the commodities produced by Third World workers tend to decline persistently relative to the prices of commodities produced by workers in the advanced capitalist countries, then, even though their own productivity may be increasing, the Third World workers will have to work longer and longer to obtain the same quantity of commodities produced by workers in the advanced capitalist countries. In short, there will be a more and more unequal exchange of labour times between the two groups of workers. (Conversely of course because the prices of their commodities are always rising relative to those of Third World workers, workers in advanced capitalist countries will have to work less and less time to obtain the same quantity of 'Third World' commodities.)

Several criticisms have been made of Emmanuel's argument. Bettelheim, in a critique appended to the English edition of *Unequal Exchange*, argued that Emmanuel's model depended upon trade unions in the advanced capitalist countries determining by sheer bargaining power the level of real wages, whereas, he argued, they are determined in fact by the rate and scale of capital accumulation and thus by the supply of labour relative to capital (Bettelheim 1972). However, it is unclear that Emmanuel's model does depend upon this assumption, and certainly it can be expressed, as above, without it. Barratt Brown argued that Emmanuel had persistently underestimated the productivity differences between labour times of First and Third World workers, and that these were great enough to explain much of the trend in the terms of trade. Hence there was no necessary 'unequal exchange' between workers equipped with the same type and degree of capital equipment (Barratt Brown 1974, p. 232). Others, however, have taken issue with this and, in defence of Emmanuel, have argued that major differences between prices and wages do exist between First and Third World workers even when they are equipped with an identical technology (Dandekar 1980).

The most serious theoretical criticism of Emmanuel in my view does not lie in these areas but in the area of his initial assumptions. In Emmanuel's model there is a free flow of capital between countries, very unequal real wages and a much more restricted flow of labour. However, theoretically at least, if there are sectors of the international economy with low real wages and there is a free flow of capital between countries, one would expect capital to flow toward the low wage sectors and countries attracted by the higher profits available. This capital influx in turn will increase the supply of capital, and as the 'excess' labour is absorbed in employment, there will be an upward pressure on wages. Thus, although there may be quite prolonged historical periods in which productivity increases (through capital investment) outpace wage increases (and thus lower prices and raise profits), it is impossible for this to continue *ad infinitum*, in a situation where labour is not perfectly mobile internationally, without upward pressure on wages within a particular economy. As a result wage levels in a rapidly developing economy will gradually rise to levels compatible with its more advanced competitors, and thus the 'unequal exchange' will terminate. That this is not merely a theoretical possibility can be seen in the case of Japan, which was a low wage ('excess labour') economy up to the late 1950s but which experienced very rapidly rising real wages in the 1960s and 1970s. Today real wages there are comparable with those in western Europe and North America. Partly as a result of this, Japanese capital has in the last fifteen or twenty years sought investment outlets elsewhere, especially in the low-wage economies of South-East Asia (Korea, Taiwan, Hong Kong, Singapore), which may themselves go through the same metamorphoses in the future (Halliday and McCormack 1973). Of course in situations where the capitalist sector is small and the supply of labour is enormous relative to capital, as for example in India, the period of 'labour absorption' (especially if industrial technology is becoming more and more capital intensive) may be so long as to maintain 'unequal exchange' relationships in being for centuries rather than decades. But the theoretical argument for seeing 'unequal exchange' relationships as products of particular stages in the uneven development of the world capitalist economy is very strong.

I wish now to note one particular implication which has been drawn out of Emmanuel's model. It has been explicitly suggested that if workers in the advanced capitalist countries benefit from unequal exchange of labour times with Third World workers, then they themselves are involved in the exploitation of Third World workers. That is, as suggested earlier, the new, refurbished theory of unequal exchange has been used as a theoretical underpinning of a concept of national exploitation, the exploitation not of one class by another but of one nation by another.

If we look closely at the situation, however, even as it is outlined by Emmanuel, it is clear that no such implication can be drawn. And if we ask how the situation he outlines comes about, we see why. For in the case both of workers in the advanced capitalist countries and in the peripheral countries, the labour time which they embody in commodities is expended for capitalists in mines or factories, plantations or ranches. Thus, in the case of the dependent economies, when productivity increases are converted not into higher wages but into lower prices and higher profits, those profits accrue to the immediate employers (whether these be local capitalists or subsidiaries of multi-nationals).

Conversely, when the 'cheaper' Third World commodities are sold to the advanced countries, the capacity of workers there to buy them as an ever smaller proportion of their rising real wages depends upon their having been successful in an economic class struggle with their employers (again, irrespective of whether these are local capitalists or multinational companies). In so far as the better bargaining position of First World workers allows them to raise their real wages by successfully struggling for an increased share of their own rising productivity, then they certainly benefit from the low prices of imported commodities, which prices have been made possible by the inability of workers in the Third World to do the same thing. However, in both cases (the Third World situation and the First World situation) the *actual agency* of exploitation is the same: national and international capital. Though workers in the advanced capitalist countries may *benefit from* exploitation of Third World workers (but only if they are relatively successful in their own class struggle), *they are not themselves an exploiting agency*. This is a simple logical distinction, but a vital one, and one which is often overlooked. It suggests that at least as a category in economic theory, the concept of 'national exploitation' cannot be sustained.

But this is not all. If capital is attracted to a dependent economy by the prospect of lower wages and higher profits, then this suggests that the transitional period of 'unequal exchange' (the period in which the export prices of commodities are falling or rising only slowly because productivity increases are ahead of wage increases) may also be a period of rapid structural transformation of a dependent economy. For this is precisely, or at least it may be, the period when excess labour is being absorbed in employment, either directly in industry or indirectly in tertiary and service employment. Rapid urbanization is occurring and the proportion of the labour force in agriculture is declining. In fact 'unequal exchange' relationships internationally will end when the internal process of structural transformation is completed.

Conversely they will persist so long as the structural transformation is incomplete. This does not mean that all countries which are experiencing 'unequal exchange' will also be experiencing structural transformation (this transformation may be blocked or retarded for some other reason). But it does mean that, theoretically at least, 'unequal exchange' and persistently negative terms of trade are not necessarily incompatible with internal structural transformation, that is, with a process of industrialization and development. So once again, just as in the case of 'surplus transfer' formulations, 'unequal exchange' directs attention away from empirical investigation of *internal changes* in dependent economies towards a rather *static* concern with exchange relationships.

That those relationships are conceived not in price or money terms, but in labour time terms, does not change matters much. For just like the concept of 'surplus transfer', 'unequal exchange' offers no convincing reasons why its existence should imply the impossibility of development in a dependent economy. In any particular case empirical investigation may reveal that *as a matter of fact* such a development is blocked, or at least that it is proceeding in a very slow or contradictory fashion, but one cannot *deduce this theoretically* either from the existence of 'surplus transfer' or from 'unequal exchange'. Both these concepts can provide tools for nationalist rhetoric, but they are totally inadequate foundations for any theory which purports to show that development in dependent capitalist economies is impossible or necessarily abortive.

Some dependency theorists have realized this, and since the late 1960s Cardoso in particular has called for a recognition that 'dependency' and 'development' are not simply polar opposites, and that there may be forms of 'dependent development'. In a recent article he suggests that there are two polar 'modalities' (or positions) among dependency theorists, and he locates himself with reference to these. He says that there are

> those who believe that 'dependent capitalism' is based on the hyper-exploitation of labor, that it is incapable of broadening the internal market, that it generates constant unemployment and marginality, and that it presents a tendency to stagnation and a kind of constant re-production of underdevelopment (thus Gunder Frank, Marini, and to a certain extent, dos Santos).

These dependency theorists are to be contrasted with

> those who think that, at least in some countries of the periphery, the penetration of industrial-financial capital accelerates the production of relative surplus-value; intensifies the productive forces; and if it generates unemployment in the phases of economic contraction, absorbs labor-power in the expansive cycles, producing, in this respect, an effect similar to capitalism in the advanced countries, where unemployment and absorption, wealth and misery coexist.
>
> (Cardoso 1977, p. 19)

Cardoso believes that the second position 'is more consistent', but he does not believe that, because there may be such a process as 'dependent development', the theory of dependency is thereby 'impugned' or rendered contradictory. He argues that because the dynamic capital goods industries and technological development in industry remain 'in the central nuclei of the multinational firms', because the international division of labour 'based on very unequal degrees of wealth' continues, and because of the indebtedness of the dependent countries and their smaller share of the international surplus, the distinction between them and the 'central countries' is not in doubt. There is no warrant in simply going over to some universal concept of 'interdependence' between capitalist countries within a world system (Cardoso 1977, p. 20). Personally, I have my doubts about this, and elsewhere (Kitching 1980b) I have suggested why, but this debate need not concern us here. We may simply note that two crucial theoretical supports of dependency theory ('surplus transfer' and 'unequal exchange') – which were supposed to demonstrate the *necessarily* abortive nature of capitalist development in the dependent countries – have been seen to be unsatisfactory theoretically and indeed have needed alteration in the light of trends in certain parts of the Third World (such as the rapidly quickening tempo of capitalist industrialization in Brazil, Mexico and parts of South-East Asia). For the simpler 'blockage' or 'stagnationist' versions of dependency theory had suggested that such trends were impossible. This indeed is why reformulations such as that attempted by Cardoso have been necessary. I have argued that these theoretical weaknesses stemmed from a basic nationalism which, just like populism, can generate powerful political rhetoric but produces rather muddled economic theory. Whether that nationalism led to demands for a genuinely national capitalist development or to visions of a socialist industrialization 'in one country', it had to base itself upon an *a priori* denial of the possibility of capitalist industrialization in the periphery. However, no such theoretical *a priori*s can be made to hold water, and so it is not surprising that in some parts of the capitalist periphery events in the real world are catching up with bad theory.

POPULISM AND DEPENDENCY THEORY

We can conclude this chapter by a brief résumé of the relationship between populism and dependency theory. They share in common, as we have seen, a denial of the possibility of capitalist industrialization in 'late-starting' nations (though the arguments adduced are somewhat different), and also a tendency to locate the source of exploitation and inequality in the realm of exchange relationships. More specifically the former bequeathed to the latter an essentially unchanged concept of 'unequal exchange', but now clothed in mathematical economic theory and doing duty in the international rather than the national realm of exchange.

We should not, however, overlook the differences between the two bodies of theory. Most importantly, most dependency theorists are determined industrializers and desire an 'independent' economic position for the underdeveloped countries so that they can industrialize. Among the leading theorists of dependency (Frank, Amin, Emmanuel, dos Santos, Cardoso) one does not find any romantic idealization of the peasantry or any belief that development can come predominantly or totally through agriculture and rural development. Conversely, the kind of theorists who are heirs of the populists in this respect (Lipton, Schumacher) would have little sympathy for 'surplus transfer' or 'unequal exchange' formulations based on some neo-Marxist concept of imperialism. In fact of the major modern theorists analysed in this book, only Nyerere comes close to *combining* an anti-urban, pro-rural, small-scale romanticism with the 'dependency' apparatus. He has at least committed himself to critiques of the advanced countries' international economic relations which echo, in a rather muted way, 'unequal exchange' perspectives (see, for example, Nyerere 1973).

However, in the world of development studies as a whole this kind of combination is not by any means uncommon. I have come across it often among Tanzanian civil servants and other representatives of the modern African intelligentsia who take up a 'radical nationalist' perspective on development. It can also be found in the writings of a number of other academics in the development studies field, notably Norman Long (1977), Steven Langdon (1980), Edward Brett (1973) and in the earlier work of Colin Leys (1975). In the final chapter of this book I will look, very briefly, at some of the wider dimensions of populism and nationalism, and suggest why they may have such an attraction for thinkers concerned with underdeveloped countries. I have suggested in this and earlier chapters that they make very unsound and misleading bases for economic theories of development and underdevelopment. But economics is by no means the whole of life, and when one looks wider than the stern demands of consistent theory, there are good reasons why both populism and nationalism have engaged the sympathy of both theorists of development and the peoples of underdeveloped countries.

7

Conclusions

These conclusions will be brief. I have presented a tradition of thought in this book, and have traced its ramifications in modern-day 'radical' theories of underdevelopment. I have suggested that as a body of economic theory, as a total alternative to a development based on industrialization and urbanization, populism and modern neo-populism are severely wanting, and indeed that they do not issue in any total alternative, but at best in some minor alterations to the conventional industrialization thesis. I have also looked at the relationship between populism and nationalism, and have traced the story of nationalist economic theory through to modern-day dependency theory. The latter, if not a direct descendant of populism, yet partakes of both a similar pessimism about capitalist development and a similar concept of exploitation (through exchange). This nationalist variant of radical anti-capitalism was also found to be inadequate as economic theory, and for reasons not dissimilar to those advanced to criticize populism.

And yet writing and reflecting upon social and economic change can serve important and 'truthful' purposes even when, subjected to the harsh test of logical or theoretical consistency, it may be found wanting. The Russian populists, for example, may have been unable to provide a consistent alternative development path to the one trodden by the Tsarist state, but they vividly described the social and human costs of that path for the peasants of Russia. By their interest in the peasantry, at first romantic but later both realistic and informed, they advanced the understanding of peasant economies and societies to new heights (with the culmination perhaps coming in the work of Chayanov). Even more importantly, they refused to let either the Tsarist government or the Russian ruling classes forget the suffering that social and economic change was bringing to the mass of the Russian people. Those who were revolutionaries justified both the demand for revolution and their use of violence by reference to that suffering. Consider, for example, the following passage from the Russian populist and revolutionary, Stepniak:

Here lies the peremptory cause, the permanent stimulant and the highest justification of the Russian revolution and of Russian conspiracies. Life is not worth living when your eyes constantly behold such miseries as these inflicted on a people whom you love. It would be a shame to bear the name of a Russian had these unutterable sufferings of the masses called forth no responsive and boundless devotion which glows in the hearts of all those thousands of Russia's sons and daughters who risk life, freedom, domestic happiness – all of which is most dear to our common nature – in the effort to free their country from a government which is the main-spring of all their woes.

(Stepniak 1888, p. 70)

One can label this passage both nationalist and populist. For the 'peremptory cause', the 'permanent stimulant' and the 'highest justification' were of course the social and economic conditions of the Russian peasantry which Stepniak had analysed in great detail in the previous sixty-nine pages. Yet neither label can detract from the passion, the idealism and the genuine concern for human suffering which both it and every word of the accompanying empirical analysis demonstrate.

And in the modern-day Third World the peasant indebtedness, hunger, disease and poverty, which Stepniak and the other populists detailed in Russia, are still to be seen. Hence theories which would put 'the peasant' at the centre rather than the periphery of the development process, which wish to raise his crop prices, improve and expand his land resources, reduce his debt and lower the mortality rate of his children, which desire him to want more and to demand more, are far from being merely the romantic daydreams of the simple-minded. They speak to a real situation of neglect, exploitation and inequality. The point of this book therefore has not been to defend a single-minded industrialism which sacrifices peasants and other small-scale producers as mere 'cannon fodder' of some inevitable process of proletarianization. The point rather has been to argue that a really effective 'agricultural' or 'rural development' effort which will improve the human well being of peasants and other rural dwellers *requires as a prerequisite a dynamic and growing industrial sector of a certain sort*. The case study of China, I believe, demonstrated that clearly, as it also demonstrated that to be effective such an 'industrially-backed' rural development effort has to occur within the context of a socialized and centrally planned economy. If this does not happen, then in certain other countries (Brazil, Mexico, possibly other parts of Latin America, parts of South-East Asia), the classical capitalist alternative – industrialization and urbanization with the effective dissolution and destruction of the peasantry – may occur, as it occurred earlier in western Europe. The social and human costs of that transformation are, and will continue to be, enormous, and they will be accompanied by massive increases in inequality.

For these reasons revolutionary movements may arise among those who are the prime sufferers from the transition. However neither effective planning for such a revolution nor indeed (if this is preferred) effective reforms to make the transition less socially costly will be served by theories of underdevelopment and dependency whose main thrust is to assert that no such transformation is occurring. Moreover, if I am right and even under socialism a process of agricultural and rural development can only occur – paradoxical as this may seem – within the context of a sustained industrialization, then it behoves opponents of capitalist development in the Third World to be thinking clearly about what, precisely, socialist industrialization implies, and how it can be made as 'humane' as possible. In particular the question of whether in a small country 'socialist industrialization in one country' can occur without even greater costs than those incurred in industrialization under international capital must be squarely faced. (The same is true incidentally of notions of development through an autonomous 'national' capitalism.) In the case of socialist development, models of an 'open socialist industrialization process', in which international trade plays an important role, are sorely needed for use in small countries which, unlike China, cannot pursue a quasi-autarchic path.

In short this book has tried to argue that industrialization cannot be avoided or run away from, either in theory or in practice. Those who try to do so, in the name of loyalty to the peasantry and the poor, are likely to end up offering no effective help to 'the people', and seeing the process of industrialization occur in any case, under the anarchic sway of international capital. A rejection of populist and neo-populist solutions then does not indicate any indifference to the real and pressing problems of development to which populist and neo-populist writers have pointed. It does not even betoken rejection of the essential populist vision – as a vision. A world of 'humanized' production, based on a small-scale but modern and scientific technology, a world of co-operation in villages and small towns, a world of enriched social relationships growing out of a process of production and exchange which is under human control rather than 'alienated' – this is by no means an unattractive utopia. In some ways, as a vision at least, it has rather more in common with Marx's vision of the Communist future than many Marxists like to pretend. Moreover it recurs so frequently in societies embroiled in the painful process of industrialization and urbanization (in western Europe and the United States, in Russia and eastern Europe, in Latin America and other parts of the Third World) that it clearly answers some deeply felt need in the people undergoing such a transition. Schumacher would argue that it offers a viable alternative even for advanced industrial societies, whilst Fiedler (1960) has claimed to see tattered remnants of old American populist visions in the images of the good life presently conjured up by American TV and other mass media.

However this may be, one must firmly insist that an attractive utopian vision is not an adequate basis for a theory of development, nor does the desirability of a state of affairs guarantee its possibility. I have argued that the central weakness of populism in theory and practice is that *it is unable to provide any coherent account of how a continuing process of rising material productivity and living standards is compatible with the maintenance of an economy in which peasant agricultural producers are the dominant social force.* In rejecting Proudhonist and other 'petty bourgeois' or 'utopian' visions of socialism, Marx clearly believed that in some way human societies could, and must, *pass through* a phase of industrialization and urbanization, of the large-scale concentration of people, forces of production (technology) and capital, in order to use the knowledge and productive power acquired in that process to create *afterwards* a smaller-scale, more democratic and less alienated world under communism. The viability of this alternative to backward-looking recreation of a rapidly disappearing world (which was how Marx saw Proudhonist ideas) must remain an open question. There are certainly a number of tensions, even contradictions, in Marx's broad sketches of the communist society. But it is also true that as an alternative development strategy to large-scale industrialism and urbanization, populism and neo-populism are not viable. Though they draw attention to the desirability of going about industrialization in a manner which does not simply sacrifice millions of peasants either to 'market forces' or to some state-directed process of crash industrialization, *in themselves* they do not provide a coherent or practicable way to do it.

Essentially the same considerations apply to nationalism. The preceding chapter was devoted to arguing that a certain sort of radical nationalism makes for weak development theory and that, in particular, it is impossible to give any coherent theoretical meaning to the idea of national exploitation, that is, the exploitation of one nation or country by another. This is because the only concept of exploitation which is theoretically defensible involves a relationship between those who own or control means of production and those who have only their labour power to sell. 'Nations' as a whole are never found totally on one side or the other of this divide; all nations under the sway of capitalism have part of their populations on one side of this divide and part on the other.

However, though it is important to insist upon this theoretical point, it should not be taken to mean that, in a broader sense, it is totally unacceptable or incomprehensible that economic domination and subordination should be expressed in national terms. Colonialism *did* allow *some* people of one nation (the imperial power) to become rich on resources forcibly extracted from people of another nation (the colonized). The economic policies of imperial and colonial government *were* often designed to protect and enhance the economic interests of industrialists/merchants/financiers in the colonizing country at the expense of other interests among the colonized – peasants, artisans, local merchants and industrialists. In some cases the working classes of the colonizing country *did* benefit from such policies (for example, the Lancashire cotton workers provided with employment by the mass Indian market). Above all the humiliations and discrimination suffered by colonized peoples at the hands of their colonial masters were real enough, and perhaps the most powerful stimulus of all to anti-imperial nationalist movements. For it was often the more educated sections of the colonized peoples, their intelligentsias, who suffered most acutely from this humiliation, and put themselves at the head of nationalist movements in India, Africa and elsewhere.

The main danger of seeing the causes of exploitation and poverty in developing countries in nationalist terms is only that in taking an understandable observation or shorthand conceptualization of the problem and turning it into a causal principle, one will be led into dangerously naive prescriptions about what must be done to end poverty and underdevelopment. At its simplest this can involve the view that it is only necessary to obtain juridical independence, to have political power 'in our own hands', and all misery and suffering will end overnight. Though never seriously believed by nationalist leaderships in European colonies, it is not inconceivable that some of the peasant peoples of India and Africa, carried away by nationalist euphoria, *did* cherish almost millenial beliefs on the eve of independence, beliefs which can make post-independence acceptance of continued sacrifice and struggle hard to popularize. Such hopes and dreams can in fact be one important source of political instability in the post-independence period, for vastly inflated expectations bring bitterness and disappointment very quickly in their train if they are not satisfied.

More subtly, however, when independence comes, when the 'blossoms are in the dust' as Kusum Nair (1961) puts it, and the immediate end of poverty and underdevelopment does not materialize, one can explain this by simple *extension* of the nationalist explanatory principle. That is, poverty and underdevelopment continue because, though 'we' have 'juridical' independence, it is not 'real' independence, and so what is required is for 'us' to have 'our' economic resources and economic decision-making power in 'our' hands. Hence the demands which were made all over Africa for the 'Africanization' of commerce and business and of the civil service. In its conservative form this ideology simply seeks an 'independent', 'national' capitalism, in which 'our people' run firms and industries, rather than 'foreigners' (Oginga Odinga 1967). More radical nationalist critiques see this as totally inadequate, and advocate a 'nationalist socialist' solution involving withdrawal, totally or partial, from the world capitalist system.

In the former case ('national' capitalism) it is difficult to see *a priori* why merely changing the nationality of industrial bosses or landlords should itself aid the situation of workers or peasants. Indeed there are some arguments for supposing that 'indigenous' capitalists, who do not experience ideological constraints deriving from national 'illegitimacy', may feel freer to be more crudely exploitative. Similarly, the effects of the 'indigenization' of commerce, finance or government service depends greatly on the goals and the levels of competence of the local people appointed to such positions. If, for example, they are (for particular historical reasons) both extremely venal and technically incompetent, then the development process, capitalist or socialist, may suffer markedly, at least in the short or medium term. In Africa, at least, examples of this are not hard to find (Killick 1978).

In the second case ('nationalist' socialism), there may be no naive belief that simple 'indigenization' of capitalism is likely to be of much benefit to peasants or workers. But there may be a not dissimilar belief that development can be accelerated markedly simply by combining a socialist form of organization of the internal economy with withdrawal from the world capitalist system. But, under capitalism *or* socialism, development requires saving and investment, and a small and poor country will not be able to obtain high rates of savings and investments (even under socialism) without marked squeezing of already low levels of current consumption. As the experience of the Soviet Union showed, the attempt to maintain social discipline in the face of the considerable unpopularity provoked by such squeezing can have profound and very damaging political consequences. The experience of China suggests that more modulated and subtle answers to this problem (which do not involve a crude squeezing of the peasantry) are possible. But the point is that many small and poor countries of the Third World do not have the 'internal' resources of either China or the Soviet Union, and must therefore look to supplement local sources of saving and investment to some degree by external resources. Once again overly simple nationalist visions of 'our own socialism' may make clear and constructive thinking about such problems difficult.

And this, in the end, is why good theory is important. For good theory helps one to identify causes and constraints accurately, while bad theory leads to simplistic conceptions of both causes and constraints. These in turn lead to simplistic prescriptions for policy and action in which some constraints are overlooked or wished away. But of course in reality the constraints remain, and when the policies or prescriptions are put into practice, *they fail*, partly or totally. In the real world the failure of development policies in turn may have undesirable political effects: unpopularity and overthrow of progressive governments or (perhaps worse) the use of repression to maintain the pretence that the failure has not occurred, or even that it is a success. Marcuse's work on *Soviet Marxism* (1958) is a brilliant analysis of an official ideology (Stalinism) which existed, partly at least, in order to define failure as success.

Postscript

As I write, it is over five years since *Development and Underdevelopment in Historical Perspective* was first published and over six years since it was written. Although I feel that nothing has happened in that period to make its central thesis less relevant or interesting (indeed the ideas which it attacks have, if anything, spread even more widely in radical development circles both in the West and in the Third World) nonetheless the 1980s have seen some important changes, both in the Third World and in the world economy as a whole, which find no place in the text and which do have implications for its central arguments. The aim of this postscript therefore is both to make some comments on these changes and to offer some further thoughts on the major themes of the book in the light of general reader reaction and of the critical reflections of friends and colleagues.

DEVELOPMENT IN THE LATE 1980s

When *Development and Underdevelopment in Historical Perspective* was published it was possible to conceive of the 'radical orthodoxy' it attacked as becoming increasingly dominant not only among radical intellectuals and Third World politicians but even in such supremely conservative international organizations as the World Bank. No sooner had it appeared, however, than the resurgence of right wing 'monetarist' economics which had already surfaced in the domestic politics of Europe and the USA began to make its mark in the international economic arena, deeply affecting both the policies of the World Bank and the International Monetary Fund (IMF) and the scholarly development literature. The general result of this has been a return to a somewhat uncritical cult of 'the market' as an agency of economic development and its usual concomitant − a blanket hostility to the state and to state intervention in the economy as necessarily productive of inefficiency, waste and as destructive of the growth potential of the 'free market'.

Such ideas, perhaps best exemplified in the World Bank's 1981 Berg Report on Africa (World Bank 1981), are neither particularly new (indeed in some respects they are as old as economic theorizing itself) nor, despite some novelties of presentation and argument, are they particularly 'revolutionary'. Nonetheless they have had a radical impact on development theory and, more importantly, on development policy in the 1980s. This has been especially true in Africa where both the World Bank and the IMF have used economic 'adjustment programmes' as a means to force African governments into major policy changes – most notably to 'roll back' state involvement in their economies and to allow 'market forces' greater play, especially in agricultural production and marketing.

This is not the place to comment at length either on the resurgence of free market economics, or on the roots of the economic crisis in Africa, both of which topics are large enough to require a monograph to themselves. It is, however, appropriate to note that the kind of weak-minded 'radical orthodoxy' which is analysed and attacked in this book, was, in my opinion, both an ideological concomitant and a justification of the kinds of development policies which played a large part in bringing Africa to the parlous state in which it could be so easily bullied into new directions by the IMF and World Bank. A sentimental cult of 'rural development' unsupported either by appropriate pricing policies or, more importantly, by proper infrastructural provision for rural areas; the pursuit of inappropriate industrialization strategies motivated more by an unthinking nationalism than by any clear development logic; and above all the erection of massively bureaucratic state structures maintained, in most cases, out of peasant-produced surpluses which were then squandered (used neither for the benefit of the peasantry nor in any other way which would assist the long-term growth of real output); all of these practices could be perfectly justified by a nationalistic populism.

Indeed, in Africa, at least, this populism became more or less the official ideology of the very state bureaucracies who were, at least for a while, the only real beneficiaries of these policies. In the 1980s however, these bureaucracies themselves have experienced even larger proportional declines in their standards of living than the peasants upon whom they depend. For it has been the withdrawal of millions of peasants all over sub-Saharan Africa from the grip of grossly parasitic state agricultural marketing systems, a withdrawal into subsistence production, domestic black markets and smuggling, which precipitated 'fiscal crises of the state' (i.e. large declines in state revenues and increased state debts acquired to meet current expenditures) in the vast majority of sub-Saharan African states from the early 1980s onwards (for details see Bates 1981, Hyden 1983, and Sender and Smith 1986).

This is not to deny that international factors, such as the severe oil price rises of 1974 and 1979 and the large increases in the prices of fuel and of nearly all manufactured goods which they provoked, have played an important part in the creation of widespread economic crisis in Africa, especially in exacerbating balance of payments problems and the severe debt problems to which these led. But it is to say that long before 1974 many African economies had been rendered peculiarly unable to withstand these balance of payments shocks by domestic economic policies which grossly weakened and undermined the agricultural sectors on which they nearly all depended for their principal exports while putting nothing even remotely as productive in their place.

It is not surprising, therefore, if the demoralized elites of Africa have proved unable to resist the logic of the IMF/World Bank 'free market' analysis (even if they have not, for political reasons, been able actually to carry out all the 'adjustment' prescriptions). It is perhaps somewhat more surprising that the Keynesian consensus which for so long dominated development economics has not been able to mount a sterner ideological resistance to the monetarist assault on the field which it had created and so long dominated both theoretically and practically. However, it may be that the crucial problem has been the same in both cases – the role and nature of the state. For both Keynesian and neo-Keynesian economists and their Marxist and neo-Marxist critics and African state bureaucrats shared a faith in what state intervention in the economy for 'development' purposes could achieve. Yet of these groups only the Marxists had any interest in analysing the social bases of the new state structures or their actual functioning (rather than their formal or putative goals). And while Marxist scholars often asked the right questions about the state in Africa, their answers were too often based on theoretical *a prioris* about 'exploitative' ruling classes, or about 'comprador' elites rather than on careful empirical analysis, the latter in any case being very difficult to undertake (see Kitching 1985).

The net result of all this was that neither Keynesians nor Marxists nor (needless to say) African state bureaucracies themselves were concerned with specifying the material and ideological prerequisites of effective (i.e. non-parasitic) state intervention in the economy. If Keynesian development economists held to the view that all states can be equally effective economic managers, Marxists (for not dissimilar reasons in fact) held to the view that all state ruling classes could be equally effective 'exploiters' (i.e. appropriators and reinvestors of a surplus product). But both these views are flawed and flawed for the same reason – that they take certain cultural and material prerequisites of effective state action as given. As a result, both Keynesians and Marxists in development studies found themselves equally ideologically vulnerable before the monetarist 'free market' assault, as vulnerable in fact as the African elites sitting atop their ruined economies. And this itself is a disaster. For in my view, the monetarist prescription for Africa is in certain respects just as naïve and ill-informed as its Keynesian predecessor, and likely, if applied in a uniform fashion, to be just as damaging. For African economies, no more than the rapid-growth economies of South-East Asia (the so-called Newly Industrializing Countries or NICs which have seemed to give the free marketeers' prescriptions such validity) cannot hope to experience any real development without systematic state intervention. The real question is about creating forms of effective, growth-oriented, non-parasitic state intervention in Africa, and this may be partly a question about restricting the role of the state in many African economies, but it is certainly not a question about totally eliminating such a role (which is politically impossible in any case).

Aside from the resurgence of free market ideologies and policies, the other great issue of development in the 1980s which found no place in this book, is of course debt – the massive and ever-increasing indebtedness of many Third World countries not only in Africa, but in Latin America and parts of Asia as well. I do not wish to reiterate here the well-known story of the roots of this problem which the reader can find in many other sources. I simply want to note two points relevant to the debt problem which abut on theoretical themes in this book.

1   To a degree the problem of Third World debt is seriously misconceived in the normal 'nationalist' discourse in which it is usually described, i.e. that 'Brazil' owes X billion dollars, or that the interest payments on its debt account for Y per cent of 'Tanzania's' GNP, etc. This is because it is inaccurate, strictly speaking, to conceive of nations or countries as contracting debts. It is governments which contract debts and the reasons for which they borrow and, more importantly, the uses to which they put the money borrowed, will be determined by the ideologies and material interests of the social groups which dominate those governments or whose interests they serve. In a slogan, debt like much else, is a class question not a national question.

Concretely this means that if ruling groups use borrowed money for purposes which are frankly unproductive and make no contribution to generating the funds with which to repay such loans when they fall due, then such debts are highly likely to escalate and become crippling. In addition, it is certain that when repayment has to be made this will be done by such ruling groups squeezing those in their populations (peasants and/or workers) who neither contracted the loans in the first place nor received any benefit from them. Indeed it is only at this point – the point of repayment – that debt does become in actuality a national question, i.e. 'everybody' pays but even then only through the use of class power.

2   However, this should not be taken as denying that some Third World debt (particularly that of the poorest countries who owe least in absolute terms but whose debt load may nonetheless be crippling for their economies) was contracted for 'essential' and 'unavoidable' reasons, principally to cover balance of payments deficits following from oil and other import price rises. In these cases in particular the acuity of Baran's distinction between 'absolute' and 'potential' surplus (see chapter 6) becomes clear. For whatever questions Baran's concept of the 'potential surplus' may beg, it is certainly true that any country which is forced to use 20 per cent, 30 per cent or even 40 per cent of its current internationally marketed output to repay interest on past debts is severely damaging its prospects for future growth by, in a sense, 'wasting' its current investible surpluses.

Having now commented on those major issues in development in the 1980s of which this book makes no mention, let me now turn to some reflections on the issues and themes with which it does deal, reflections to which I have been stimulated by comments and events since its publication.

CRITICAL REFLECTIONS AND AFTERTHOUGHTS

These can perhaps best be dealt with under two heads, empirical issues and theoretical issues, of which the former can be treated more briefly.

Empirical issues

Empirically, the major issues are the case studies of Tanzania and China (see chapter 5) and events and processes taking place in those countries since 1982. In the case of Tanzania it does not seem to me that any subsequent events there have seriously invalidated the analysis offered. On the contrary, if this section of the book errs in any way, it is in not being critical enough of the Tanzanian experiment. In particular, were I rewriting this section now I would be much more sceptical of Tanzania's official figures for economic growth and I would want to emphasize how far even Tanzania's achievements in the provision of mass social services (education, health, water supply) have been deeply damaged in practice both by acute foreign exchange shortages (of what use are dispensaries without drugs, schools without books, paper or pencils, or bore holes with broken pumps?) and by rampant inflation which has so devalued official salaries that school teachers, for example, cannot afford to devote all their time to teaching school but must be chicken farmers or fruit growers to survive (see Cheru, 1987).

It also seems that the broad thrust of my analysis of Tanzania's problems was correct, and that the principal mistake has been the nominal concentration on rural development and agriculture unsupported by an effective provision of necessary infrastructure and inputs and vitiated by the *de facto* budgetary priority given to utterly irrelevant and wasteful forms of industrialization. However, if I were rewriting the analysis now, I would probably give more emphasis to the role of the state crop marketing system and somewhat less to the *ujamaa* experience in damaging Tanzania's agricultural sector.

In the case of the section of chapter 5 devoted to China, however, matters are somewhat less satisfactory. My feeling now is that the case study was right in its intuitions but quite radically mistaken in some parts of its analysis. That is to say, I believe I was correct in seeing the Chinese model, at least prior to 1978, as in essence an orthodox Communist development model focused on central planning with a consistent priority given to industrialization and especially to heavy industry. I erred, however, in underestimating the extent to which this was true, and in particular I greatly overestimated the benefits to the Chinese peasantry from China's development path prior to 1978. It certainly seems that the urban-rural income gap was far greater than I thought and that the real income growth in rural areas from China's collective-based rural development was far less than I had supposed (see Lardy, 1986).

However, one should perhaps beware of drawing too hard and fast conclusions on these matters. Despite the rhetoric of the Deng regime, developments in China since the death of Mao are perhaps best interpreted not as demonstrating that the previous development strategy was an absolute failure but that it was not enough of a success. That is, the major problem was not that real incomes did not grow but that they did not grow fast enough, given China's huge absolute increases in population and rapidly rising popular aspirations (themselves of course a product of previous successes). As a result, a new leadership has opted for a strategy which may raise rural incomes faster (they more than doubled between 1978 and 1983 alone) but will also certainly increase income inequalities both within rural areas and between rural and urban areas (see Griffin 1984, Lardy 1986). Certainly to an outsider the dominant impression is still, as it was in 1982, of China's astonishing overall development achievement since 1949 given her severe shortage of cultivable land and the enormous population pressure on that land.

Toward the end of the China case study I noted:

> To put the matter paradoxically, the Chinese peasantry appears to have been 'saved' by being abolished. A total loss of individual peasant autonomy (in the use of land and labour power) has been the price of a continual rise in living standards and of greater equality both among peasants and between peasants and others. However, a desire to separate these two phenomena is precisely the hallmark of populist and neo-populist visions of development.

Chinese realities have changed, but this theoretical point still seems valid, indeed in a sense it is confirmed by those changes. For under the Deng regime, the Chinese peasantry has, as it were, 'reappeared' from its Maoist abolition, with power of decision over use of its land and labour power being increasingly returned to the Chinese peasant household through the 'contract responsibility' system (see Crook 1986 for details). Through this system the peasant household can now sell a considerable part of what it decides to produce into a free market rather than being bound by Commune controls and the grain quota demands of the state. As a result of the increased specialization which has resulted and the greater productive effort by peasants which the prospect of higher returns and a more direct link between effort and reward seems to have stimulated, both agricultural output and incomes have risen sharply since 1978. However, these average increases disguise rapidly increasing income inequalities both between peasant households and between different areas of rural China. To that extent it remains true that what I term the 'populist vision' is incoherent for China as elsewhere. For such a vision always seeks to deny the existence of a trade-off between the rate of growth and inequality which all development experience, including the Chinese, appears to confirm (though the severity of the trade-off can be altered by state policies). Indeed, it is clear that worries about these kind of consequences of the new strategy continue to exercise part of the Chinese leadership, and conflicts over this will no doubt continue to affect Chinese development policy in the future as they have done in the past.

Theoretical issues

In retrospect, and in the light of the comments of both students and colleagues, it seems to me that *Development and Underdevelopment in*

Historical Perspective has two major theoretical weaknesses. These are: (i) its treatment of industrialization, and (ii) its treatment of populism as an ideological tradition.

In the first case the fault is largely one of omission rather than commission. Since the main polemical aim of the book was to provide a critique of an ideology of development which denied the centrality of industrialization in raising material standards of living, it is almost entirely concerned with explicating the theoretical and practical weaknesses of that ideology. Throughout the book, the analytical technique adopted is one of highlighting the questions which are unanswered or begged in the 'new' (1970s) 'radical orthodoxy' of development and thereby demonstrating – by negation as it were – the superiority of the 'old orthodoxy' (whether in its Marxist or non-Marxist form) in facing and answering these questions.

As a result of all this, the necessity of some form of industrialization is more or less plausibly demonstrated, but nothing is said about the specific form or forms of industrialization which may be possible or desirable in any given context. This omission, together with some remarks on the Dobb-Sen thesis on choice of techniques (chapter 5) left some readers with the impression that I favoured the universal application of some Stalinist 'heavy industry' model of development across the world. Let me state explicitly here that this is not so. The form and sequence of industrialization which is appropriate in any given context depends on a host of factors, including the demographic and geographical size of the economy involved, its resource endowment (including its 'human capital' endowment) and its role in the world economy at the point at which industrialization is attempted. For small, resource-poor Third World countries a development sequence which begins with the expansion of primary product exports, moves to the manufacture of simple inputs and basic consumption goods for the primary producers (usually, though not always, peasant producers) and from there to the manufacture of labour-intensive consumer and producer goods for export *and* domestic consumption, is a particularly appropriate strategy. Certainly it is a more appropriate industrialization strategy for small peripheral economies than either 'crash' heavy industrialization under state auspices or luxury 'import substitution' industrialization undertaken under the auspices of multi-national corporations. Such a strategy is particularly desirable in that it can accommodate forms of rural 'agro-industry' which can act as a counter-balance to over rapid urbanization. It should be noted in this context that the term 'industrialization' as used in this text incorporates the industrialization of agriculture (i.e. its conversion into a commodity-producing industry rather than a source of direct subsistence), as well as of non-agricultural production.

The second and much more serious theoretical weakness in the text lies in its treatment of populism as an ideological tradition. As Henry Bernstein in particular noted (Bernstein, 1984), *Development and Underdevelopment in Historical Perspective* hovers uneasily between a form of discourse familiarly known as the 'history of ideas' (in which a set of ideas are analysed in terms of their temporal sequence, their logical coherence and their practical implications, but in abstraction from the shifting social and historical contexts in which they are produced and reproduced) and a more Marxist or materialist analysis of ideas as ideologies, as the products of particular social interest groups and as expressions of their material interests.

The net result of this somewhat ambiguous approach is that it is asserted in a general way that in populism we are dealing with some sort of ideological tradition or constantly reproduced ideological syndrome, but it is left very unclear whose tradition or syndrome this is, or whether indeed populism in, say, nineteenth century Russia is an expression of the same set of material interests as in, say, twentieth century Tanzania.

Subsequent reflection on this issue has led me to the three following conclusions:

First, the present-day 'syndrome' as I analyse it – a combination of commitments to anti-industrialism, rural development, appropriate technology and a rather crude 'dependency' version of anti-imperialism – is mainly an ideology of western intellectuals and aid professionals. As such it is mainly found in western higher education and development research institutions and in parts of the international agency world colonized by the graduates of such institutions (including people who may be of Third World origin). This syndrome, which I term 'populism' (sometimes/often with the addition of a feminist strand) is particularly omnipresent in such institutions as UNESCO, ILO, WHO, and the less technicist parts of the FAO.

Second, however, this syndrome is also to be found in many Third World bureaucracies, mainly because of its transmittal through western education and technical assistance programmes, and because of its continual reinforcement by the interaction of such bureaucrats with the international agencies enumerated above. However, in the case of Third World bureaucrats, the particular parts of the syndrome which are emphasized depends largely on the occupational role of the individual involved.

Some form of dependency perspective is almost omnipresent, but the rural development/appropriate technology strand is likely to be particularly strong among those who work in relevant fields, i.e. agriculture, community development, rural health, etc. It should be noted, however, that the material and occupational interests of such bureaucrats nearly always mean that the contemporary populist syndrome is given a distinct statist twist. Is trade and industry too dominated by foreign capital? The state must act to diminish its role. Is more rural development required? Three more state institutions must be set up to provide it. Is the development of an appropriate agricultural and manufacturing technology necessary? The state must set up another two research institutes to undertake the task. The net result of all this of course may be that the material beneficiaries of such programmes are anybody but the rural or urban poor people whose welfare provides their nominal ideological justification.

Such indeed are the complexities of the relationship between ideology, policy formation and policy outcomes, and as a result it is always dangerous to 'read off' any one of these things from any one of the others, which may be in turn a partial justification for treating ideologies in an analytically separate way both from policy formation and from the analysis of the material beneficiaries of policy.

Third, another justification of this procedure, and one which allows me to end this postscript on a rather more positive note, is that it is possible to learn something of importance from the analysis of ideas alone. It is for this reason that I set out in *Development and Underdevelopment in Historical Perspective* to take a 'world view' or 'syndrome' which I sensed was increasingly influential amongst my peers in the development field and (more importantly) amongst the students for whose education I was partially responsible, and to subject it to sympathetic but searching scrutiny. I wanted to show that ideas which they thought were new and revolutionary were certainly not new, and that their 'revolutionary' potential for assisting or liberating the most poor or oppressed people of the world might be vitiated by certain confusions and evasions which lay at their heart – confusions and evasions which could easily lead to very damaging outcomes if they came seriously to influence the making of development policy.

Above all, I wanted to show that a sincere and passionate commitment to the welfare of the 'wretched of the earth' – to those people who, if the world has progressed, have certainly been the principal victims of that progress – whilst it is often an important and admirable motive for involvement in development studies and issues, is not in itself enough. And it is not enough whether we are considering western 'radical' students and intellectuals, aid or international agency personnel, Third World civil servants, or the ideas of such a sincere and admirable man as Julius Nyerere.

It is not enough because economic development as a long-term process of structural change, as a historical process, poses awful and awesome moral and political dilemmas, dilemmas which, even to be confronted adequately, require hard and informed thinking and, for the policy makers themselves, considerable moral and political courage and self-discipline. It is my view that the hardest and clearest thinking about development always reveals that there are no easy answers, no panaceas whether these be 'de-linking', 'industrialization', 'rural development', 'appropriate technology', 'popular participation', 'basic needs', 'social-ism' or whatever. As I have had occasion to say repeatedly in speaking on and about this book, development is an awful process. It varies only, and importantly in its awfulness. And that is perhaps why my most indulgent judgements are reserved for those, whether they be Marxist-Leninists, Korean generals, or IMF officials, who, whatever else they may do, recognize this and are prepared to accept its moral implications. My most critical reflections are reserved for those, whether they be western liberal-radicals or African bureaucratic elites, who do not, and therefore avoid or evade such implications and with them their own responsibilities.

It is perhaps in this regard, with respect to these hard realizations, that, judging at least from many readers' reactions, this book has been a success – a limited pedagogical success. For it does seem to have stimu-lated those who have read it to a greater appreciation of the difficulties of development as a process and to a greater understanding of the profound limitations of good intentions as a grounding for development policies. This seems to have been true moreover, irrespective of whether its basic thesis has elicited agreement or disagreement. Since, therefore, a teacher's greatest desire and reward is to deepen understanding, and since I consider myself above all as a teacher, this book has certainly achieved the major objective in the modest list of those which I set for it. I hope that it will continue to do so for further generations of readers.

Bibliography

Albertini, R. von (1980) 'Colonialism and underdevelopment: critical remarks on the theory of dependency', in Blussé, L., Wesseling, H. L. and Winius, G. D. (eds) *History and Underdevelopment*, Leiden University Press.

Allen, W. (1972) *A Short Economic History of Modern Japan 1867–1937*, London, Allen & Unwin.

American Rural Small-Scale Industry Delegation (1977) *Rural Small-Scale Industry in the People's Republic of China*, Berkeley, University of California Press.

Amin, S. (1976) *Unequal Development: An Essay on the Social Formations of Peripheral Capitalism*, Hassocks, Harvester.

Awiti, A. (1972) 'Class struggle in the rural society of Tanzania', *Maji Maji* (Dar es Salaam), Special Research Publication, 7.

Bandyopadhyaya, J. (1969) *The Social and Political Thought of Gandhi*, Bombay, Allied Publishers.

Baran, P. (1957) *The Political Economy of Growth*, New York, Monthly Review Press.

Baran, P. and Sweezy, P. (1966), *Monopoly Capital: An Essay on the American Economic and Social Order*, New York, Monthly Reivew Press.

Barratt Brown, M. (1974) *The Economics of Imperialism*, Harmondsworth, Penguin.

Bates, R. H. (1981) *Markets and States in Tropical Africa: The Political Basis of Agricultural Policies*, Berkeley, University of California Press.

Beer, M. (1919) *A History of British Socialism*, London, Allen & Unwin.

Bennamane, A. (1980) *The Algerian Development Strategy and Employment Policy*, University College of Swansea, Centre for Development Studies Monograph Series, 9.

Bernstein, H. (1984) 'A Natural History of Populist Economics,' *Third World Book Review*, vol. 1, no. 1.

Bettelheim, C. (1972) 'Theoretical comments', Appendix I of

Emmanuel, A., *Unequal Exchange: A Study of the Imperialism of Trade*, London, New Left Books.

Blussé, L., Wesseling, H. L. and Winius, G. D. (eds) (1980) *History and Underdevelopment*, Leiden University Press.

Boesen, J., Moody, T. and Madsen, B. S. (1977) *Ujamaa: Socialism from Above*, Uppsala, Scandinavian Institute of African Studies.

Booth, D. (1975) 'Andre Gunder Frank: an introduction and appreciation', in Oxaal, I., Barnett T. and Booth, D. (eds) *Beyond the Sociology of Development: Economy and Society in Africa and Latin America*, London, Routledge & Kegan Paul.

Braverman, H. (1976) *Labor and Monopoly Capital*, New York, Monthly Review Press.

Brett, E. H. (1973) *Colonialism and Underdevelopment in East Africa*, London, Heinemann.

Broadbridge, S. (1966) *Industrial Dualism in Japan: A Problem of Economic Growth and Structural Change*, London, Frank Cass.

Bukharin, N. (1917) *Imperialism and World Economy*, English translation, London, Merlin Press (1972).

Byres, T. J. (1979) 'Of neo-populist pipe-dreams: Daedalus in the Third World and the myth of urban bias', *The Journal of Peasant Studies*, 6 (2), 210–44.

Cardoso, F. H. (1977) 'The consumption of dependency theory in the United States', *Latin American Research Review*, XII (3), 7–24.

Chayanov, A. V. (1925) *The Theory of Peasant Economy*, Moscow; English version edited by Daniel Thorner, Basile Kerblay and R. E. F. Smith, Homewood, Illinois, Richard C. Irwin for the American Economic Association (1966).

Chenery, H. *et al.* (1974) *Redistribution with Growth*, Oxford University Press for the World Bank.

Cheru, F. (Nov. 1987) 'Adjustment Problems and the Politics of Economic Surveillance: Tanzania and the IMF' (Paper to the US African Studies Association Conference), Denver, Colorado.

Chou Chin (1977) 'Mechanisation: fundamental way out for agriculture', *Peking Review*, 20 (9).

Clark, C. (1957) *The Conditions of Economic Progress*, London, Macmillan.

Clark, C. and Haswell, M. (1964) *The Economics of Subsistence Agriculture*, London, Macmillan.

Cohen, S. F. (1973) *Bukharin and the Bolshevik Revolution: A Political Biography 1888–1938*, New York, Vintage Books.

Coulson, A. (1977) 'Agricultural policies in mainland Tanzania', *Review of African Political Economy*, 10, September–December 1977, 74–100.

Cowen, M. P. (1972) 'Differentiation in a Kenyan location', Provisional Council for Social Sciences, East Africa Annual Conference Paper.

Cowen, M. P. (1975) 'Wattle production in the central province: capital and household commodity production 1903–64', Working Paper, Nairobi, Institute of Development Studies.

Crook, F. W. (May 1986) 'The Reform of the Commune System and the Rise of the Township-Collective Household System' in *China's Economy Toward the Year 2000*, vol. 1, *The Four Modernizations* (Papers submitted to the Joint Economics Committee, US Congress): 354–75.

Currie, R. and Hartwell, R. M. (1965) 'The making of the English working class?', *Economic History Review*, 2nd series, XVIII (3).

Dandekar, V. M. (1980) 'Unequal exchange: imperialism of trade' and 'Bourgeois politics of the working class', *Economic and Political Weekly*, XV (1) and (2), 27–36 and 75–85.

Danielson, N. (1902) *Histoire du développement économique de la Russe depuis l'affranchissement des serfs*, Paris.

Digby, W. (1901) *'Prosperous' British India: A Revelation from Official Records*, republished by Sagar Publishers, New Delhi (1969).

Dobb, M. (1955) *On Economic Theory and Socialism: Collected Papers*, London, Routledge & Kegan Paul.

Eckstein, A. (1977) *China's Economic Revolution*, Cambridge University Press.

Edie, J. M., Scanlon, J. P. and Zeldin, M. B. (eds) (1965) *Russian Philosophy*, Chicago, Quadrangle Books.

Emmanuel, A. (1972) *Unequal Exchange: A Study of the Imperialism of Trade*, London, New Left Books.

Engels, F. (1895) Letter to George Plekhanov in Geneva, 26 February 1895, in Marx, Karl and Engels, Friedrich, *Werke*, vol. 39, Berlin, Dietz Verlag (1968), 416–17.

Epstein, T. S. (1962) *Economic Development and Social Change in South India*, Manchester University Press.

Fanon, F. (1965) *The Wretched of the Earth*, New York, Grove Press.

Fernandez, R. A. and Ocampo, J. F. (1974) 'The Latin American revolution: a theory of imperialism not dependence', *Latin American Perspective*, 1 (1), 30–61.

Fiedler, L. A. (1960) *Love and Death in the American Novel*, New York, Criterion Books.

Field, R. M. (1975) 'Civilian industrial production in the People's Republic of China 1949–74', in *China: A Reassessment of the Economy*, Joint Economic Committee, US Congress.

Frank, A. G. (1971) *Capitalism and Underdevelopment in Latin America*,

Harmondsworth, Penguin.

Freyhold, M. von (1979) *Ujamaa Villages in Tanzania: Analysis of a Social Experiment*, London, Heinemann.

Friedland, W. H. and Rosberg, C. G. (1964) *African Socialism*, Stanford University Press.

Gammage, R. C. (1854) *History of the Chartist Movement 1837–1854*, reprinted by Merlin Press, London (1969).

Gellner, E. (1964) *Thought and Change*, London, Weidenfeld & Nicolson.

Gerry, C. (1979) 'Poverty in employment: a political economy of petty commodity production in Dakar, Senegal', Leeds University Ph.D.

Gerschenkron, A. (1962) *Economic Backwardness in Historical Perspective*, Cambridge, Mass., Harvard University Press.

Green, R. H. (1979) 'Tanzanian political economy: goals, strategies and results 1967–74', in Mwansasu, B. U. and Pratt, C. (eds) *Towards Socialism in Tanzania*, University of Toronto Press.

Green, R. H. (1980) 'The political economy of Tanzania 1979–81', *Bulletin of Tanzanian Affairs*, December 1980.

Griffin, K. (1984) ed., *Institutional Reform and Economic Development in the Chinese Countryside*, London, Macmillan.

Halliday, F. (1979) *Iran: Dictatorship and Development*, Harmondsworth, Penguin.

Halliday, J. and McCormack, G. (1973) *Japanese Imperialism Today: Co-prosperity in Greater East Asia*, Harmondsworth, Penguin.

Hammond, J. L. and Hammond, Barbara (1911) *The Village Labourer*, 1978 edition, London, Longman.

Harrison, M. (1975) 'Chayanov and the economics of the Russian peasantry', *Journal of Peasant Studies*, 2 (4), 389–417.

Hekken, P. M. van and Velzen, H. U. E. Thoden von (1972) *Land Scarcity and Rural Inequality in Tanzania: Some Case Studies from Rungwe District*, The Hague, Mouton.

Herzen, A. J. (1956) *From the Other Shore* and *The Russian People and Socialism*, trans. Moura Budberg, London, Weidenfeld & Nicolson.

Heyer, J. *et al.* (1976) *Agricultural Development In Kenya: An Economic Assessment*, Nairobi, Oxford University Press.

Hilferding, R. (1910) *Finance Capital: A Study of the Latest Phase of Capitalist Development*, Vienna; English edition edited with an introduction by Tom Bottomore from translations by Morris Watnick and Sam Gordan, London, Routledge & Kegan Paul (1981).

Hill, C. (1972) *The World Turned Upside Down: Radical Ideas during the English Revolution*, London, Temple Smith (1972) and Harmondsworth, Penguin (1975).

Hill, P. (1972) *Rural Hausa: A Village and a Setting*, Cambridge

University Press.

Hobson, J. A. (1902) *Imperialism: A Study*, London, Allen & Unwin, 6th impression (1961).

Honey, M. 'Gloomy outlook for Tanzania's peasants', *Guardian*, 2 December 1980.

Hyden, G. (1980) *Beyond Ujamaa in Tanzania: Underdevelopment and an Uncaptured Peasantry*, London, Heinemann.

Hyden, G. (1983) *No Shortcuts to Progress: African Development Management in Perspective*, London, Heinemann.

IESHR (1968) *Indian Economic and Social History Review*, V; see piece by Morris (pp. 1–15), replies by Matsui (pp. 17–33), Chandra (pp. 35–75) and Raychaudhuri (pp. 77–100), and a reply to replies by Morris (pp. 319–88).

International Labour Office (ILO) (1970) *Towards Full Employment: A Programme for Colombia*, Geneva.

ILO (1971) *Matching Employment Opportunities and Expectations: A Programme of Action for Ceylon*, Geneva.

ILO (1972) *Employment, Incomes and Equality: A Strategy for Increasing Productive Employment in Kenya*, Geneva.

ILO (1973) *Employment and Incomes Policies for Iran*, Geneva.

ILO (1974) *Sharing in Development: A Programme for Employment. Equity and Growth for the Philippines*, Geneva.

ILO (1976a) *Employment Growth and Basic Needs: A One-World Problem*, Geneva.

ILO (1976b) *Growth, Employment and Equity: A Comprehensive Strategy for the Sudan*, Geneva.

Ionescu, G. and Gellner, E. (eds) (1969) *Populism: Its Meanings and National Characteristics*, London, Weidenfeld & Nicolson.

Kautsky, K. (1899) *The Agrarian Question*, Hanover; selections translated by Jarius Banaji from the French edition of 1970 in *Economy and Society*, 5 (1), 1976, 2–49.

Keller, W. (1977) *Strukturen der Unterentwicklung Indiens 1757–1914, Eine Fallstudie über abhängige Reproduktion*, Zurich.

Kiernan, V. (1981) 'Development, imperialism and some misconceptions', University College of Swansea, Centre for Development Studies, *Occasional Papers*, 13.

Killick, T. (1978) *Development Economics in Action: A Study of Economic Policies in Ghana*, London, Heinemann.

King, K. (1977) *The African Artisan: Education and the Informal Sector in Kenya*, London, Heinemann.

Kitching, G. N. (1972) 'Mabadaliko: politics and social change in Northern Tanzania', University of Oxford, D.Phil.

Kitching, G. N. (1980a) *Class and Economic Change in Kenya: The Making of an African Petite-Bourgeoisie 1905–1970*, London, Yale University Press.

Kitching, G. N. (1980b) 'The Role of a national bourgeoisie in the current phase of capitalist development: some reflections', in Lubeck, Paul (ed.) (1981) *The African Bourgeoisie: Capitalist Development in the Ivory Coast, Kenya and Nigeria.*

Kitching, G. (1985) 'Politics, Method and Evidence in the Kenya Debate' in Bernstein, H. and Campbell, B. K. (eds) *Contradictions of Accumulation in Africa*, California, Sage Publications: 115–51.

Kuznets, S. (1966) *Modern Economic Growth: Rate, Structure and Spread*, New Haven, Yale University Press.

Landes, D. S. (1969) *The Unbound Prometheus: Technological Change and Industrial Development in Western Europe from 1750 to the Present*, Cambridge University Press.

Langdon, S. (1980), 'Industry and capitalism in Kenya: contributions to a debate', in Lubeck, Paul (ed.) (1981) *The African Bourgeoisie: Capitalist Development in the Ivory Coast, Kenya and Nigeria.*

Lardy, N. R. (1978) *Economic Growth and Distribution in China*, Cambridge University Press.

Lardy, N. R. (1986) 'Overview: Agrarian Reform and the Rural Economy' in *China's Economy Toward the Year 2000*, vol. 1: 325–35.

Leng Chuan Sheng and Palmer, N. (1961) *Sun Yat Sen and Communism*, London. Thames & Hudson.

Lenin, V. I. (1899) *The Development of Capitalism in Russia: The Process of the Formation of a Home Market for Large-scale Industry*, 1908 edition, Moscow, Progress Publishers (1977).

Lenin, V. I. (1912) 'Democracy and Narodism in China', *Collected Works*, vol. 18, 163–9, London, Lawrence & Wishart (1963).

Lenin, V. I. (1917) *Imperialism: The Highest Stage of Capitalism*, 11th impression, Moscow, Progress Publishers (1963).

Lewin, M. (1966) 'Who was the Soviet kulak?', *Soviet Studies*, 18 (2).

Lewin, M. (1968) *Russian Peasants and Soviet Power: A Study of Collectivisation*, London, Allen & Unwin.

Leys, C. (1975) *Underdevelopment in Kenya: The Political Economy of Neo-Colonialism 1963–1971*, London, Heinemann.

Lipton, M. (1977) *Why Poor People Stay Poor: A Study of Urban Bias in World Development*, London, Temple Smith.

List, F. (1841) *The National System of Political Economy*; English translation by Sampson Lloyd, London, Longman (1904).

Long, N. (1977) *An Introduction to the Sociology of Rural Development*, London, Tavistock.

Luxemburg, R. (1913) *The Accumulation of Capital*, trans. Agnes Schwarzschild, Introduction by Joan Robinson, London, Routledge & Kegan Paul (1963).

Mapolu, H. and Phillipson, G. (1976) 'Agricultural cooperation and the development of the productive forces: some lessons from Tanzania', *Africa Development*, 1 (1).

Marcuse, H. (1958) *Soviet Marxism: A Critical Analysis*, London, Routledge & Kegan Paul.

Marx, Karl (1846) letter to P. V. Annenkov, 28 December 1846, in Marx, Karl and Engels, Frederick, *Selected Correspondence 1846–1895*, ed. D. Torr, London, Lawrence & Wishart (1943).

Marx, Karl (1847) *The Poverty of Philosophy*, Paris; New York, International Publishers (1963).

Marx, Karl (1887) *Capital: A Critical Analysis of Capitalist Production*, vol. 1, Moscow, Progress Publishers (1965).

Mascenharas, A. (1979) 'After villagization – what?', in Mwansasu, B. U. and Pratt C. (eds) *Towards Socialism in Tanzania*, University of Toronto Press.

Maxwell, N. (1979) (ed.) *China's Road to Development*, 2nd edn., Oxford, Pergamon.

Mehmet, O. (1978) *Economic Planning and Social Justice in Developing Countries*, London, Croom Helm.

Mendel, A. P. (1961) *Dilemmas of Progress in Tsarist Russia: Legal Marxism and Legal Populism*, Cambridge, Mass., Harvard University Press.

Millar, J. R. (1970) 'A reformulation of A. V. Chayanov's theory of the peasant economy', *Economic Development and Cultural Change*, 18 (2) 219–29.

Mitrany, D. (1930) *The Land and Peasant in Rumania*, Oxford University Press.

Mitrany, D. (1951) *Marx against the Peasant: A Study in Social Dogmatism*, London, Weidenfeld & Nicolson.

Mwansasu, B. U. and Pratt, C. (eds) (1979) *Towards Socialism in Tanzania*, University of Toronto Press.

Nair, K. (1961) *Blossoms in the Dust: The Human Element in Indian Development*, London, Duckworth.

Nyerere, J. K. (1962) 'Ujamaa – the basis of African socialism', *Freedom and Unity: Uhuru na Umoja*, London, Oxford University Press (1967).

Nyerere, J. K. (1965) 'The importance and pleasure of reading', *Freedom and Socialism: Uhuru na Ujamaa*, Dar es Salaam, Oxford University Press (1968).

Nyerere, J. K. (1967a) 'The Arusha declaration', *Freedom and Socialism:*

Uhuru na Ujamaa, Dar es Salaam, Oxford University Press (1968).

Nyerere, J. K. (1967b) 'Education for self-reliance', *Freedom and Socialism: Uhuru na Ujamaa*, Dar es Salaam, Oxford University Press (1968).

Nyerere, J. K. (1967c) 'The purpose is man', *Freedom and Socialism: Uhuru na Ujamaa*, Dar es Salaam, Oxford University Press (1968).

Nyerere, J. K. (1967d) 'Socialism and rural development', *Freedom and Socialism: Uhuru na Ujamaa*, Dar es Salaam, Oxford University Press (1968).

Nyerere, J. K. (1967e) 'After the Arusha declaration', *Freedom and Socialism: Uhuru na Ujamaa*, Dar es Salaam, Oxford University Press (1968).

Nyerere, J. K. (1973) 'Interview with David Martin', *New Internationalist*, May.

O'Brien, P. (1975) 'A critique of Latin American theories of dependency', in Oxaal, I., Barnett, T. and Booth, D. (eds) *Beyond the Sociology of Development: Economy and Society in Africa and Latin America*, London, Routledge & Kegan Paul.

OECD (1977) *Science and Technology in the People's Republic of China*, Paris.

Oginga Odinga (1967) *Not Yet Uhuru*, New York, Hill & Wang.

Open University (1978) *Choosing Appropriate Technology*, Milton Keynes, Open University Press.

Oxaal, I. (1975) 'The dependency economist as grassroots politician in the Caribbean', in Oxaal, I., Barnett, T. and Booth, D. (eds) *Beyond the Sociology of Development: Economy and Society in Africa and Latin America*, London, Routledge & Kegan Paul.

Oxaal, I., Barnett, T. and Booth, D. (eds) (1975) *Beyond the Sociology of Development: Economy and Society in Africa and Latin America*, London, Routledge & Kegan Paul.

Palmer, R. and Parsons, N. (eds) (1977) *The Roots of Rural Poverty in Central and Southern Africa*, London, Heinemann.

Pratt, C. (1979) 'Tanzania's transition to socialism: reflections of a democratic socialist', in Mwansasu, B. U. and Pratt C. (eds) *Towards Socialism in Tanzania*, University of Toronto Press.

Preobrazhensky, E. (1926) *The New Economics*; English translation by Brian Pearce, Oxford, Clarendon Press (1965).

Proudhon, P. J. (1840) *What is Property? An Inquiry into the Principle of Right and Government*; trans. Benjamin Tucker, London, Reeves (1898).

Proudhon, P. J. (1970) *Selected Writings*, edited with an introduction by Stewart Edwards, trans. Elizabeth Frazer, London, Macmillan.

Pushkarev, S. (1963) *The Emergence of Modern Russia 1801–1917*, New York, Holt, Rinehart & Winston.

Raikes, P. L. (1972) 'Wheat production and the development of capitalism in North Iraq', Dar es Salaam Research Paper.

Rawski, T. G. (1979) *Economic Growth and Employment in China*, Oxford University Press for World Bank.

Redfield, R. (1956) *Peasant Society and Culture: An Anthropological Approach to Civilization*, University of Chicago Press.

Ricardo, David (1817) *On the Principles of Political Economy and Taxation*; Harmondsworth, Penguin (1971).

Rodney, W. (1971) *How Europe Underdeveloped Africa*, Dar es Salaam, Tanzania Publishing House.

Rostow, W. W. (1960) *The Stages of Economic Growth: A Non-Communist Manifesto*, Cambridge University Press.

Schram, S. (1966) *Mao Tse-Tung*, Harmondsworth, Penguin.

Schumacher, E. F. (1973) *Small is Beautiful. Economics as if People Mattered*, New York, Harper & Row.

Sen, A. (1962) *Choice of Techniques: An Aspect of the Theory of Planned Economic Development*, Oxford, Blackwell.

Sender, J. and Smith, S. (1986) *The Development of Capitalism in Africa*, London, Methuen.

Shanin, T. (ed.) (1971) *Peasants and Peasant Societies*, Harmondsworth, Penguin.

Shanin, T. (1972) *The Awkward Class: Political Sociology of Peasantry in a Developing Society: Russia 1910–25*, Oxford, Clarendon Press.

Shivji, I. G. (1976) *Class Struggles in Tanzania*, London, Heinemann.

Simonde de Sismondi, J. C. L. (1815) *Political Economy*; Reprints of Economic Classics, New York, Kelley (1966).

Smith, Adam (1776) *The Wealth of Nations*, eds R. H. Campbell and A. S. Skinner, Oxford, Clarendon Press (1976).

Smith, A. D. (1971) *Theories of Nationalism*, London, Duckworth.

Sorrenson, M. P. K. (1967) *Land Reform in the Kikuyu Country: A Study in Government Policy*, Nairobi, Oxford University Press.

Stepniak (S. Kravchinsky) (1888) *The Russian Peasantry: Their Agrarian Conditions, Social Life and Religion*, New York, Harper & Brothers.

Stirling, P. (1965) *Turkish Village*, London, Weidenfeld & Nicolson.

Stokes, E. (1978) *The Peasant and the Raj: Studies in Agrarian Society and Peasant Rebellion in Colonial India*, Cambridge University Press.

Tanzania, United Republic (1969) *Tanzania Second Five-Year Plan for Economic and Social Development 1969–74*, vol. I, 'General Analysis', and vol. II, 'The Programmes', Dar es Salaam.

Tanzania, United Republic (1974) *Economic Survey*, Dar es Salaam.

Tanzania, United Republic (1976) *Third Five-Year Plan for Economic and Social Development 1976–81*, Dar es Salaam.

Tanzania Food and Nutrition Centre (1980) *Data Report on the Food and Nutrition in Tanzania 1973–78*, Dar es Salaam.

Thompson, E. P. (1963) *The Making of the English Working Class*, London, Gollancz; Harmondsworth, Penguin (1968).

Thompson, E. P. (1967) 'Time, work-discipline and industrial capitalism', *Past and Present* (38), 56–97.

Thompson, N. (1979) 'Ricardian socialists/Smithian socialists: what's in a name?', University of Cambridge, Faculty of Economics and Politics, Research Paper.

Thorner, D. (1962) 'Context for co-operatives in rural India', *Economic Weekly*, February.

Thorner, D. (1971) 'Peasant Economy as a category in economic history', in Shanin, T. (ed.) *Peasants and Peasant Societies*, Harmondsworth, Penguin.

Todaro, M. (1977) *Economics for a Developing World*, London, Longman.

Venturi, F. (1966) *Roots of Revolution: A History of the Populist and Socialist Movements in Nineteenth Century Russia*, New York, Grosset & Dunlop.

Walicki, A. (1969) *The Controversy over Capitalism: Studies in the Social Philosophy of the Russian Populists*, Oxford, Clarendon Press.

Walicki, A. (1975) *The Slavophile Controversy: History of a Conservative Utopia in Nineteenth-Century Russian Thought*, Oxford, Clarendon Press.

Wallerstein, I. (1974) *The Modern World-System: Capitalist Agriculture and the Origins of the European World-Economy in the Sixteenth Century*, New York, Academic Press.

Warren, W. (1980) *Imperialism: Pioneer of Capitalism*, London, New Left Books.

Whittaker, E. (1950) *A History of Economic Ideas*, London, Longman, Green & Co.

Whittaker, E. (1960) *Schools and Streams of Economic Thought*, Chicago, Rand McNally.

Widstrand, C. G. (ed.) (1970) *Cooperatives and Rural Development in East Africa*, Uppsala, Scandinavian Institute of African Studies.

Williams, R. (1973) *The Country and the City*, London, Chatto & Windus.

Wolf, E. R. (1966) *Peasants*, Englewood Cliffs, Prentice-Hall.

World Bank (1980) *World Development Report 1980*, Oxford University Press for World Bank.

World Bank (1981) *Accelerated Development in Sub-Saharan Africa: An Agenda for Action*, The Berg Report, Washington, World Bank.

Youngson, A. J. (1959) *Possibilities of Economic Progress*, Cambridge University Press.

Index

Vorontsov, V. P., 37–9, 42, 60, 91,
150–3, 155, 158, 163

Walicki, A., 35, 38, 43, 44, 146, 148,
150–2

Warren, B., 154, 161
Witte, Count, 37, 150–1
World Bank, 7, 60, 84, 103